WOMEN
ON DUTY

WOMEN ON DUTY

A HISTORY OF THE FIRST FEMALE POLICE FORCE

SOPHIE JACKSON

FONTHILL

Fonthill Media Limited
Fonthill Media LLC
www.fonthillmedia.com
office@fonthillmedia.com

First published in the United Kingdom and the United States of America 2014

British Library Cataloguing in Publication Data:
A catalogue record for this book is available from the British Library

Copyright © Sophie Jackson 2014

ISBN 978-1-78155-362-6

Typeset in 10pt on 13pt Sabon
Printed and bound by CPI Group (UK) Ltd, Croydon, CR0 4YY

CONTENTS

Acknowledgements

The greatest acknowledgement for this volume has to go to those women who pioneered policing and proved that it was not a role exclusively available to men. Where possible I have used their personal accounts to build a picture of their work and lives, but many of them have simply vanished from history, forgotten in time. To those pioneers who created the first women patrols, putting both themselves and their reputations at risk, this work must be dedicated.

The images within this book are taken from a range of sources and wherever possible their original copyright sources have been stated.

Introduction

The history of modern policing is surprisingly short. Law enforcement is a natural and logical part of most civilisations, stemming from a need to control abnormal or disruptive behaviour; systems of punishment are instigated to act as deterrents to the behaviour or behaviours a society has deemed unacceptable. Policing, as we understand it, is only one part of that system: at its simplest it is a method for maintaining order and apprehending those who purposefully disrupt it. However, this is a very modern view.

For much of the history of Britain, policing has been the duty of all citizens—there was no distinct force that specialised in it. Therefore the Norman sheriff would expect the ordinary men of his parish to raise a 'hue and cry' to catch a wanted felon who had escaped. He had his own men as well, but by and large catching a criminal was the duty of the population, particularly when it came to lower level crimes that did not affect the state—so theft from a farmer's home would raise little notice, unless it directly affected the Crown or the Church.

Policing is also about keeping the peace in a neighbourhood, and once again this duty had to fall on the ordinary man or woman before a true police force existed. The prosecution of a criminal after he or she has been detained is another matter entirely, which has a much longer and more convoluted history. For much of history the prosecution of criminals has been a more important part of law enforcement than actual policing, involving the Justices of the Peace, magistrates, Clerical Courts, and even the King in high-priority trials.

However, prosecuting a criminal cost money, and for many crimes the victim was expected to foot the bill. Things had become so bad by the eighteenth century that householders would come together in special 'crime clubs', paying in a set fee each week or month as a form of insurance against crime. The crime clubs would cover the cost of prosecuting an offender who had committed a civil offence against one of their members; but even this insurance could not cover all cases of crime, and anyone who could not afford to pay could also not afford justice. Clearly the problem was becoming ridiculous, while the rise in population numbers—especially in cities—made old systems of self-regulation impossible. Changes were needed, but they would be slow.

The appointment of special constables, done by two or more Justices of the Peace, was one way forward. However, by necessity they were volunteers, who fitted policing around their regular work and often had only limited training for the role. They could not provide a regular police force. Equally, eight hundred years or so of making and changing laws had left Britain with a convoluted and at times archaic legal system, meaning it was not always plain what was—and what was not—a crime. Relying solely on themselves, the special constables could really only be a stop-gap measure.[1]

It was in the capital, London (where more and more people were emigrating to, to escape poverty in the country, often only to find more poverty in the city), where real progress came first. The Bow Street Runners were created in 1749 by the author Henry Fielding. They were a revelation as they were attached to the Bow Street Magistrate's offices and paid out of their funds. Thus they could help ordinary people for free. Up until 1839 the Bow Street Runners were a common sight on London streets, and though funding for them had been intermittent, they had paved the way for the future of policing.

London still required an effective full-time police force, as crime figures demonstrated. Sir Robert Peel was outlining plans for six police districts in 1826, but it was not until 1829—when the first Metropolitan Police Act was passed—that the 'Peelers' took to London's streets. In the same year, Commissioner of Police Sir Richard Mayne said:

> The primary object of an efficient police is the prevention of crime: the next that of detection and punishment of offenders if crime is committed. To these ends all the efforts of police must be directed. The protection of life and property, the preservation of public tranquillity, and the absence of crime, will alone prove whether those efforts have been successful and whether the objects for which the police were appointed have been attained.[1]

The Peelers were certainly going to make their mark, but for the time being they had to compete with the Bow Street Runners. In 1839 the Metropolitan Police would absorb their rivals, and so policing fell for the first time under one state-funded body.

Outside London, police forces were slow to take hold in some provinces, but eventually every county could boast its own force—though often, in the case of serious crime, these county forces had to be bolstered by the arrival of police from London.

There remained one very significant omission in the ranks of this new police force—women. The history of law enforcement has been male dominated; women could play minor roles in the background, but any influential role was to remain in male hands until the twentieth century. It would be a shock for a modern woman to discover how one-sided the court system was and how poorly-served women criminals or their victims were. This is made even clearer by the double standards found in the legal system—adultery by a husband was not grounds for a divorce unless coupled with cruelty, however, adultery by a wife was. Women could be arrested and taken to court for soliciting the opposite sex, but there was no similar law for men. The list of grievances goes on; in court women often found themselves alone with no support, whether they were the victim or the defendant. Rape victims would be accused of leading a man on and would be badgered mercilessly to admit they were to blame for their own abuse. With no female back-up, women often found their testimony undermined and their cases dismissed.

The unlucky female criminal was regularly demonised for crimes which were considered almost excusable for men. Sent to prison, she would find herself bundled in with male criminals and the consequences of having 'mixed' prisons can all too well be imagined.

It was the suffragettes who first started to make a loud noise over conditions for women. It was long overdue, but hammering on the closed doors of the male-controlled legal system was far from easy. Along with votes for women, the issues of prison reform and better support for women in court became hot topics for suffragettes.

A brief pause must be taken to define the suffragette and her cousin the suffragist. In loose terms, the suffragist avoided militant actions through protest and constant demands for reform. The suffragette came face-to-face with the law by instigating acts of criminal damage and violence towards the police. At their height, certain suffragette organisations had reached a level of violence which we would today call terrorism. Bombs and arson, rather than placards and petitions, became their means of protest. This clarification is necessary because both the suffragettes and suffragists are integral to the story of the women police, but often the terms were badly misused by the media and even the government, which could naturally lead to confusion. The ladies involved felt aggrieved by the popular press's carelessness, which would even infiltrate reporting on women's police work, with irritating consequences.

For many of these modern ladies the Victorian period seemed to favour men too heavily, while women were pushed to one side, advised by etiquette and fashion to be silent creatures. Even worse, certain old rights women had once enjoyed had now been removed, thus stripping them of what little power they had. But it was the Defence of the Realm Act (DORA) which really made women feel they were being persecuted. DORA had various parts to it, but it was those that specifically singled out women for penalisation that angered so many. The Act was designed only to play a significant role in garrison towns where problems had arisen from venereal disease; wherever a garrison town existed prostitution was rife. Women were attracted to the camps where soldiers with a little spare money—and a lot of free time—would happily pay for their company. VD was a huge bugbear to the military as it put men out of action, and with no real treatment for the condition it could effectively ruin an army. Statistics for VD indicate that it was at its highest in the Victorian period among the military; even during the First World War the figures were nowhere near as extreme. This contradicts the hype generated by the media and government surrounding the problems VD was causing between 1914 and 1918.

Desperation launched DORA; through the auspices of the Act, curfews could be imposed on women in certain towns and any woman suspected of prostitution could be taken for an examination. If she refused she would be sent to prison. The heavy-handed nature of the decrees and the ease with which women could be accused of prostitution (it only required the word of one police officer) appalled not only suffragettes and suffragists, but men also, who recognised its lop-sided nature. The soldiers who were half of the problem had no preventative methods imposed upon them, and there was a great deal of talk that men could not be punished or regulated for such behaviour as it was natural, and they couldn't help themselves. On the other hand, it was expected that women could. DORA's social stigma, not to mention the humiliation and indignity meted out to women under its name, resulted in at least one suicide; enough was enough. It took several years, but DORA was repealed to much celebration—though she would raise her ugly head again in the First World War and cause a great deal of problems for the first female police.

The various women's movements recognised that while women were prevented from being in a position of any real power DORA or something similar was always a potential risk. Suffrage started to battle on a number of fronts, including the need for women police. The case was logical enough –women victims found it hard to talk to men, and male police often suffered embarrassment trying to take statements on a crime of assault. Prosecutions were hampered by this reticence, when it could be easily combated by having women sworn in to take statements. The problem was then compounded by women being abandoned in the courtroom with no support from their own sex. It was common practice to banish women from the courtroom when a crime of indecency came up, so the unfortunate victim was usually the sole member of her gender in the courtroom. The legal system had failed women and so it needed to be challenged; going for the head was almost impossible, but further down there was the police force, not even a century old, which could perhaps be infiltrated.

Whatever goals the suffrage organisations had, they were turned on their heads with the outbreak of the First World War. A ceasefire between the suffragettes and the government was wisely announced; there is no knowing how far the extremism of certain women within the movement could have taken them, possibly to the detriment of the entire suffrage cause. But the respite was only short-lived because women soon recognised the potential opportunities war was offering them. For some suffragettes, and even those not involved in the movement, the upheavals caused by war were viewed as a potential opportunity, even offering a political advantage. This is not to say that they were unmoved by the sufferings of the soldiers, as there were many who offered genuine patriotic and philanthropic services; but they were hardly blind to the political possibilities now available to them, even in the first months of war. What decades of campaigning had failed to achieve, the horrors of the First World War would push forward in a sudden burst. Old arguments decayed in the face of desperation, shown up for the nonsense they were. Women took a dominant role for the first time, and once there, refused to go back to being in the shadow of men. The world would never be the same after the horrors of war, and neither would women's suffrage. Through four years of hardship and conflict women had proved their worth and demonstrated their equality to men. Integral to this change were the women police, who showed that maintaining law and order was not just the preserve of men.

Considering its part in the suffrage movement, it is surprising that the rise of women police is a neglected subject; in fact the history of policing as a whole is rather under-studied. Former police officers, such as Joan Lock, have made attempts to right the balance and reveal the convoluted origins of modern policing, in particular of the modern policewoman. However, there still seems to be a lack of understanding of how significant those first policewomen were, how fundamental to changing the way women were perceived, and above all, how tough a journey for them it was. The strains and stresses took their toll: the woman recognised as the first female police constable with arresting powers committed suicide, and the founder of one of the first women patrols died of a heart attack, thought to be stress-related, only a few months after seeing women police accepted. Great pioneering work rarely comes without cost, and many of the early women police paid with their lives or reputations. No records remain to tell us the number of women who used all their wealth to maintain the fledgling forces. Margaret Damer Dawson came close to bankrupting herself despite being a lady with a considerable fortune; we do not know how many others gave without thinking because they believed in the women police, and thus forced themselves into poverty. However, it is an indicator of the passions and fierce emotions the women police generated that so many would be prepared to give up all they had for the cause.

The policewoman was not born easily—she came with enough struggles and pain to have daunted most. She was persecuted, ridiculed, and openly mocked. She was called abnormal by magistrates who felt no respectable woman could possibly want to join the police; insinuations were made about her sexuality; and she was derided as a spinster, looking for something to do to fill her time because she had failed to find a husband. Bad as the insults were, the policewoman then had to go out onto the streets and take on the drunk and the dangerous, risking assault, and patrol on the darkest, coldest, wettest and snowiest of nights. It took a certain kind of woman to face all these lashes happily.

The story of the policewoman is one of courage, determination and difficulty, and the war shaped it all. This is the history of her first steps in those frantic years of war, how conflict created and changed her and how it took a monumental upheaval to bring women to centre stage. It is not often that war generates new life, but in the rise of the policewoman, its influence was vital and unforgettable.

1

Origins of the Policewoman

At the dawn of the twentieth century the hot topic on many people's minds was female suffrage. It was hard to ignore; the movement had gained momentum through the 1890s, and by the turn of the century the suffrage leaders were pushing for political reform. This female-led revolution almost seemed to have come from nowhere. In 1914, when collecting together her memories of her brief but tumultuous time with the Women's Social and Political Union (WSPU), Lady Constance Lytton wrote:

> We do not know how it sprang to life, no one explanation is entirely satisfactory, certainly not the theory that it was the work of 'leaders.' It began all over the country, in silent, lonely places. It was a spiritual movement and had fire, not form... it released vast stores of unconscious energy... it was not premeditated or controllable—it *happened*.[1]

Lytton had been a suffragette who believed that actions spoke louder than words. She had been imprisoned several times and had gone on hunger strike, resulting in a breakdown in her health and a severe stroke that left her partially incapacitated. After a life of luxury and contentment it was a severe shock, but she was motivated by her own personal experiences of the disregard shown to women:

> I realised how often women are held in contempt as beings outside the pale of human dignity, excluded or confined, laughed at and insulted because of conditions in themselves for which they are not responsible, but which are due to fundamental injustices with regard to them, and to the mistakes of a civilisation in the shaping of which they have had no free share.[2]

Lytton described the movement as 'not premeditated'. In reality the suffrage movement had begun over a hundred years before Lytton's lifetime, in small, isolated ways. However, it was the push for male suffrage in the nineteenth century that spurred large numbers of women into action. Intrinsic to female suffrage was the belief that women should be entitled to have some say in how they were governed. The Victorian world was dominated by men; men made the rules by which women had to abide, whether they were fair or not. Various heavy-handed acts introduced in the nineteenth century had made women realise that they were at the mercy of men and whatever whims that took their fancy. So the call for female suffrage began in earnest, and with it the notion that women were best placed to 'police' their own gender.

A number of organisations were formed to heed this call. For some of these suffragettes or suffragists (the terms were interchangeable) they saw their task to be not so much about gaining equality between the sexes, but about proving their natural superiority to men. Others were more practical in their aims.

For instance, The National Union of Women Workers (NUWW) was created in response to calls among suffragists for trade unions to support women workers, following examples set in America. The NUWW formed in Bristol under the auspices of a parent organisation, the Women's Protective and Provident League (WPPL). Established by Anna Maria, Mary Priestman, and their friend Mary Estlin, it was soon sprouting branches across Yorkshire. The union operated as a sort of friendly society, providing club facilities and opportunities for self-improvement, but their main goal was to improve the limited protective legislation for women workers. They would later prove themselves fundamental in the formation of women police.

However, it was the militant WSPU, led by the formidable Emmeline Pankhurst, that became the main force for female suffrage in twentieth-century Britain—or so it seemed from their headline grabbing antics. For better or worse, the militant actions of the WSPU would shape the way that suffragettes were perceived.

The Women's Social and Political Union

Emmeline Pankhurst had a rebellious streak which showed itself long before she became interested in women's suffrage. While she was a member of the Independent Labour Party (ILP) she had become embroiled in a minor scandal. The ILP had been banned from holding Sunday meetings at Boggart Hole Clough by the Manchester Parks committee; but Mrs Pankhurst and two male colleagues ignored the ban repeatedly and were eventually arrested. Only the men received jail terms. Mrs Pankhurst was excused, probably on account of her husband's position within the ILP and his prominence in local politics. In fact the whole matter soon became a sore point for the council and they backed down, removing the ban and releasing the two men. Mrs Pankhurst and her husband were trumpeted as heroes, which delighted her.

But even the ILP was not immune to chauvinistic behaviour, and this was soon to cause a clash between the party and Emmeline. In 1903 she was a widow with four children, including a sickly son. She was working as a registrar and supplemented her income by selling prints and other forms of modest art. Her daughter, Sylvia, had trained as an artist and that year had received a commission to decorate the Dr Pankhurst Memorial Hall in Salford for the ILP. The family was delighted to have a place named after the late Mr Pankhurst, but when Sylvia learned that the Hall was to be used as a male-only social club, and not even her mother and sisters would be able to enter and see the work she had done for her father, she was mortified. Emmeline was furious. She had been considering a split with the ILP for some time, but Sylvia's news tipped her over the edge. Within a week of the Hall being officially opened, she had founded the Women's Social and Political Union (WSPU).

'We must have an independent women's movement!' she told her friends, and summoned them to her house for the first meeting. Missing from this gathering was her eldest daughter Christabel. Christabel later became one of the figureheads of the WSPU, but at this early stage she was completely uninterested in the cause.

Emmeline had grand plans for her association, and they were not to be muddled or complicated by outsiders. From the outset she was very much in charge:

> There was little formality about joining the Union. Any woman could become a member by paying a shilling, but at the same time she was required to sign a declaration of loyal adherence to our policy... But, you may object, a suffrage organisation ought to be democratic. Well the members of the WSPU do not agree with you. We do not believe in the effectiveness of the ordinary suffrage organisation. The WSPU is not hampered by a complexity of rules. We have no constitution and by-laws; nothing to be amended or tinkered with or quarrelled over at annual meetings... The WSPU is simply a suffrage army in the field... no one is obliged to remain in it. Indeed we don't want anybody to remain in it who does not ardently believe in the policy of the army.[3]

Emmeline always intended her union to be different from the suffragist societies that already existed. She wanted to persuade the ILP to support women's suffrage and believed the only way to do that was through direct action. 'Deeds not words' was her motto. From the very beginning the WSPU was set on a path for violent protest and militancy. To differentiate these new women protestors from the previous campaigners, a new term was coined—Suffragette. Though the term was often muddled with suffragist, in general it was understood that a suffragette was a woman who campaigned through militancy, while a suffragist used traditional, law-abiding means of lobbying

MPs. These two opposite means of protest were quick to divide women who believed in the same cause. Suffragists believed their militant rivals threatened the entire legitimacy of the women's cause, while the suffragettes wanted to know what exactly their quieter counterparts had achieved in the last fifty years.

The problem became so divisive that in 1897 the National Union of Woman's Suffrage Societies was formed to try and bring together the disparate women's groups. There was a danger of the various organisations beginning to fight among themselves. The two main national suffrage societies of the day were divided over support for the Liberal party. The NUWSS, led by Mrs Fawcett, had one purpose: '[votes for women] on the same terms as it is, or may be granted to men.' Some were disappointed the society was not pushing for greater reforms, but Mrs Fawcett believed in focussing on one cause and slowly building support for female suffrage among MPs. She was a Suffragist, meaning she favoured non-militant action, and her persistence in lobbying had paid off in 1897 as the Commons consistently voted in favour of women's suffrage. Yet MPs still felt there was little importance or necessity in pressing for reforms and constantly ignored the Suffragist demands.

Despite their initial aims, the NUWSS had failed to bring the warring women's groups together. While some women attempted to support both the NUWSS and WSPU, it wasn't long before the two factions polarised, and to be a member of one instantly excluded a person from membership of the other.

Emmeline, who ruled the WSPU with autocratic authority, was not interested in working with other societies. The only person she could work with was her daughter Christabel, who had finally joined the WSPU. The pair were soon recognised as the official leaders of the cause. Emmeline and Christabel were initially completely in step with one another, to the exclusion of the other Pankhurst children. This was nothing new, as Emmeline's daughters Sylvia and Adela had always felt on the outside of their mother's love, while Christabel was always favoured for affection and attention. However, the power the Pankhursts displayed over the WSPU started to unsettle some of its mainstays.

From its foundation in 1903, the WSPU had spread across the country so that, by 1907, a number of branches had been set up—especially in the north of England. This had put further pressure on Emmeline and Christabel's autocratic rule, and the latter feared she might be challenged at the WSPU's annual conference. She was right. WSPU member Teresa Billington-Grieg drafted a constitution which was ratified at the conference, reducing the power of the Pankhursts. She wanted to turn the WSPU into a democracy, but Emmeline would not relinquish control. With Christabel upset and calling Teresa a 'wrecker', Emmeline snatched the fledgling constitution out of Teresa's hands and tore it to shreds. She cancelled the conference and immediately formed a new committee from her most loyal and devoted followers. Teresa was cast out; furious, she became the catalyst for a split within the party, the first of seven—largely caused by Christabel—before the war. Unhappy WSPU members went with her to form the Women's Freedom League (WFL), a society that would work closely with the Labour Party. Though militant, the WFL operated as a democracy and was opposed to the increasing violence displayed by the WSPU.

The WSPU briefly became the NWSPU (the N standing for National) to distance themselves from the dissidents. In 1908 the NWSPU organised a barge to sail up the Thames to surprise members of the House of Commons who were almost impossible to reach by any other means. The MPs happened to be sitting on a balcony overlooking the river, having afternoon tea with their lady friends (described as such by the suffragettes, but one wonders if it was a tongue-in-cheek comment). At 4 p.m. a little steamer barge with a white funnel, adorned with bunting and banners proclaiming the women's movement, approached them. At the prow of the barge was Flora Drummond, affectionately nicknamed the 'general' for her love of attending marches in pseudo-military uniform. She loudly introduced herself and her comrades to the MPs, inviting them to attend a women's demonstration in Hyde Park that Sunday. 'I am very glad you have got lady waiters,' she said, 'but are you not afraid that some of them might be suffragettes?' Her listeners responded with laughter, but the police were already on their way in their own river barge. With her message given, Mrs Drummond ordered her crew to turn the barge around and head off before the police could reach them. It was a sore point for the Metropolitan forces that they had been out-foxed on that particular June afternoon.

During the war the WSPU agreed to a temporary ceasefire, and Emmeline turned her talent for public speaking towards condemning the Germans and promoting her own form of unflinching patriotism. She encouraged women into war work and, as might be expected from a militant suffragette, made her distaste for pacifism clear.

This went directly against the beliefs of her daughter Sylvia, who actively spoke out for pacifism and continued to push for women's votes throughout the war. She had split from her mother and Christabel and formed the East London Federation of Suffragettes, which in 1915 became the Workers Suffrage Federation. Sylvia spent the war looking after the poorest, who were most affected by the loss of their men folk. She set up mother and infant welfare clinics in the East End of London and inexpensive restaurants. Her organisation opened factories to employ women who had lost their jobs with the outbreak of war, and helped those women suffering the worst both economically and emotionally. But her mother and sister were unimpressed, and became furious that Sylvia would not take the same stance as them. From this point on they effectively cut ties with her.

The suffrage movement had been striven by internal debates and rivalries in the decade before the war. Efforts for reconciliation among the main parties had been ineffectual. This pattern of conflict would continue into the women's police movement, and would at times threaten to completely undermine it. As bad as this lack of unity was, there was an even worse hurdle to overcome. In their decade of campaigning, the suffragettes had often gone to great lengths to mock, deride, and denigrate the male police. The resentment this had generated would not be easily smoothed over or quickly forgotten, especially now those same women desired to join the police force.

2

Suffragettes versus Police

The early Edwardian police force had been in something of a shambles when the women's movement began to make its big push for votes. Driven by the Pankhursts, peaceful protests turned into aggressive demonstrations, with women going deliberately out of their way to break the law and cause chaos or damage to the government wherever possible. When the women began their militant campaign the Metropolitan Police were 2,000 constables understrength and hard-pressed to keep order in London, let alone command respect among the inhabitants. The situation was not much better for the understaffed provincial police forces. Incompetency among the police led to the press sensationally suggesting corruption.

Problems between the police and suffragettes soon arose. In June 1906 the WSPU had been pursuing the then Chancellor of the Exchequer, Herbert Asquith, heckling and abusing him whenever they had the opportunity. This brought them into confrontation with the police in Cavendish Square. Teresa Billington (as yet unmarried so she had not added Grieg to her name), was among a protest party of women who objected to the police striking at the protestors to drive them back. As a result she was seized, struck, and throttled. When she retaliated by slapping and kicking the police officer, she was arrested and brought to court, where she refused to testify. Lady Constance Lytton tried to explain the situation in a manner that would not alienate the police forces:

> The police, of course, in turn came under the influence of those in authority over them, and when under orders would knock us about in the streets, and accuse us in the courts, according to the requirements imposed upon them. Under this pressure, individual policemen would occasionally act with brutality and unfairness, but in the main their treatment of Suffragists was in striking contrast to that of the magistrates, the Homes Office and the Government.[1]

This she wrote in 1914, when some of the furore had died down, but she could not completely ignore the police brutality that had been meted out:

Another time a policeman turned me round and, holding my arms behind me, drove me ahead of him for several yards at a great pace. So that his violence would not land me on to my face I exerted what pressure I could to steady my feet.... Twice again I was thrown as before described. I offered no resistance to this whatever, and being of light weight for my size, I fear that I was becoming a specially desirable victim for the experts in this line. Each time I was thrown to a greater distance and the concussion on reaching the ground was painful and straining, though in each case the crowd acted for me as sort of buffers.[2]

One of the worst incidents caused by a clash between suffragettes and police occurred on 18 November 1910, a day that went down in suffrage history as 'Black Friday'. On that day Asquith made a statement in the House of Commons before it was dissolved until 28 November. He made no mention of female suffrage, nor of the recently proposed Conciliation Bill which might have started the ball rolling for full female suffrage. Members of the WSPU were holding a conference as Asquith spoke and, learning that once again they had been side-lined, they determined to send a deputation to the House of Commons. Three hundred women marched for the Houses of Parliament, Mrs Pankhurst at their head. Asquith had expected as much and the police were waiting for them.

The orders of the Home Secretary were, apparently, that the police were to be present both in uniform and also in plain clothes among the crowd and that the women were to be thrown from one to other. In consequence of these instructions many of the women were severely hurt and several were knocked down and bruised.[3]

Suffragettes often complained of rough-handling by the police, who would throw them to the ground and sometimes resort to kicking and beating persistent women. There were also attacks of a sexual nature where a woman was grabbed from behind and her breasts held. One woman told of what had occurred to her:

For hours I was beaten about the body, thrown backwards and forwards from one to another, until one felt dazed with the horror of it.... Often seized by the coat collar, dragged out of the crowd, only to be pushed helplessly along in front of one's tormentor into a side street ... while he beat one up and down one's spine until cramp seized one's legs, when he would then release one with a vicious shove, and with insulting speeches, such as 'I will teach you a lesson. I will teach you not to come back and more. I will punish you, you—, you—,' ... once I was thrown with my jaw against a lamp-post with such force that two of my front teeth were loosened.[4]

Another complained of indecent assault:

> Several times constables and plain-clothes men who were in the crowds
> passed their arms round me from the back and clutched hold of my breasts
> in as public a manner as possible, and men in the crowd followed their
> example. I was also pummelled on the chest, and my breast was clutched by
> one constable from the front.... I was also very badly treated by a PC ... my
> skirt was lifted up as high as possible, and the constable attempted to lift me
> off the ground by raising his knee. This he could not do, so he threw me into
> the crowd and incited the men to treat me as they wished.[5]

If anything, this treatment made the women even more determined to persist.
On Black Friday 115 women (and four men) were arrested.

Relations between the suffragettes and the police were becoming more and
more complicated. While the WSPU was intent on showing women as victims
and thus justifying any resort to violence –no matter the extremes—the police
were viewing them as dangerous troublemakers. This came to a head in 1912
when the Metropolitan Police felt it necessary to report that at one suffragette
meeting, a certain Miss Gilliatt had made a remark about murdering a
politician. 'As regards the possibility of killing a Cabinet minister,' said Miss
Gilliatt, 'attend their political meetings and you will find out for yourselves
what an easy matter is their destruction.'

Though not a direct declaration of murderous intent, it certainly implied
that killing was a possibility. Rumours that suffragettes had been practicing
with pistols had troubled politicians for years. Asquith in particular felt
vulnerable to these women.

Lesbianism

To counteract the bad publicity the police—and thus the government—were
suffering, a new campaign was launched to directly denigrate the suffragettes.
It was a smear campaign, with its main target being the feminine qualities
of the suffrage women. In essence it was suggested that no 'normal' woman
would ever consider joining the suffrage movement, and that only those
women who were abnormal (and unfeminine) would want to be part of a
suffragette organisation. This was attacking women at their most vulnerable
point—femininity, one of the most prized Victorian attributes. And, it has to
be said, certain women within the movement played straight into the hands of
the slanderers, dressing and acting in a decidedly masculine fashion. Though
it was never blatantly stated, the enemy was implying that suffragettes were
women with perverse sexual tastes.

Homosexuality within the suffrage movement is a complicated question. There can be no doubt that some of the women involved were more comfortable surrounded by members of their own sex. Claims of lesbianism are sometimes levelled at the suffrage movement to undermine it and give it an ulterior motive. Whilst there is no doubt that certain leading figures in the cause showed lesbian inclinations, many more were or had been married. Emmeline Pankhurst, for instance, was a widow, though her daughter Christabel has been accused of being aggressively opposed to men.

Trying to turn the suffrage question into one of homosexual equality simply doesn't work, as it implies a conscious knowledge among all the women involved that they were promoting lesbianism. For many women at the time this would have been a shocking thought, and it is quite clear that some were deeply concerned about leaders who displayed homosexual inclinations. At most protests, participants were reminded to dress femininely to oppose the stereotypical views of their denouncers.

What is plain from the suffrage movement is that women formed strong friendships with each other. At that period it was not considered homosexual for two women to live together or to talk of one another affectionately. For the suffrage women, united in a bond of suffering and grievances, close friendships were to form naturally and there was nothing unusual in telling a friend you loved her.

The suffrage movement was also very empowering for women: for some it gave them a role in life which they never previously had. Women were heavily defined by their association with men, and so the unfortunate spinster, who had failed to secure a spouse, was looked on with derision and deemed worthless. For such women the attraction of the suffrage cause was obvious— it gave them a purpose and made them feel useful. It was also easier for single women to regularly participate in the cause rather than married women, who had a household to look after. It was therefore logical that members would be largely unmarried or widows, who had no attachments to prevent them regularly participating in protests. Anti-suffrage movements feared that this implied that women were intending to do away with men—they would simply function without them. If a woman could find companionship and love with another woman, what use—other than procreative—did a man have? The terror of becoming worthless fuelled many men to denounce the suffragettes and level new accusations of homosexual behaviour at them, cries that have dogged women's rights movements ever since.

3

Enter Mary Allen

Mary Allen started life in a traditional middle-class family, one of ten children born to Thomas and Margaret Allen. All the children were driven and ambitious, but this was most prominent in the Allen girls, partly because at that period it was unusual for a woman to aspire to anything other than a satisfactory marriage. Certainly Mary's sister Margaret Anne—'Dolly'—achieved this, though she also played her part in the founding of the women police movement. It is also safe to say a certain eccentricity ran through all the girls; the youngest girls, Janet and Christine, became involved in a quest for the Holy Grail, Christine practiced automatic writing, and both believed in mysticism.

The Allen boys also had their talents. Denys Allen invented things, and Herbert Allen became a master mariner before being killed in First World War, although in general the Allen boys were slightly quieter and less extroverted than the sisters. The Allen girls seemed to attract attention, good or bad, with an eagerness that knew no bounds.

Even so, Mary's early life was peaceful and fairly typical for a well-bred young lady. She dressed in the latest fashion for wasp waists and big picture hats, and showed few signs of her later inclinations. Thomas Allen was an old-fashioned patriarch who had little time for women's politics and the agitation of the suffragists. Mary was raised to dismiss 'with a delicate shudder the whole subject of Women's Suffrage'. Like other suffragettes (including Constance Lytton) Mary held a strong view that her health was fragile. Her childhood was haunted by illness and therefore her parents, fearing she would grow up a semi-invalid, allowed Mary a certain latitude that the other children did not enjoy. Mary was not expected to marry, so she drifted through her days of early adulthood reading and absorbing what she could.

Thomas Allen may have wished to ignore the suffrage issue, but even in his quiet corner of England the rallying voices of the women's movement could be heard. As closeted as she was, Mary could not avoid knowing of the movement—she began to learn about it, overcoming her 'delicate shudders'. Mary was curious enough to broach the subject with her father, perhaps hoping for a better understanding of why he disapproved. From what she had read and heard, Mary was already a committed suffragette when she approached her father in his study and asked him to explain the subject to her.

Thomas Allen drew down thick white brows and glowered at his daughter: 'I cannot discuss such folly! As for you, I wish you to think no more about it.' Mary was implacable; she had come to her father to try and understand his feelings, perhaps even to reproach him. But his flat refusal to talk only made plain to her how strong her own thoughts on the movement were. She would not ignore the subject, and she would not deny women's suffrage.

'Either you give up this Suffragette nonsense absolutely and for good or you leave this house!' Thomas Allen blustered, no doubt entirely certain his frail daughter would consent to his will. He misjudged Mary. The thought of a young, respectable Edwardian girl leaving home on her own, without an occupation to support her, was shocking enough that Thomas thought his daughter would concede defeat. Indeed the idea caused Mary a great deal of terror, but she was not prepared to give in. Quietly, but firmly, she agreed to leave home.

Thomas must have been stunned; as much as he tried to control his children, he was also deeply fond of them. Before Mary had packed her things he had agreed to maintain—and even increase—her allowance, ensuring she might live with ease, without having to earn money. Ironically, considering the early actions that sent Mary off into the world, she did not always agree with young women who had purposefully disobeyed their fathers. In fact, Thomas had raised more of a puritan than he had imagined. Mary had strong, almost archaic views on the relationship between men and women, which would influence her work as a policewoman. She firmly believed that women should respect and obey men, as in general men knew best, especially fathers. It just happened that this view did not extend to Mary herself—she was a special case, and as such she did not fall under her own conservative views on womanhood.

Mary had been inspired by the pretty, working-class Annie Kenney to join the Women's Social and Political Union (WSPU). From the start it was plain she would not be drawn to the peaceful protesting of the suffragist cause—she wanted action, and her strong rebellious streak naturally directed her to the more militant side of the women's movement. She was soon heavily involved in the cause and making headlines. On 24 February 1909 Mary was part of a deputation of women headed for the Houses of Parliament with a petition. With long skirts swishing and huge hats pinned to their heads, the congregation of forty women approached the House of Commons and tried to force their way through the cordon of police set up to prevent them getting any closer. The result was arrest.

Mary, along with her fellow protestors, was taken to Cannon Row police station and charged with obstructing the police. Emmeline Pethick-Lawrence, who (along with her husband) was a staunch supporter of the WSPU and helped produce its magazine, bailed them out. They were released once the House of Commons had safely been discharged for the day. On 26 February Mary was in the Bow Street Police Court being told, 'It was greatly to be regretted that educated ladies should disgrace themselves in this way.' Mary was unmoved, and having refused to be bound over, she was sentenced to a month's imprisonment in Holloway.

This was all to the joy of the suffragette leaders. Ladies such as Emmeline Pankhurst realised the publicity value of imprisoning women for protesting: it caused debate, especially when the women were not confined in the first division (where political prisoners were normally kept and which allowed certain privileges—including the retaining of their own clothes) but were placed in the second or third division with the ordinary inmates. Various tales of the conditions endured by suffragettes—and, it should be remembered, by ordinary female prisoners—filtered into the press and caused criticism of the government over its heavy-handed treatment. Imprisonment won the suffragettes supporters, particularly when hunger strikes were met by force-feeding and the suffering of suffragette prisoners increased tenfold.

On her first visit, however, hunger strikes had not become WSPU policy and Mary was preoccupied with her meals and food allowance. She was still convinced that her sickly childhood had permanently weakened her and she regularly pleaded for special treatment. In this Mary was not a typical, self-sacrificing suffragette: she wanted the privileges both her social rank and her precarious health (or at least her perception of her health) allowed her. In contrast, when Lady Constance Lytton (also a WSPU member) went to prison, she went to great lengths to ensure she was not accorded special treatment. Her successes were limited until she disguised herself as a working-class woman. In her case she actually deserved special treatment due to a heart condition, though she refused to play on this. Shortly after her last imprisonment she suffered a stroke which paralysed her right arm; the strictures of the prison regime, coupled with Lytton's determination to take part in a hunger strike and endure the horrors of forced feeding, are very likely to have caused the stroke. Her heart condition was certainly worsened and Lytton would die relatively young, having never fully recovered from her prison ordeal.

Mary was arrested again in July 1909 for smashing a pane of glass in a door at the Home Office. She was sentenced to yet another month in prison, in the second division. Shortly before her arrest another suffragette, Marion Dunlop, had gone on hunger strike in protest of being held in the second division rather than the first. Suffragettes on hunger strike were initially released, and this spurred WSPU headquarters to instruct all imprisoned suffragettes to go on hunger strike; and so Mary began her first period of deliberate starvation.

She refused food and drink, and after two days she was beginning to feel desperate:

...they brought in a kettle of boiling water, a teapot, some creamy milk and some lump sugar. They made the tea; they held the steaming teapot under my nose. It almost drove me mad. My tongue was like leather with thirst, and the hot, fragrant smell, started the saliva running at the back of my throat. I shook my head and shut my eyes.

After two more days they brought mincemeat and chicken into my cell. Slices of white chicken's breast in savoury brown gravy were offered to me. They clattered teacups, poured milk with a bubbling sound, and tinkled bits of ice in a bowl.

I shut out the thought of the delicious dainties—the healing ice for my burning throat, the rich gravy which could end my terrible exhaustion.[1]

Mary was released after five days, claiming she had existed without food or water for the entire period—the latter is debatable as the human body cannot last for extended periods without fluids. The release was seen as another suffragette triumph; victorious hunger strikers were now issued with medals. But this game could not carry on indefinitely as there was a limit to how long the government would be held over a barrel. If suffragettes refused to eat they would be forced to, rather than be able to gain their release by such expedience. In reality there was little else the government could do; releasing a prisoner on hunger strike was giving in to their demands, whereas allowing them to continue the strike—possibly until death—would cause the government to be accused of neglect and cruelty. While the suffragettes believed this would push the government into always releasing striking prisoners, they failed to realise that there was another option—forced feeding.

Mary discovered the horrors of forced feeding on her third and final arrest. This time she had broken windows at the Inland Revenue offices in Bristol. On a cold November day she was sentenced to yet another month in prison. Mary started her hunger strike at once, but this was no longer a ploy that favoured the suffragettes. She was at once taken to the prison hospital, and after two days of refusing food and drink the prison doctors came to force feed her. It was a brutal ordeal:

...while six wardresses held me down, the prison doctors beat up an egg in one and a half pints of milk, and forced it into my stomach, through the nose in two minutes.

One and a half pints in two minutes! Of course I was violently sick, getting rid of all the nourishment which had been so brutally shovelled into me. I developed a shivering terror whenever I thought of my next forcible meal. But I would not give in.

Finally they made me so very ill that I had to be released, my digestion being permanently affected.[2]

Forced feeding involved a rubber tube being shoved down the throat of the victim, either via the mouth (if it could be opened) or via the nose. Just getting the tube into a person was a violent and painful procedure. A metal gag was used to try and force open the mouth, cutting flesh and gums, and if this succeeded the gag wedged the prisoner's mouth open for the entry of the tube. When prisoners proved too resilient for the gag and the mouth could not be opened, the tube had to be forced up a nostril and then down the throat into the stomach. The whole procedure would often require the assistance of several wardresses to hold down the struggling patient.

Doctors often inflicted undue suffering by forcing the tube deep into the stomach and overloading the organ with fluid; invariably the patient was sick as soon as the tube was removed, making the effort a complete waste from a nutritional standpoint—but was that the point? Yes, force feeding might have prevented starvation, but the haphazard nature of the operation and the careless, rough handling by doctors seemed to make it less about feeding the patient and more about torturing them into submission. As Mary soon discovered, the doctors' methods were often counterproductive; the prison still had to release their prisoners, who then gained support for the suffragettes by asking how a government could be so cruel in their treatment. Mrs Pankhurst naturally used her suffering, and the suffering of other suffragettes, to her advantage and equated force feeding to a form of rape, a term of reference designed to encourage righteous outrage in suffrage supporters.

Mary's health had suffered badly during the November she was imprisoned. She slowly recovered, but Mrs Pankhurst told her bluntly that she must not risk imprisonment again. Thus from now on Mary was behind the scenes as an organiser, and away from the active violence that was becoming more extreme each year. By 1912 the suffragettes had turned themselves from a political nuisance into a terrorist organisation; aside from window smashing, works of art were now vandalised and houses were set on fire. These new measures, a natural escalation of previous minor offences, did more harm to the cause than good. People started to turn away from supporting these women who sliced up paintings and set homes aflame. A backlash began and, in the run up to the First World War, much of the good work achieved by both suffragist and suffragette causes suffered greatly; there was a danger that the entire suffrage cause would be seriously undermined and set back.

It was almost a saving grace when war broke out. Suffragette violence was officially placed on hold as Emmeline Pankhurst declared her patriotic stance and her support for the government. With the WSPU taking a back seat for the time being, Mary found herself adrift and wondering what her purpose might be during the war. She wanted a role in uniform—uniform had been part of the suffragette cause in colours of purple, white, and green, with some of the higher ranking suffragettes adopting military-style attire for parades. Mary found uniform distinctly appealing, especially when it echoed the masculine uniform of the military. The only uniformed women's military organisation at the time was the FANY (First Aid Nursing Yeomanry), but this was work that did not appeal to Mary—she was not the nursing type.

While Mary was hunting around for an occupation that suited her, she learned that another suffragette, Nina Boyle, was trying to establish a voluntary women police force. Constance Antonina 'Nina' Boyle was born in 1865, making her almost fifty when war broke out. Daughter to a Royal Artillery captain (who died when she was four), she had two brothers who served in the Boer war. Nina was living in South Africa at the same time and did hospital work before becoming involved in women's rights, forming a Women's Enfranchisement League in Johannesburg.

Nina returned to England in 1911, bringing with her strong opinions on the empowerment of women in society. It was also around this time that a splinter group had formed from the WSPU, calling itself the Women's Freedom League. Founded by former WSPU member Teresa Billington-Grieg, the WFL ran itself as a democracy and attracted Nina to its ranks.

In 1913 Nina took part in a demonstration that echoed an earlier one made by Flora Drummond. Mounting a pleasure barge and sailing down the Thames, Nina paused before the terrace of the Houses of Parliament and interrupted afternoon tea with a speech. Four fellow passengers had unfurled a Women's Freedom League flag as Nina raised her voice and addressed startled ministers.

'You are quite ready to accept the help of women at election times,' she reminded the MPs, wobbling slightly as passing traffic caused the barge to bob in the swells, 'and yet, when elected, just as ready to refuse them their rights!'

She was referring to the recent efforts suffragette organisations had made to help their chosen party candidates succeed in the elections. They had done this in the belief that their chosen MPs would promote their cause but, inevitably—once securely in power—MPs who had been favourable to the suffrage cause quietly began ignoring it. Nina soundly criticised the ministers for their two-faced behaviour, remarking on how ridiculous they were. The members were impressed by her courage and spirit, and some greeted her words with cheers. The police on the balcony, however, were hissing for the women to leave—a pointless exercise since the ladies had no intention of going until they were forced.

The police launch was summoned and when it finally appeared (after much delay) the ministers gave it a mocking cheer; Nina's lookouts had spotted it first, and they were already on the move. Just before leaving, a young, bright-faced woman stood up beside Nina. She smiled to her large audience and thanked them for listening.

'Should it be thought necessary for your education on the subject the Women's Freedom League will return,' she told them, tossing a bundle of leaflets onto the terrace, before signalling for the captain to leave. This lady was Edith Watson, who was later to become a significant figure in the women's police movement. As the WFL's barge sped away, the police launch arrived— too late to intervene and not inclined to give chase. The newspapers would enjoy noting how the women had outwitted them. This was hardly conducive to the other cause that Nina Boyle and Edith Watson were pushing—the need for policewomen.

Edith had been attending court cases for the last year, and would continue to do so into 1914. Her notes on the cases she witnessed were compiled into a column, '*The Protected Sex*', for the WFL's official paper, *The Vote*. Edith had seen and heard an awful lot over the last few months and much of it had made her deeply aware of how badly women and children were treated by the law. No matter whether they were in court as the victim, the accused, or purely as a witness, the handling of women and children during the alleged process of justice was both shoddy and rough. Cases involving indecency were particularly hard on the victims, who often found themselves being accused of luring their abuser into his crime. No matter what the age of the victim, counsel implied that they were sexually experienced and had seduced the accused. The situation was made all the worse when the presiding judge or magistrate in an indecency case would come over exceptionally prudish, and dismiss all female spectators from the court. Even if the victim was a young child, their mother would be banished and they would have to face questioning alone.

Both Edith and Nina found the practice deplorable and even illegal. They protested to the Home Office who gave vague promises to do something about it, but in reality 'something' was very little. Edith did her best by refusing to leave court during a case, thus providing an ally for the women in the dock. She could not be everywhere at once, however.

These attempts to change the court system outraged many men, but in particular Mr Frederick Mead, a conservative and old-fashioned magistrate at Marlborough Street Police Court, who point-blank refused to have women sit in on 'filthy and disgusting cases'. He was also vehemently against the suffrage movement, believing judgements against suffragettes to be too lenient. During the trials of accused suffragettes, he would sometimes take on their cross-examination himself. In 1914 Mead was sixty-seven and badly behind the times (though he would continue to serve until he was eighty-two). He had been called to the bar in 1869 and served as a magistrate at the Marlborough Street Police Court from around 1889. In that time he had overseen a cosmopolitan catalogue of crimes and criminals 'of every type and every nationality'. Whether it was the years of serving a court in the West End of London, where many of the debauched, destitute, and morally degenerate appeared on a regular basis, or whether he was naturally cynical and harsh, even his supporters had to admit that Mead was often criticised for the severity

of his judgements. Mead was vehemently against the suffragettes and would do all in his power to undermine the movement. He would also prove a thorn in their side when it came to the issue of women police.

However, the campaigners would not be dissuaded. Edith had witnessed injustice first-hand. A woman arrested for soliciting was sentenced to nine months' hard labour, but there was no similar offence or punishment for a man doing the same. Male criminals often got off lightly, especially for crimes against women. A man found guilty of grievous bodily harm to a woman was sentenced to only three months in the second division—the division most suffragettes found themselves in. The absurdity of this made women cry out— it seemed the law was determined to punish women harshly and turn a blind eye to male offenders.

With the Home Office failing to take the women's complaints seriously, Nina and Edith opted for action. Though the WFL did not believe in violence, they did believe in protest, and Mead's courtroom became the focus for their campaign. In the summer of 1914, Nina Boyle became 'Ann Smith' and Edith Watson became 'Edyth Smythe'. Accompanied by three fellow WFL women (Lillian Smith, Annunziata Smith, and Louisa Smith—also obvious pseudonyms), the women placed themselves in the waiting room of Marlborough Street Police Court and then, using a chain attached to a ring on a leather belt around their waists, wove a barricade from the court door to themselves. Anyone trying to pass the women and reach the door was confronted by a network of chain, looped from one woman to the next. Naturally the women were arrested.

When 'Ann Smith' appeared in court she offended the magistrate (very probably Mead himself) by asking him to refrain from speaking into his waistcoat and raising his voice so everyone could hear. She then turned on the police sergeant and said, 'I know it is not fashionable in this court to tell the truth, but do try.'

Edyth Smythe was equally truculent and began cross-examining the police witnesses with great success on her part, and great embarrassment on theirs— it might not have led to an acquittal, but it made the police look distinctly foolish. Nina Boyle felt these attempts had been a huge triumph, labelling them 'Obstruction Protests', and she planned a series of campaigns based around them, all designed to disrupt court business for as long as possible. However, the outbreak of war scuppered everybody's plans.

4

Oh, What a Lovely War!

Seven days after Nina Boyle's triumph in court, Germany declared war on Russia. Two days later, on the August Bank Holiday Monday, they declared war on France. For a brief spell Britain existed in a glorious bubble of delusion, thinking this was not a war that could possibly concern them, and that it was something to do with foreign countries alone. The public awoke to the bitter reality the following day when the British Government announced the country was at war with Germany.

The strangeness of the moment, and the tragedy that followed, have created a golden haze over those last few days of the Edwardian era (which continued beyond the death of King Edward VII to the start of the First World War). Somehow that summer became set in stone as something magical, and the worries that had occupied so many minds prior to the war began to seem mundane, even petty. The various groups of suffragettes and suffragists responded to this new disaster with surprisingly alacrity and diplomacy. Almost at once many of them realised that to continue waging war against their own government would be detrimental to both themselves and society. Instead they offered a hiatus, and rallied around those ministers and officials once deemed the enemy, to help support patriotism and recruitment.

The start of the First World War changed everything. Even the Pankhursts could not justify militant action when Britain and her young men were in peril. As the first brave souls set off for Belgium, many never to return, the suffragettes found themselves calling a momentary ceasefire—but what were the women's associations to do with themselves during the war? Mrs Fawcett, head of the NUWSS, believed that all must be done to avert war, and called for pacifism and negotiation. This was naturally unrealistic in the face of an enemy intent on conflict. She quickly changed her tune, and by the second day of the war she was calling on all British women to do their duty and prove themselves worthy of British citizenship.

Christabel Pankhurst had an entirely different spin on the war: she saw it as a judgement upon men. 'A man-made civilisation, hideous and cruel enough in time of peace, is to be destroyed,' she wrote in *The Suffragette*. '...That which has made men for generations past sacrifice women and the race to their lusts, is now making them fly at each other's throats and bring ruin upon the world....' Men deserved this, Christabel added, for their subjugation of women.

Initially Emmeline made similar gloating comments ('War is not women's way!'), but her tone changed as the government offered a truce. Emmeline saw the way public opinion was turning—if she tried to continue battling or denigrating the country's leaders, the WSPU would face destruction. A ceasefire was agreed, suffragettes were released from prison, and Emmeline and Christabel began a new campaign promoting patriotism and support for the war. Soon suffragettes had exchanged stones for white feathers, which they handed to men not in uniform with the same boldness they had displayed when smashing windows.

The NUWSS took a temporary hiatus as well, and did not resume campaigning for female suffrage until 1916 when Edward Carson, among others, was pressing for a new voting register based on war service. Mrs Fawcett wanted women included on the register and pressed Asquith on the matter. Though it would be two years before a partial success of the suffrage campaign was achieved, the work women had done throughout the war had cast aside the last arguments against their equality with men. They had served in factories, made munitions, acted as police and porters at train stations, gone to France to act as nurses, driven lorries, worked on farms and taken on countless roles once reserved for men. They had done things previously thought impossible for women and had earned unexpected respect. The last barriers had been broken down and a partial vote for women was at last achievable.

There was one benefit from the outbreak of war no one realised at the time. The WSPU had become highly violent in their activities during 1912–14, with some of their members falling into the category of extremists. Their attacks on individuals, homes, and works of art had caused a backlash against women's suffrage. The war had come at just the right moment to prevent this deadly tide of criticism from completely destroying the movement; instead women could come to the fore and prove themselves in a way that would finally win them the vote.

In 1914, however, the main thought on everyone's mind was coming together and seeing the war over and done with by Christmas. The Home Secretary announced a remission of Suffragette prison sentences, effectively holding out an olive branch. Both the WSPU and the WFL reciprocated, the latter agreeing to abstain from militant action for the duration of the war and instead busying themselves with the formation of the Women's Suffrage National Aid Corps to give help to women and children.

By September 1914 Mr George Cave MP and Sir Edward Ward were working on behalf of the Home Secretary to form a division of special constables for the Metropolitan Police District. Nina wrote to Ward asking if he would consider able-bodied women for the role; in addition she suggested that women on other branches of the WFL offer themselves to the local constabulary as 'specials'. The first success of this scheme came at Sandgate, Kent, when two ladies, Miss Mumford and Mrs Burke, were enrolled as special constables. They were mainly responsible for keeping a look-out for suspicious persons or lights on the beach.

Nina also created the Women Volunteer Police, which she advertised in *The Vote*, calling for 'healthy, self-reliant and reliable, punctual and regular and not undersized' women. Nina was hopeful that with time the WVP would develop a uniform and become a recognised authority. She was also smart enough to realise the potential these women would have as pioneers for greater equality between the sexes. 'If we *now* equip every district in the country with a body of women able and willing to do this class of work, it will be very difficult for the authorities to refuse to employ women in such capacity after the war'—or at least she hoped it would be difficult. Sir Edward Ward saw things differently. He had instructions to raise a force of 20,000 able-bodied *men*, not men and women, and so he declined Nina's offer. Soon it would become impractical to deny women a role in policing, but at the start of the war there were still plenty of men available to fill the void. Undaunted, Nina continued recruiting for her own force.

The outbreak of war brought new concerns to WFL members and other women with the unopposed passing of the Defence of the Realm Act (DORA) in the House of Commons on 8 August 1914. Under DORA the government extended its social controls, including censorship, and gave itself powers to create new criminal offences. Though the Act seemed petty on occasion (for instance when banning the flying of kites or feeding wild animals bread) it was based on logic and a desire to keep morale up on the home front, as well as preventing invasion by the enemy. For instance, to stop important information leaking to the enemy, censorship of journalism limited what newspapers could say about troop movements or numbers. Anyone breaching the regulations to deliberately assist the enemy could face a death sentence and, in fact, ten people were executed under this clause of DORA. Other provisions of the Act were designed to keep people safe: flying kites, for instance, might attract the attention of zeppelins, while feeding wild animals when food was scarce was a waste of resources. But it was how the provisions of the Act might be used against women that worried individuals such as Nina Boyle.

The vague wording of DORA's provisions could be exploited in regards to prostitution. Nina and others were particularly concerned that the notorious Contagious Diseases Act might be reintroduced in garrison towns.

The Contagious Diseases Act had been a response to the growing problem of prostitution and resulting venereal diseases in the army. In 1824 an estimated two-thirds of the patients in a military hospital at Baroda, India, were suffering from some form of venereal disease. In 1828, 31 per cent of the army in Bengal was believed to be infected. Little was done to turn the tide and the incidents of VD began to rise. During the Crimean War (1854–56) the British found themselves with more soldiers in hospital than on the battlefield, and among the causes for this (of which there were several including poor sanitation in barracks) was a high incidence of VD. By 1864, one in three cases of illness in the army were a direct result of VD; in the navy the ratio was one in eleven. It was ridiculous that so many fit soldiers were being put out of action because of sex.

Armies had always been easy prey for prostitutes. Vast numbers of men without wives or lovers for comfort and with a great deal of free time on their hands (not to mention money, since they did not have to pay for things like food) provided fertile ground for ladies of the night. Not all of them began as prostitutes: some were respectable young women simply attracted to uniform. These naïve young girls would flock to an army camp to dance with the soldiers. Some would end up getting carried away and disgracing themselves. After this, many had no option but to continue down a life of prostitution as there was no returning home.

However they found themselves among the army camps, once there the girls found plenty of work and profit. The spread of venereal disease naturally followed within this close community of soldiers and harlots. Armies were decimated by the spread of debilitating illnesses, some of which, like syphilis, had no cure. Patients were treated with mercury, which was nearly as nasty as the disease and fatal in large enough quantities.

Syphilis has a remission phase during which a person can appear healthy. During this period a soldier might marry and this could easily result in the spread of the disease to an innocent wife. Many women were frightened by this scenario, especially as syphilis could then be transmitted to an unborn baby or cause miscarriages. Fear turned into resentment of the prostitutes who were indirectly infecting other women with this horrible disease.

Prostitution in Victorian Britain was widespread, particularly among the cities and near the garrison towns where soldiers congregated. Few took the time to consider the unfortunate soul who cast herself into such an unhappy occupation; in the worst slums girls as young as ten would turn to prostitution to earn a few pence for supper. Legal occupations were limited for women and often poorly paid. Respectability often came at the price of starvation; girls sometimes prostituted themselves for nothing more glamorous than a loaf of bread, a bottle of gin, or even so that they could sleep indoors for the night. The conditions for these women were appalling, not least because once caught in this spiral of decline, they were trapped until illness or old age carried them off.

Venereal disease was rife, and it was not long before a new prostitute contracted something. This was made worse by the urban legend that a young virgin was the best cure for syphilis. Unscrupulous men would pay a high price for such a girl, whether she was willing or not, expecting to be cured by sex with her. When they were not, they simply believed that the girl had lied about her virginity. Prostitutes lived out a pitiful existence, always on the verge of hunger, subject to all manner of abuse and in various stages of VD. Many turned to drink which exacerbated the problem, as now they worked to buy alcohol rather than food. They wasted away; at Aldershot prostitutes were reported to be living in the sand caves outside the military camp, insensible from drink and semi-naked. One expert on sexual diseases visited the Aldershot prostitutes and described them as being 'very dirty—in fact, filthy, covered with vermin, like idiots in their manner, very badly diseased; they almost burrowed in the ground like rabbits, digging holes for themselves in the sandbanks.'

The government decided something must be done to protect the fighting forces. The men escaped any legislation, but the prostitutes came under scrutiny; in a sparse House of Commons, the Contagious Diseases Act of 1864 was passed without debate. The Act related to certain garrison towns and gave the local police the power to arrest a prostitute and send her for internal examination. If she was found to be diseased she would be detained until 'cured'. If she refused to be examined she could be jailed and face a trial where she had to prove herself virtuous. The heavy-handed nature of the Act upset many women, as it opened any female in a garrison town to suspicion. In 1866 the Act was extended to include compulsory three-month examinations for suspected prostitutes, who could be accused on the word of one policeman alone. By 1869 all garrison towns were under the provision of the Act and a woman could be held for up to five days before examination without even a trial. The feeling of persecution among women was strong, as was the fear of being suspected and examined. Although, naturally enough, it was the lower classes who were most at risk, it also upset middle and upper class women that others of their sex could be accused of immorality and subjected to humiliation on the word of one policeman.

The examination itself caused a great deal of consternation. Part of it was conducted using a vaginal speculum, a hollow cylinder with a rounded end that was hinged and split into two parts. Once inserted into the body it would be opened to widen the vaginal canal and enable a doctor to see inside. The procedure was undignified, and for a virgin extremely painful. Even doctors argued the speculum was an unnecessary tool for examination: professor of midwifery Robert Lee had been agitating against use of the speculum since 1850, stating the horrific case of one woman suffering from paraplegic symptoms who was also a virgin. Her doctor believed inflammation of the uterus was the cause and insisted on using a speculum. The poor woman's screams under examination echoed through the house.

No wonder some called the use of the device akin to medical rape. With deep Victorian taboos about modesty and the sensitivity of female parts, the use of such of a device did not sit well with many. Some even blamed its frequent use among the poor for the increasing immorality in the land.

Not all women protested against the Act—some saw it as the only way to reduce VD, completely ignoring the flagrant misuse of the law and the repercussions it might have had on innocent women. However, in 1869 everyone was getting jumpy when the government discussed extending the Act to cover the entire country. Petitions were signed, debates held, and more agitation than ever was organised to prevent this further harassment of women. Despite such vehement disapproval, the Act was not repealed until 1880, though it never entirely proved a successful means to reduce VD.

The Tragic Case of Mrs Percy

The case of Mrs Percy illustrates why so many women opposed the Contagious Diseases Act, and why its threatened reintroduction undermined much of what women had worked for over the last fifty years. Mrs Percy was a singer and actress, and in Victorian Britain this was a profession that teetered on the brink of respectability. On the one hand celebrity performers such as Jenny Lind were the starlets of the age, featured in high-class magazines and treated with a degree of respect. On the other, there were numerous women in the lower echelons of the world of theatre who struck out a career through performing either on stage or in bed. Prostitution and acting had always gone hand-in-hand: an actress might be adored from afar by kings and lords, but she was not fit to be in their intimate company, and certainly not fit for marriage (certain notable cases excepted).

Exactly where Mrs Percy fit in this descending scale of respectability is debatable. Up until 1875 it seems she had etched out a reasonable career on the stage. Her husband was a playwright, mainly working on pantomimes in which his wife always performed. They had three children: a daughter and two sons. The daughter, Jenny, having turned sixteen, became an actress and singer in her own right and, according to Mrs Percy, had never been out of work. This was vital for the family as Mr Percy had died from consumption in 1874, throwing them into desperate times. After the death of her husband, Mrs Percy's mental state appears to have deteriorated. Financially strained, she took a job performing at Aldershot in the Red, White and Blue Music Hall. The name sounds grand, but the papers state it was part of the Alliance Inn, so it was probably a rather humble setting. Mrs Percy performed there with her daughter, but in her spare time she was noted to participate in amateur performances at the nearby army camp. To some this suggested immoral conduct.

At some point the police began to take an interest in Mrs Percy and her daughter. Under the Contagious Diseases Act they were required to keep track of women who might be acting as prostitutes, and so they watched Mrs Percy over the course of several weeks, noting her visits to the camp.

Around 11 March 1875 Mrs Percy received an unexpected visit from Inspector Godfrey of the police. He informed her that due to her and Jenny being seen with several different soldiers, and her allowing two soldiers to stay in her lodgings until midnight, the police required her to visit Lock Hospital under the Contagious Diseases Act. The implication couldn't be plainer. Mrs Percy and her daughter were suspected of being prostitutes and were required to submit to an examination. Mrs Percy was naturally horrified; whether or not she had been acting as a prostitute, a visit to the hospital for such a purpose would ruin her reputation. She would have to consent to adding her name to a list of suspected women of the night and so would her daughter Jenny. If knowledge of this got out, neither she nor Jenny would be able to find reputable work in Aldershot. Prostitution might have been an occasional side-line for an actress, but it had to be discreet, or else the theatre owners would ban them from their stages.

This was not to mention the horrors of the examination itself. For a private Victorian woman to be examined with intrusive instruments by a male stranger, and often before gawping witnesses, was a sickening thought. In some instances examinations were performed in a room with a street window, where passers-by could gather to watch. For Jenny, if she was a virgin, the experience would have been particularly painful. The doctor would probe deeply enough to break the hymen, effectively 'ruining' an innocent girl.

Mrs Percy simply could not face such an ordeal. She grabbed up Jenny, reneged on her engagement at the Red, White and Blue (where she had been performing for twelve years) and fled to Old Windsor where she had relatives. As she cancelled her engagement at the Red, White and Blue she learned from the theatre proprietor that he had also had a visit from the police, to inform him that if he continued to employ Mrs Percy his license would be in jeopardy. This was another blow to Mrs Percy: before she had even been examined she was deemed guilty and her work, let alone her reputation, was jeopardised.

Safety was to be found at Old Windsor, but not employment. Around this time Mrs Percy had fallen in with a gentleman by the name of Mr Ritson, whose own character did not aid her respectability. Mr Ritson was an actor, estranged from his wife who he claimed had committed bigamy. He wanted to marry Mrs Percy, but could not because of his previous vows, so he occasionally stayed with her, masquerading as her husband. Ritson, on learning what had happened to his lover, composed a letter pretending to be Mrs Percy and sent it to the local press complaining about the behaviour of the police. Though no name was mentioned, there were enough clues in the letter for Aldershot residents to identify the writer as Mrs Percy. Ritson, instead of assisting, had made the matter worse: now everyone knew that Mrs Percy had been confronted under the law of the Contagious Diseases Act.

Poor Mrs Percy felt more desperate than ever: she had little money and there were no opportunities for her in Old Windsor. Mr Ritson finally persuaded her to return to Aldershot alone and resume her acting and singing. Mrs Percy was soon employed at a music hall run by a Mr Childs and attached to the Queen's Tap. Before long the police knew she was back and paid a call to Mr Childs, informing him that he should release her from his employ if he wanted to keep his license. They mentioned she had failed to appear under a summons for the Contagious Diseases Act. Mr Childs wanted no trouble, nor an alleged prostitute on his stage. He dismissed Mrs Percy.

The unfortunate woman's mental state quickly declined. She had very little money now she was unemployed and no means of making more—suggesting the police were wrong about her side-line activities. Depression and cheap drink started to take their toll.

The following Saturday Mrs Percy went to the Artillery Arms with a friend and had a cup of tea and bread and butter. As she handed over three-pence to the proprietor's wife, Mrs Styars, she asked, 'Have you heard the scandal about me?'

Mrs Styars admitted she had.

'I'm innocent of all the charges. I'd rather drown than go to that hospital.'

Mrs Styars tried to laugh off the comment and cheer her up—they had been friends for several years.

'That threepence is all I have in the world,' added Mrs Percy.

'Then take it back.'

Mrs Percy shook her head and bade her farewell. As she headed for the door she said, quite clearly, 'I will never live to go into the hospital.'

A short time later Mrs Percy, now alone, stumbled upon an old friend Mr Solly Lewis and his wife. She had played in pantomime with Solly at the Crystal Palace. It was plain to Solly that Mrs Percy had been drinking. She made a point of telling him and his wife that she would do all in her power to clear her good name. Solly bade her goodnight and thought no more of it.

By eleven o'clock Mrs Percy was very drunk. She had been with Ritson, but when she wanted to go home to her lodgings it was a soldier who said he would escort her. It was plain Mrs Percy could not make the trip alone, but it seems her lover, despite lodging with her, had no inclination to see her safely indoors. Ritson let the soldier escort her, later stating that he did go after her to see she was alright but never found her.

Mrs Percy walked a short way with the soldier. She stumbled once and fell to the ground, grazing her cheek. The soldier and a passer-by helped her to her feet. The soldier intended to see her home but he met an acquaintance and Mrs Percy insisted on going on alone. After parting from the soldier Mrs Percy was not seen again until 10.15 Sunday morning, when an army driver saw her walking along the towpath quite alone. No one could say what she had been doing for almost twelve hours, and Mr Ritson was adamant she had never returned to their lodgings.

At one o'clock two lads were rowing on the river when someone shouted from the bank they could see a black skirt just beneath the water. The boys, in the confusion of the moment, clipped something with an oar just beneath the surface of the river. A body floated up: it was Mrs Percy. She had drowned a mere 100 yards from where the army driver had last seen her. There was no sign of violence and she had not been in the water long. At her inquest Mr Ritson repeated to the court over and over that it was the heavy-handedness of the police, and the fear of being examined under the Contagious Diseases Act, that had caused Mrs Percy to cast herself into the water. There was no evidence to suggest it was anything other than suicide. He also accused the police of depriving her of legitimate work. He then lowered himself in the jury's opinion by admitting that after Mrs Percy's death he had found himself without a roof over his head, so had spent a night or so with a prostitute.

Ritson was a loathsome character, but Mrs Percy earned the jury's sympathy. Even the coroner admitted he disliked the new Act. Mrs Percy's tragic demise seemed to sum up its failings: she had been persecuted until her back was against a wall, facing ruin one way or another, until ultimately she saw only one way out. The case of Mrs Percy struck a chord with every suffragette and made it all the more plain why the Contagious Diseases Act had to be abolished. Fifty years on, talk of reintroducing it was anathema to many women, but not all. Some actively supported the Act and even promised to enforce it if asked.

Nina believed that the only way to curb such excessive uses of the Act (as typified by the case of Mrs Percy), and to help women in general during the war, was to have voluntary women police patrolling certain areas. This was far from a new idea, as others had been suggesting the possibility for months, if not years. Many women (and men) felt that the police failed in their duty by not employing women who could deal with vulnerable individuals of their own sex. Nina approached Sir Edward Ward, Commissioner of Special Constabulary, with the idea of recruiting female special constables in the Metropolitan area. She was turned down.

5

Enter Margaret Damer Dawson

While Nina was clashing with Sir Edward Ward, another woman was musing on the need for women police. Margaret Damer Dawson was living in Chelsea in August 1914 when she first became aware of the push for female police. Unlike many of her contemporaries in the policewoman campaign, Margaret had avoided the suffrage movement because in many ways it simply did not concern or affect her. She was a big-hearted person who worried over the less fortunate and preferred to act directly to help others rather than to dabble in politics. However, politics was rapidly catching up with Margaret. For a long time she had been concerned about the rumours of a white slave trade operating out of Britain. Her concerns grew after she joined a committee formed by local people, which had the sole ambition of helping refugees from Belgium who were spilling over the Channel to escape the Germans. Margaret had been appointed Head of Transport for the committee and regularly attended London train stations to greet the latest batch of refugees. While she stood waiting for her refugees it occurred to her that this group of people was extremely vulnerable to exploitation by white slavers.

One particular evening at a London train station, she noted a woman loitering nearby who seemed vaguely familiar. As with all such passing fancies she quickly forgot about it, until her group had arrived and she was organising them into a party so they might head to waiting cars. It was then she saw the woman talking to two female refugees, and the penny dropped—she had spotted the woman around the station at least twice earlier that afternoon, but each time in different clothes and with a different hair colour. She also recalled that on a previous occasion she had mysteriously lost two of her party. Margaret suddenly became certain the stranger was working for white slavers and was luring away Belgian women from under her very nose. There and then she realised the only way to assuage such danger was to have a body of uniformed, trained women guarding the refugees. For a number of years organisations such as the Criminal Law Amendment Committee (CLAC) and the National Vigilance Association (NVA), both of which Margaret was connected to, had been campaigning for women police who could fight against the white slave trade.

The white slave trade had troubled the suffragettes too. Many women (and men) believed there was organised trafficking of white women into prostitution abroad. Some of this was led by scandals in the Victorian period concerning young girls being sold to Dutch brothel owners. Though the stories sparked wholesale panic about the foreigners infringing on British virtue and purity, and no doubt the trade was despicable and had to be stopped, the actual extent of the trafficking was limited.

That did not stop groups such as the NVA pressing for legislation against white slavery, with a particular emphasis on the 'nasty foreigner' who was clearly responsible for converting British women to immorality. Jews came in for a backlash that in some regards could be compared (though in a much milder form) to the early years of their persecution in Nazi Germany. All brothel owners were Jews, or so the xenophobic paranoia went, and prostitutes (unless forced into the trade) were also Jews. In the minds of the puritans, no real British woman would demean herself in such a way.

Such utter nonsense was strangely attractive to many Brits and led to the 1905 Aliens Act, which was passed far more easily, under pressure from social purity and eugenics campaigners, than anything for female suffrage. The idea was to prevent Jewish prostitutes coming to Britain, as if that was going to deal in any degree with the home-grown problem. The NVA wanted to go further and have foreign Jews repatriated to their home countries, despite many having recently fled from the Tsarist pogroms in Russia.

It was these same campaigners who were most concerned about the supposed trafficking in white women. The general idea was that unfortunate, misguided girls would be lured away by shifty foreigners into a life of debauchery. If luring failed there was always kidnap, and to be fair to the campaigners there had been such cases, usually involving children or teenagers. Just two years before the war the government, under pressure from feminists, social purists, and Liberal ministers, passed a new Criminal Law Act called the White Slave Act, which further tightened laws concerning prostitution. The Act was something of a sop to the puritans fearful for British female virginity. The Metropolitan Police, who had a White Slave Traffic Branch, were less impressed. Evidence for such trafficking was very limited and the police complained that the tales of such crimes had 'been aroused by a number of alarming statements made by religious, social, and other workers, who spread the belief that there was a highly organised gang of 'White Slave Traffickers' with agents in every part of the civilised world, kidnapping and otherwise carrying off women and girls from their homes to lead them to their ruin in foreign lands.'

The police may have been nonchalant, but when women started to patrol London's streets white slavery was very much prevalent in their minds. Damer Dawson was convinced women were being snatched away in their hundreds and told her ladies to be on the look-out for suspicious characters.

However, not all women believed in the white slave trade as staunchly as Mary and Margaret. Teresa Billington-Grieg wrote in 1913:

> ...almost entirely by the statement that unwilling, innocent girls were forcibly trapped; that by drugs, by false messages, by feigned sickness, by offers of or requests for help and assistance, girls were spirited away and never heard of again; that these missing girls, often quite young children, were carried off to flats and houses of ill-fame, there outraged and beaten, and finally transported abroad to foreign brothels under the control of large vice syndicates ... these dabblers in debauchery by word of mouth have given us a shocking exhibition of unlicensed slander. That this exhibition had been possible is due in no small measure to the Pankhurst domination. It prepared the soil; it unbalanced judgement; it set women on the rampage against evils they knew nothing of, for remedies they knew nothing about.[1]

Some of Billington-Grieg's words were said in spite, but it was true that a furore had been built up on the basis of very little evidence. There *had* been cases of girls being sold to foreign brothels by parents, but building these sad stories into an entire international criminal trade was rather far-fetched. Teresa attempted to investigate the trade and swiftly found herself confronted with very few facts; all the stories she heard were second or even third-hand, and eyewitness reports were not forthcoming. Teresa had to conclude there was no real trade as such, only opportunists who would whisk away a girl if the chance presented itself. To imply that any unmarried girl was in daily risk of kidnap and abduction by such men was stretching the limits of plausibility, though the fear of white slavery continued to be prevalent in the public mind, fuelled by scare stories in the press.

It was at this time that Nina Boyle heard that Margaret Damer Dawson, a friend of Sir Edward Henry, Commissioner of the Metropolitan Police, was setting up her own police organisation: the Women Police Volunteers (WPV). Nina decided to join forces with Margaret to avoid overlapping their organisations, while at the same time Mary Allen was growing interested in the WPV. What Nina could not know at the time was how willing Margaret Damer Dawson was to observe and even enforce the provisions of DORA.

Margaret Damer Dawson is one of the forgotten names of the campaign for policewomen, and has somewhat slipped out of history. Born in Sussex in 1873, she was the daughter of a surgeon, Richard Dawson, who had married Agnes Baird Hemming. After her father's death her mother married Thomas de Grey, sixth Baron Walsingham, and became Lady Agnes Walsingham. Margaret's early life is obscure, but it is known she had a passion for music and studied under Benno Schoenberger and Herbert Sharpe, winning a gold medal and diploma from the London Academy of Music. Another of her early passions was for animal rights and Margaret joined the campaigns for anti-vivisection. In 1911 she was living with two women who were prominent campaigners for animal welfare: Countess Emilie Augusta Louise Lind and Leisa Schartau, both formerly of Sweden. They were involved in the 'Brown Dog Affair' of 1903, which lasted seven years and caused a national scandal, exposing the use of live, non-anaesthetised dogs in experiments which involved cutting open the animal.

Margaret travelled abroad to promote the better treatment of animals, visiting slaughter houses with her camera to capture shocking cruelty. She later said that she was only able to maintain her composure by digging the heel of one foot into the instep of the other, until her boot filled with blood. Her work was well-recognised and she was awarded medals from both the King of Denmark and the Finnish Society for the Protection of Animals.

Unfortunately for Nina, there was a dark side to Margaret Damer Dawson, and also to her new friend Mary Allen. Margaret had always moved in high-ranking circles and had been brought up to recognise a difference between her own class and the working classes, and particularly those in the poorest sections of society. Like so many of her age and social origins she believed working class women who fell into prostitution had done so out of their own folly. She did not consider that for many of them there was little other choice. She laid the blame for prostitution and the resulting diseases firmly at the door of the women involved in the trade, while men escaped her wrath as she considered them unable to control their base desires. It was the poor women who must be controlled and monitored, for it was they who were ruining the menfolk of the country.

Such views would have appalled women like Nina (and later, when she learned of Margaret's opinions, she broke from the WPV), but they were common enough at the time. After all, Margaret was a member of the National Vigilance Association (NVA) which had promoted the deportation of foreign Jews. She was also a member of the Criminal Law Amendment Committee (CLAC) and was concerned with 'social purity'. She and Mary shared the opinion (not uncommon among suffragettes) that they had a duty to protect women from their own foolishness and the base desires of men, if they were ever to achieve full suffrage and female emancipation.

The Edwardian police force, little reformed from its Victorian days, left much to be desired when it came to cases involving rape and violation, particularly against children. The lack of justice for these crimes had led suffragettes to argue that there was a great need for female police, and male minds were also being persuaded of the advantages of women on the force. War merely pushed the argument forward faster. Margaret argued that what was needed were solid, respectable women to patrol public parks, open spaces, and areas near garrisons and army camps, to discourage immoral behaviour. In many instances they would be intercepting girls just starting out on a life of vice and directing them to safe places where they might gain legal employment. In other instances they were simply watching out for the old guard of prostitutes and moving them on before they could cause too much trouble. They would also inspect female lodging houses.

Despite Margaret's connections, there was no certainty that the WPV would be officially accepted. It was not as well received among MPs as some of the other organisations being set up independently, partly because Margaret's views were so repressive towards the working class woman and so concerned with social purity, that they troubled more liberal-minded men. Equally, support from her most important ally was hardly guaranteed. Just a couple of months before Margaret approached Sir Edward Henry about the possibility of her women recruits being able to train and patrol in London—purely on a voluntary basis, of course—he had declared he did not believe in the idea of women police, 'especially in view of the strained relationships between the sexes, or some portion of the sexes, in connection with the agitation over the suffrage question.' This was naturally understandable considering the antagonism that had existed between the suffragettes and the police over the last decade. On more than one occasion the police had been made to look like fools in public, not least by Nina Boyle. Sir Henry found her presence on the WPV committee unwelcome, and this may partly explain why there was discrepancy in the roles of Nina and Margaret, as it would look better to men such as Sir Henry for Margaret to be chief, even if Nina was technically in the role. Fortunately Margaret could ease Sir Henry's worries, and it helped enormously that she was not requesting that the women would become an official part of the Metropolitan Police. However, he still distrusted Nina, who he deemed 'an intransigent and in opposition to constituted authority'.

Permission for the WPV to begin recruitment and patrols was finally given, but beyond that very little help was offered to the women except the titles of a few textbooks and the name of an ex-sergeant who could teach them about police procedures (including the giving of evidence and basic self-defence in the form of ju-jitsu). The ladies were very much on their own.

The very first WPV policewoman to appear in uniform in public may have been Edith Watson, who had stood not so many months before on a barge in the River Thames to hail ministers. Like so many of the suffragette women, aside from her political activities, Edith's life story has almost vanished. She refused to take part in the 1911 census as part of the mass protest by suffragettes to boycott what they deemed to be information gathering by an illiberal government. Therefore Edith is difficult to trace in a personal sense: she is a shadow in history, like so many women of her period, yet she was playing a significant role in the cause of suffrage and women's rights. When she donned WPV uniform in September 1914, it was to convey authority in her role as an observer of court proceedings. Nina Boyle was keen that her new recruits spend a lot of time at court, observing the way the legal system functioned and, of course, casting a watchful and rebuking eye over certain magistrates. When Edith strolled outside the Old Bailey in full uniform, this ordinary cockney lass naturally attracted attention and was photographed by the press. Needless to say, this was delightful for the WPV.

Meanwhile, the NUWW set up voluntary female patrols to work near military camps, concentrating on welfare. In fact the NUWW's work proved so appealing to those in charge, they were approached by Scotland Yard in 1914 to create the Women Voluntary Patrols (WVP), which would operate in the Metropolitan Police area and watch out for the many girls and women arriving daily in the capital, attracted by the numerous soldiers stationed all around.

Rivalry between the two organisations was heightened by the similarity of their names, which caused confusion not only among the public but also within the press—work done by the WVP would be erroneously attributed to the WPV and vice versa. When the WVP was formalised, Mrs Sofia Stanley was appointed to supervise thirty-seven special patrols in London, which rapidly grew to fifty-five. Their relationship with the Metropolitan Police was complicated: on the one hand, they were given a subsidy from the police authorities and described as auxiliaries to the traditional force, but on the other they were not 'formally' connected to the police and did not have powers of arrest. The *Times* described them as 'neither police nor rescue workers, but true friends of the girls, in the deepest and holiest sense of the word.' However, the women themselves felt that the subsidies and support from the police gave them official approval, especially over their rivals at the WPV.

Another bone of contention between the two sets of women were their differing attitudes towards the future of female police. The NUWW, in forming its voluntary force of policewomen, was clear that it expected them to operate only during the war. They made no demands on male politicians for maintaining a female police force after the conflict was concluded. This was anathema to Margaret Damer Dawson. In her mind, war was merely a stepping stone to the full establishment of women police.

Mary Allen gave a description of Margaret in her book *Lady in Blue*, an account of the first policewomen:

> She had remarkably diverse and contradictory gifts, was keenly interested in sport as well as in all the arts, an experienced Alpine climber, an expert motorist, an enthusiastic gardener, a passionate lover of animals.[2]

In *The Pioneer Policewoman* she gave further indications of Margaret's temperament: 'Danger steeled her; she was encouraged, even inspired by difficulties.'

On Mary's first meeting with Margaret she was struck by her spirit and vitality. A century later, the exact nature of the ladies' relationship is difficult to ascertain. The two women were soon living together and within months Margaret had altered her will to leave Mary her entire estate. It is very likely they were lovers, though not necessarily in a physical sense, but certainly spiritually, as Mary was drawn to Margaret. They shared the same opinions, the same goals, and now the same fledgling police force. They would remain together until Margaret's untimely death in 1920, when Mary would learn that the Damer Dawson family were not comfortable with her close relationship with Margaret.

But that was five years off, and in the meantime the WPV was just beginning to flourish. Several former suffragettes had joined the cause, including Mary's sister Dolly, now married and called Mrs Hampton. The women who rallied to Margaret's cause were all older (Mary was the youngest at thirty-six), with a stocky or strong physique. Margaret would have it no other way; her 'constables' had to be able to look after themselves and present an intimidating appearance to criminal elements—small, delicate ladies were not made of the 'right stuff'. They also all had to be of independent means. This had been the bane of the suffragette movement as well, meaning most of its active participants were ladies of a certain class with a disposable income. Working class women who often had to earn a living, along with looking after a household, simply did not have the time to aid the suffragette cause—albeit with odd, notable exceptions who were supported by the movement. There was practically no other option; social divides extended to the suffragettes, and certain members retained their class-based attitude of 'us' and 'them'. This would have its impact on the way in which the women police dealt with lower class female problems, and in the way DORA went unchallenged in some quarters.

6

Women in Blue

By no means had the war suddenly created the idea of female police. Campaigners had been agitating over the matter for some time, but the very first police woman (though this is always a debatable term dependent on context and definition) was appointed in Liverpool on 3 April 1914. She was Mrs Hughes, a 'police inspector' appointed by a commission to protect the interests of children in the city. *Votes for Women* (the famous WSPU suffrage magazine) proclaimed her 'the first English policewoman', yet it also stated 'although policewomen have not yet been appointed in this country, the movement in their favour goes ahead.' So what exactly was Mrs Hughes? *Votes for Women* suggested she would be getting a salary for her work, and they hoped it would be equivalent to a man's (unlikely), but it seems Mrs Hughes was not official. She was attached to the Liverpool force in, presumably, a supervisory role, giving advice on children's matters and possibly being available as support for child victims or criminals. She was not technically a police inspector, because the government did not recognise her as one. But it is important to recognise that women like Mrs Hughes were breaking down barriers, they were sneaking in by the back door. When they were already doing the job of policewomen unofficially, it was hoped that it was only a small step to have them properly recognised.

The woman commonly recognised as the first *official* policewoman, accepted almost on a level with men, came a little later.

The WPV, having failed to gain the recognition of the WVP, soldiered on nonetheless with Nina Boyle at the reins. Mary Allen later suggested that Margaret Damer Dawson was in charge during this period, when the organisation was rebuffed by Sir Edward Henry—'You will get yourselves knocked on the head, and you surely don't expect me to look after a lot of women'—though in fact, she took charge slightly later. But from Mary's perspective the omission was necessary to ensure that the future would recognise Margaret as the true founder of the WPV, and not that turncoat Nina Boyle!

In 1915 *Votes for Women* reported that Nina Boyle was chief of the fledgling WPV, but it was not to last. Nina was at odds with Margaret and the vast majority of her volunteer policewomen, who had formed the opinion they should be policing morals as much as policing criminal behaviour. Nina detested this idea, saying it was just the sort of tyrannical behaviour they were aiming to stop. Constant arguments with Margaret over her views on policing divided the chief and her deputy. Margaret was happy to follow any remit, no matter how repressive, that the male chief constables ordered. Nina was not. Finally, in desperation, Nina demanded that Margaret resign her position. Feathers ruffled, Margaret immediately summoned a meeting of all the WPV and put the case to a vote: out of fifty policewomen present only two took Nina's side; the chief was ousted. Margaret took control and changed the name of the organisation to the Women's Police Service. Despite the name change and a reshuffling of its infrastructure, the WPS was still struggling alongside the more popular WVP.

On the surface their intentions were very similar. Both organisations were determined to watch over and protect vulnerable women and children, the portion of society that for many years the suffragettes had felt were badly let down by men. Margaret made her own concerns very plain:

> ...there was no place more dangerous for the British child than the public park, and it was not safe to allow a small girl to stray more than a few yards alone, for these places were haunted by men with criminal tendencies.[1]

Margaret was influenced by her belief in the white slave trade, but there was also no denying that children were molested and abused, and the perpetrators rarely brought to justice. Mary Allen, on the other hand, was concerned over the effect the 'indiscriminate enlistment' of men into the army was having on home life. The one thing that all the fledgling policewomen agreed on was that the existing police force was struggling and needed assistance.

They were not alone; the *British Journal of Nursing* informed its readers that they, or at least the editor, fully supported the formation of women police forces. The journal argued that nurses in particular would make excellent policewomen. It was only to be expected that this enthusiasm was double-edged, and before long the women were criticising them not so much for being underpowered but for lacking in moral fibre. There was talk of the brute force used by men, echoed eagerly by former suffragettes who had experienced it first-hand. It was remarked how difficult it was for a woman to approach a male officer when seeking advice on a delicate matter, particularly as—in the words of the journal's editor—some police officers had 'misled girls into bad houses'. He went on to say, 'The woman police officer in uniform will be a light-house preventing in some cases the wrecking of a life.' Male police were characterised as cynical monsters, unopposed to corruption. It is difficult to establish the extent of their corruption; while it was certainly present, it was probably less common than the advocates of female police made out. Regardless, the police force had a poor reputation at this time. People felt that justice depended on your rank in life rather than your crime. Having female police would not change the justice system swiftly, however much their supporters suggested it would.

Women might have been supported verbally, but financially they had to maintain themselves as best they could. A suitable headquarters had to be rented, where recruits could be trained in first aid, ju-jitsu for self-defence, and police court procedures. Volunteers also had to buy their own uniforms. The WPS began with a budget of £5, which was wholly inadequate for their needs, and Margaret was always trying to raise more money by giving talks to potential supporters. In 1916 the government relented slightly and gave them a small grant, although even this was inadequate to cover their costs. Financial shortages prevented the recruitment of women without independent means until the last year of the war, when an anonymous donor came forward and gave the WPS substantial sums. The donor—a woman of wealth—had lost two sons in the war, and wished to donate to the WPS the money which would have been their share of her considerable estate. Naturally the WPS accepted the money without hesitation.

The identity of this anonymous donor was not revealed until a decade later, at the time of her death. She was Anne Maria Trouton, wife of a surgeon, who had first met Margaret in 1916. She was passionate about the work of the WPS, and when she lost her two sons in the war (Eric in 1915 and Desmond in 1917) it helped to ease her grief to donate money, on their behalf, to the cause in which she ardently believed. However, Mrs Trouton had two other sons who were unimpressed that their mother had given away a large chunk of their inheritance. There was little they could do at the time, but when Mrs Trouton died in 1929 and left her entire estate (consisting of £55,000) to the WPS in a will she had made in 1920, her surviving sons could not let the matter go unchallenged. They contested the will, producing an earlier version from 1909 that divided Mrs Trouton's money between her two living sons and three daughters. One son, Rupert, insisted his mother was not of sound mind when she made the later will and produced a doctor who had examined her in 1921 and considered her unfit to make a will. A second doctor who had examined her appears not to have given evidence, perhaps because he would have contradicted the first. The case rested on the mental condition of Mrs Trouton after the loss of two sons. In her grief, she was said to have given away large sums of money she simply didn't have. The WPS, headed by Mary Allen, could do little on their part to challenge the case, and the judge ruled in favour of upholding the 1909 will. Mary Allen bowed out graciously, but it was a hard blow for the volunteers to weather.

The WPV/WPS was run along military lines, and thus Margaret and Mary agreed it required a uniform to make them identifiable in the street. A design was submitted to Sir Edward Henry for approval and was accepted. The ladies adopted a practical outfit of skirt and tunic-style jacket, sewn with many pockets, and a sturdy felt hat based on a riding hat ('We thought it would stand the weather and might stand a fairly sharp knock on the head if necessary,' wrote Margaret Damer Dawson). Black boots completed the outfit and were visible beneath the skirt, which defied Edwardian standards by stopping well above the ankle. On occasion both Mary and Margaret adopted trousers beneath their military-style great coats and at a casual glance could easily have been mistaken for men. The cloth was dark blue and 'business-like', as Mary described it, and WPV (later WPS) was spelled out in silver letters on the shoulder straps. Members of the WPV were convinced the uniform had a deterrent effect on the would-be offender and garnered respect for the women. They did indeed prove popular, not least for identifying the women police, and soon other voluntary patrols were adopting the outfit.

By 1917 new sophistications were added to the basic uniform, and senior officers wore flat caps with silver braid rather than the bowl-shaped hats of ordinary volunteers. The addition of motorcycles to the force provided Margaret and Mary the excuse they needed to wear trousers. For those who were concerned that acting as a police officer was an unfeminine activity, these new dress codes only seemed to prove it. There was no denying Margaret, Mary, and many of their fellow officers went out of their way to appear masculine, and this troubled the sensibilities of conservative souls. Bessie Spencer, a New Zealander in London looking for war work in 1916, described Mary Allen as 'aggressively uniformed'. Wearing a uniform was also a form of freedom for the women; before the fashion revolution of the 1920s, the only way a woman could wear masculine clothes legitimately and without risk of reprimand was to be in a uniformed service such as the WPV. Many women were attracted by this.

Mary Allen took her new dress a step further, with Bessie Spencer again offering a description: '[She wore a] peaked hat, navy-blue breeches, knee-high shiny black boots and a monocle.' The monocle had become something of a code among women for lesbianism, and Mary's later appearance—akin to such openly gay women as Radclyffe Hall—certainly suggests her sexual inclinations ran in that direction. Her cross-dressing grew more extreme with age, but its origins lay with the opportunity to wear a uniform with the WPS.

Once a female police division (albeit voluntary) had been established, the only question that remained was exactly how, and more significantly, upon whom, they would operate. There was no question of women interfering with the male domain of policing, or of them actually confronting male offenders. Women had been supported in those new roles so that they might deal with other women, and that was to be the extent of their influence. In fact it was expected that women police would deal exclusively with prostitutes. A writer to *The Times* in August 1914 explained the problem clearly:

Everyone is aware that large bodies of troops, Territorials and others, are now quartered in unaccustomed places up and down the country. Their distribution is not recorded in the press, but it is perfectly well known to those among whom they are living; and many, like myself, must be aware of the dangers inherent in their sudden change of life. Little or no provision has been made for their entertainment when their military duties are over. Very often the usual places of healthy amusement, such as the public halls, have been commandeered for military purposes. The result is that the men are literally thrown upon the streets for their recreation—in other words they are exposed to all the temptations of the prostitute and the public house.[2]

It is interesting to note how little concern the letter writer has for the prostitutes themselves, many of whom had been 'literally thrown upon the streets' by the greater evils of poverty and desperation, rather than just mere boredom. But the soldiers were heroes (and male) and could not be criticised for their lack of will in resisting the charms of women. During the Victorian and Edwardian period there was a belief among many, including from within the suffrage movement, that men were intrinsically less able to control themselves than women. This was offered as one explanation as to why women required the vote, as they would have a beneficial influence on men and encourage moral purity. Yet this argument has its flip side; men were acquitted of charges of rape or sexual abuse because they claimed to be physiologically unable to control themselves. It also meant that when dealing with issues of sexual vice, prostitutes came off worse as women were viewed as morally superior to their male clients, who simply could not help themselves.

In another example of the two-faced attitudes of some, a letter published in *The Times* in October criticised drunkenness among women:

Why not close the public houses entirely to women during the war? It is humiliating to think that while our soldiers are fighting and dying for us abroad this state of things should exist at home.[3]

Once again the Tommy was dealt with sympathetically for his drinking problems, but local women—often from impoverished areas—with sons, husbands, or fathers now serving at the front, were treated with scorn and the suggestion of a blanket ban.

Concern over these moral issues saw the foundation of other women's organisations for policing. Among these was the Voluntary Women's Patrols, presided over by one Mrs Creighton, the widow of a London Bishop. Supported by the Mothers' Union, the Church Army, the Girls' Friendly Society and the YMCA, who were already offering various voluntary work to troops in garrison towns, it was run through the NUWW, who—despite their name—were like all suffragette movements, with their members coming from the middle and upper classes. Before long they would change their name to The National Council of Women, and give up the pretence of being a women workers' union run by women workers.

Mrs Creighton was complicated. Before the war she had been staunchly anti-suffrage, but as early as July 1914 she was representing many of the societies who joined forces to form the VWP in their petitions to have women employed as police. Having slightly modified her views on suffrage, her real passion remained in campaigns against immorality, and she was an important member of the International Bureau for the Suppression of White Slave Traffic, giving lectures on purity when she had the chance. In that aspect she was very similar to Margaret Damer Dawson, with whom she also shared a certain narrow-mindedness when explaining the role of women police as she perceived it.

Perhaps it would be simplest to describe the early movements as morality policing, focussed on those women who were letting the side down. They wished to protect 'our girls from the results of the very natural excitement produced by the abnormal conditions now prevailing.' The current Bishop of London was all for it, and he felt it was the VWP's duty to 'send out the young men in the right spirit, free from moral stain'.

On 31 December the following article appeared in *The Times:*

> The movement known as Women Patrols for looking after the welfare of girls in the neighbourhood of the military camps, has been highly commended for its good work by the military and police authorities. Started in October by Mrs Creighton ... and directed by a committee of ladies experienced in social work, it has rapidly developed.... Advice as to the work had been sought from places near and far, such as the Channel Islands and South Africa. There has been a general recognition of the value of the plan, both for the good of young recruits and soldiers and for the safeguarding of girls from the results of the excitement aroused by the war.
>
> [The organisers] duty is to train the women patrols constituted by the local committees in districts where troops are encamped or billeted, to assign them their 'beats,' and generally to supervise their work in cooperation with the military and police authorities. Each patrol is given an authorisation card, signed in the London area by the Chief Commissioner of Police, and in the counties by the Chief Constables.... They also wear a distinctive band. But they have no uniform and they act quietly and without parade. Every effort is made to provide recreation for the girls. Clubs and Guilds have been opened, and in some places rooms have been provided as places of pleasant resort for the girls and their men friends in the winter evenings.[4]

Not everyone felt enough was being done; in Parliament, Lord C. Hamilton of Kensington asked 'whether the Government would pass a measure empowering magistrates to issue warrants for summary arrest of women of notorious bad character who were infesting the neighbourhood of the various military camps in the United Kingdom?' This was close enough to a request for reintroducing the Contagious Diseases Act that had divided women in the suffrage movement sixty years previously. Fortunately Lord Hamilton was turned down by Mr McKenna of Monmouth:

> While the Government recognises the serious nature of the evil to which the noble lord alludes, I fear it would not be possible to deal with effectively by such legal legislation as he recommends. We must rely partly on the organised efforts which are being made by voluntary women workers and partly on the firm enforcement of the existing law by the police and magistrates.[5]

7

Going against the Grain

Nina Boyle was deeply concerned by what she viewed as anti-female propaganda. Worse still, many of her fellows in the WPV were supportive of harsher measures for offending women. Of course, part of the problem was that soldiers were valuable and, if crippled by venereal disease or imprisoned for consorting with a woman of the night, they were no use to the army and thus the war effort. Women, on the other hand, had no real use, and were numerous enough to be expendable. It was simply easy and convenient to attack prostitutes or women deemed to have low moral character, rather than the soldiers, who were at least half of the problem. Nina was troubled by this turn of events, not least because the horrors of the Contagious Disease Act had been imprinted on the minds of many suffragettes. It had taken a concerted effort by women and sympathetic men to have the Act repealed in the first place, after the consequences of such a subjective law had been made abundantly clear in the tragic case of Mrs Percy.

Mrs Percy's story was the case that always sprang to mind when whispers were going around of the Contagious Disease Act being reinstated. Nina was derided by some of her sex, but her concerns suddenly became very real when the Plymouth Watch Committee proposed that the Act be revived. With Mrs Despard at her side, Nina went straight to the Prime Minister to voice her fears. It was no surprise he was too busy to see them, but Mr Bonham Carter, his secretary, was prepared to entertain them for a while. This in itself was remarkable considering that for most of the previous decade, various deputations of women had come up against massed ranks of policemen whenever they attempted to enter the Houses of Parliament. War had certainly changed a good deal, yet on the other hand it threatened to undermine all the good work women had so far achieved. Bonham Carter tried to sooth Nina and Despard, suggesting they commit their concerns to paper and submit them to him. The ladies hardly needed prompting and the letter was swiftly written, Nina noting that perhaps it would be possible for soldiers to be asked to show a little self-control and for commanding officers to keep better discipline in the camps. With the letter written she stormed off to Plymouth and confronted the Town Council where, faced with her indomitable spirit for common sense, they agreed to defer the decision for consideration. Shortly afterwards the Prime Minister responded to Nina's letter, assuring her that there was no intention of reviving the controversial Act, even if Plymouth wanted it, since it would require an Act of Parliament.

Nina could breathe a little easier, but she knew she could not stop. On 16 November 1914 she was in Sheffield, giving a stirring speech on the need to maintain women's rights, to prevent misplaced patriotism eroding what women had gained so far, and to keep supporting the women police. She was also campaigning for women to support large firms and manufacturers, rather than attempting to do voluntary work that might take away the income of these companies. Her logic for this argument was that big companies employed women and were liable to employ more when demand outstretched supply. If misguided volunteers were to impose on the work of these companies (for instance when ladies made their own clothes from patterns, or rolling bandages for hospitals) they would in fact be harming their fellow women by potentially taking away their business. Nina was very keen to remind women of the same social rank as herself that rushing into voluntary work without thinking—just to ease their conscience—might do more harm than good. Naturally that could not apply to policing, since there were no official women police to displace, only men, and Nina was quite happy for them to look after themselves.

The first policewomen who actually performed police duties in uniform and were employed for such a purpose were from the WPV and operated in Grantham in November 1914. Grantham was then a small market town in Lincolnshire with a population of 20,000. Though its inhabitants largely concerned themselves with farming, Grantham could boast a history of important achievements. Isaac Newton went to school there, and Oliver Cromwell's first success over the royalist army was at nearby Gonerby Moor. The first running diesel engine was produced in Grantham in 1892, and was followed by the first tractor in 1896. However, it was the creation of the Machine Gun Training Centre, built just outside the town at Belton Park in 1914, which attracted attention to the town. Belton Park had an instant impact on Grantham with the arrival of thousands of troops, and this was followed by the concomitant problem of hundreds of prostitutes. Mary Allen was unusually generous to these camp followers considering her normal, venomous attitude towards prostitutes:

A serious problem was provided by numbers of workless or unstable girls who hung about the outskirts of the camp. They were in no sense of the word criminals; often they were simply carried away in a hysteria of patriotism, and wished to give something—anything, even themselves—to the men who were so shortly going out to fight for England...[1]

That was an optimistic and rather naïve sentiment. Most of the women were in fact professional prostitutes who saw rich pickings at any military camp. Prostitution was one of the hidden consequences of war; driven by many factors into the trade, women flocked to the newly formed military camps knowing the men there would be lonely and ready for a little feminine company.

The problem was quickly apparent to the local authorities, among them Staff Captain Kensington, brother-in-law to none other than Margaret Damer Dawson. He suggested to his commanding officer, Brigadier-General Hammersley, that the WPV could be approached to supply women patrols to help control the growing number of camp followers. Early on it was agreed these women would have to be employed, and this would require some form of funding. Policemen were paid out of the local rates, but there was no similar provision for policewomen, so a voluntary committee was set up by Lady Thorold to provide funds for two policewomen. The Association for the Help and Care of Girls was about to enable a vital step forward for policewomen.

On 27 November Margaret Damer Dawson left London for Grantham, accompanied by Mary Allen and Ellen Harburn. Ellen was the oldest of the three at fifty, from a middle-class Manchester family, a former intimate of the Pankhurst women, and an experienced suffragette. Ellen's passion was children and education, particularly among the most vulnerable in Edwardian society—the disabled. Having abandoned the autocratic Pankhurst regime for the WFL, she spent time as a school manager for the LCC, as well as working with schools for the deaf or mentally handicapped. She was a natural choice for acting as a policewoman in an area where young girls would be at risk. However, her selection was not without difficulty; Ellen's real family name was Haarbliecher, but the vehement anti-German attitude of the public had made it prudent to anglicise her name to 'Harburn'. Many women would have felt vulnerable with a German second name, but Ellen was made of sterner stuff—you had to be, to have enjoyed the hard days of pre-war suffrage.

First impressions of the town, which were made in the middle of a rainy day, were not good. Mary noted a 'general aspect of squalor'. A crowd of locals had gathered at the train station to inspect the new arrivals and more than a few were aghast to see three rather butch women stepping into their town in navy-blue masculine uniforms and pudding-basin hats. Few resisted the urge to shout their disapproval. Margaret, Mary, and Ellen faced it all with 'the proscribed official demeanour of stony unconcern', but they were not impressed. Trudging through large swathes of mud, they faced a mean looking town and were pursued everywhere by a gawping audience of children and adults. Mary, who had had nerves about the assignment before being chosen, found herself wondering what they had let themselves in for.

The press came out to welcome the women and a photograph was taken. It accompanied an article published on 19 December, under the title 'Women Police for Grantham Streets'. Margaret only remained a few days to settle in her two companions before leaving them alone; they were still nervous about their new roles when she departed. Mary and Ellen had an awesome task in trying to bring some level of control to the prostitution surrounding Belton Park, and also to represent the WPV in a good light. At the back of their minds was the constant nagging worry that they were pioneers who *must* do well for the sake of future policewomen. They were forging a path and failure was simply not an option.

The soldiers at Belton park were unsupervised once outside the camp and very little was done to control them by the military police who, under martial law, had taken over from the ordinary constabulary. Mary and Ellen were to take instructions from the military police, but it was clear the men were unsure what to do with them. They were advised to keep an eye on poorly lit areas where assignations might occur. With 20,000 troops in the area, Mary acerbically noted that they only needed to watch 10,000 apiece. The chief constable was even less helpful, informing the women he didn't care what they did as long as they kept out of his way.

Grantham's population had swelled enormously not just because of the influx of soldiers and prostitutes, but also because there were plenty of other opportunists ready to make money from those destined to fight, and perhaps die, for their country. Soldiers had a ready supply of cash and too much time on their hands. Travelling merchants turned up in Grantham by the dozen, setting up shop wherever they could find a small scrap of pavement. Temporary shops and stalls littered every street, blocked alleys, and caused consternation to the resident shop-owners. Anything was available, from souvenir cards that could be sent to a loved one, to socks and caps for warmth at the front. This is to mention the pernicious problem of drug-dealers flitting about the darker alleyways. Tension was high and outbursts were common between the soldiers and stallholders, with one side feeling extorted and the other feeling hard-done-by. Ellen and Mary were expected to somehow maintain order among this sprawling network of traders and customers.

Local attitudes to the soldiery did not make things any easier. Anyone in uniform was treated as a hero about to serve King and country, and thus indulged no matter what crime they might commit. Before Margaret left Grantham she came upon a scene that typified the situation. Driving home late one night she came across a woman desperately trying to prop up her hopelessly drunk son against a wall. The mother was greatly distressed, and as they helped the boy into Margaret's car she cried, 'He's like this almost every night, and the magistrate won't give him anything because he's a soldier.' It has to be wondered if the lad was purely a drunk, or whether thoughts of going to the front had so overwhelmed him that he had resorted to drink.

The women police quite naturally felt out of their depth. Whenever they stopped in the street, they were surrounded by a crowd of gawkers. But sometimes their reception was surprising. Years later, Mary described Ellen's first experience of inspecting a public house:

> Wondering what her reception would be like, she entered in fear and trembling. Public houses, it may be inferred, had not entered into her previous experience. The necessity to conceal an extreme nervousness gave her manner an incisiveness not at all characteristic of her somewhat airy and inconsequential approach, and she was quick to perceive not only that she had impressed the publican but that he was, if anything, more frightened than she was, most anxious to meet her halfway, eager to demonstrate that all in his power was being done to keep his place in order.... No resistance to the inspection was ever again anticipated, nor was any ever offered.[2]

The locals of Grantham were uncertain what to expect from these women, but in general they were respected, if not necessarily welcomed. Silence often fell when they marched into a public house in full uniform and cast a keen eye over the occupants, but as the weeks passed, people began to recognise that they were there not to persecute, but to help. Parents sought out Mary and Ellen to discuss anxieties they had about their sons or daughters. Young girls asked advice and even prostitutes occasionally took a moment to stop the policewomen and chat about the possibility of a better future. The women were helped by the unconscious deference working class men tended to show their betters, be they male or female; because Ellen and Mary were well-educated and from a higher social class, the working class men and soldiers, who they tended mostly to deal with, treated them with a certain—ingrained—level of respect. The war would quickly dismantle this old system, but in 1914 it still prevailed, and Mary noted that it was easier for her and Ellen to deal with trouble-making workers and infantrymen than it was to deal with officers, who often tried to send them packing.

In dealing with the rougher elements of society, at least, Ellen and Mary found they had a chance to make a difference, particularly among young girls who were considered most likely to lose their common sense (and virginity) around the soldiers. A large chunk of their time was spent advising the parents of these girls, or tracking down daughters who had escaped into the military camps, and keeping a general eye on intoxicated ladies who were in difficulties. Over time the military and ordinary police became more accepting of the women, and with the support of Lady Thorold, more women police were soon drafted from London to Grantham.

In the background, Nina Boyle was learning that her early concerns about the powers over women being given to authorities were not as unfounded as she had been told. Yet again women were being penalised under a new piece of legislation through the Defence of the Realm Act (DORA). The power of DORA was truly frightening: incepted initially as emergency legislation, by 12 December it was noted by the media that DORA had 'been extended into a kind of penal code'. As its name suggested, the Act was designed to protect the country against the intrusion of spies or subversives, but it was rapidly being used in a heavy-handed manner, causing great distress.

On 19 January 1915 *The Times* reported on the inquest of Mrs Smith of Suffolk, a recent widow, whose husband had slit his throat after being informed by the police that under DORA he was required to leave the country. There was a rumour that his son—who had studied languages in Germany years ago—was serving in the German Army as a lieutenant. Not only was the rumour false, but the police made no effort to trace the son (who was actually in Guatemala) and ascertain the truth. They simply acted, and the result was not only the death of Mr Smith but also that of Mrs Smith, who, distressed by the loss of her husband and the shame cast over her, hung herself.

Despite such tragedies, many promoted DORA as though it was the only way to save the country from destruction. 'Every loyal citizen must cheerfully submit to burdens and inconveniences unknown in normal circumstances,' wrote the editor of *The Times* in reference to DORA. 'Our enemy is unscrupulous, vigilant and quick to take advantage of every opening given to him by carelessness or inadvertence on our part.'

Nina was particularly concerned about how DORA was being used against working class women, because, aside from children, they were the most vulnerable in society and were often persecuted by the authorities. On 29 November 1914, such a case was reported in *People*:

Yesterday a novel court martial was held at Cardiff, when five women of a certain class were tried under the Defence of the Realm Act, 1914, for being out of doors between the hours of 7 pm and 8 am—An order had been issued by Colonel East, commanding the Severn Defences, closing public houses in the city to women customers between the hours of 7 pm and 6 am, accused women, who pleaded guilty, had been arrested in various parts of the city during prohibited hours.

It was stated that officers who had served notices upon the women read and explained the order to those who were themselves unable to read. The president pointed out that the women were liable to punishment not exceeding three months' imprisonment. It was intimated that the sentences of the court would be submitted to the General commanding the district and would be promulgated in the due course, the women being meanwhile detained in custody.[3]

Effectively, any woman outside her home at night, even for the most mundane and legitimate of reasons, was at risk of arrest, despite the order only prohibiting women from being in pubs. Nina was outraged that women were officially deemed more dangerous to the safety of the country than men. She saw this as an attempt to sneak in the Contagious Diseases Act without anyone realising, despite the assurances of the Prime Minister only weeks before. Utterly furious, Nina wrote a scathing report for *The Vote*:

> The sight of women, and women whom a hypocritical cant calls 'unfortunate', tried by a court martial in England—all this distance from the seat of active operations; their poor rights snatched away from them, their persons pilloried in ways that no man consents to for his own sex, is utterly sickening and makes one wonder how military men can so degrade their uniform and stain their boasted record as 'officers and gentlemen.' Let us remember that, when the Criminal Law Amendment suggestions tried to provide more safety for girls of sixteen, gentlemen in office protested on behalf of men who might be blackmailed; but none of these gentlemen protest against power being put in the hands of men to blackmail girls to provide safety for—not boys of sixteen but grown men! The trade called 'unfortunate' was not called into being by women; no woman had contributed one penny to its profits; it has been defended, when its practice was convenient, as 'necessary' and has received official sanction, official protection from prosecution, and official encouragement of every sort.[4]

The Shells Fall

After the war had broken out the name of the WSPU magazine, *Suffragette,* had been changed to *Britannia* in order to demonstrate the Pankhurst patriotism. On 17 December 1915 the offices of the WSPU were raided and copies of *Britannia* were seized under DORA. No exact reason for this seizure was given at the time, but the WSPU was convinced it was because its members had recently criticised Sir Edward Grey and the Foreign Office for removing troops from the Balkans. This action was considered seditious and the government wanted no more attacks on its war policies. It was now difficult to question government policy without risking serious personal injury.

Nina Boyle was still a few months away from being usurped as leader of the WVP, and she had deep concerns about the activities of her officers. Mary Allen and Ellen Harburn had been granted the right to enter any building within a six mile radius of the Army Post Office. This measure was designed to provide police with the ability to monitor soldiers and girls, but it also invasively disrespected their privacy. Nina was even more worried when General Hammersley announced a curfew—from between 6 p.m. and 7 a.m. each night—on women of loose character. He used the latitude DORA allowed to impose his personal orders and the policewomen were expected to enforce them. Mary was content to follow orders as it earned her praise (and the indirect vindication of women police officers) but it also gave her power—and Mary liked nothing better than that. Nina was troubled: the curfew sounded much like a revival of the Contagious Diseases Act, which suffragists had so heartily fought against fifty years earlier. Mary and Ellen happily acquiesced to these new requirements and began conducting searches of lodging houses and billets, expelling those suspected of immoral behaviour. Homes were inspected to make sure that women and girls were in bed at a suitable time and, slowly, a war of moral purity began.

The women police were also called upon to search homes for deserters. This might have made many feel uncomfortable (for the fate of a deserter was usually a firing squad), but there was an iron core in Mary and Ellen. A man could not desert his duty; there was to be no sympathy when they went on 'deserter raids':

Women answering the sharp military knock on their doors would assume an air of shocked and surprised indignation, vehemently denying that any men so much as crossed their thresholds, while dimly discernible in the background, huddled in some corner, would be overcoats, unmistakenly [*sic*] masculine and military. Myriads of nephews and first cousins sprang up, and were claimed by women or girls with angelic faces of injured innocence.[1]

Many of these men had simply loitered too long at a lover's house, but coy smiles and apologies were not enough for Mary and Ellen. They saw vice and debauchery everywhere and before long they were pushing the limits of their authority to deal with it. On one occasion a WPV constable visited the home of a woman with a bad reputation. Despite being married, with her husband away at the front and seven children in the household, the woman was caught with a soldier in her home. Though the report states the woman was alarmed by the spot inspection, she had enough confidence in herself to stand up to the WPV constable and insist the soldier have his supper before she sent him away. Not to be deterred, the WPV constable returned at 11 p.m. and, finding the soldier still present, drove him away.

It is unclear who had given the WPV the authority to search these homes. If the soldier was not in breach of military laws, and the woman was not obviously charging him for her services, what right did the WPV have to interfere in their private lives? It might have been discomforting to the purity vigilantes, but these affairs were completely outside the remit of the police. The WPV had overstepped its own boundaries, although they often tried to conceal their misuse of power by demonstrating—after the fact—how right they had been to enter a house. For instance, in the home of another woman who was entertaining a drunk soldier, several children were found in a dirty and diseased state and handed over to the NSPCC inspector. This did not take anything away from the fact that they had entered the woman's home with no authority—and certainly not to rescue the children. The discovery of these incidences were coincidental to the women's moral crusade.

Nina was appalled. As her ladies were employed by Lady Thorold's committee, and not by the state, they were under no obligation to follow the orders of General Hammersley. By doing so they were effectively condoning his actions—demonstrating that the WPV supported his archaic and heavy-handed regulations. The discord that followed resulted in the heated argument between Nina and Margaret which led to Nina's resignation.

The actions of the WPV were soundly criticised by other suffragettes such as Sylvia Pankhurst, who still devoted herself to women's issues despite her falling-out with her mother and sister. The WPV was rapidly bringing itself into disrepute among women and earning a reputation as an organisation that pandered to male authority. The curfew actually worked very badly, as women were entertaining more soldiers and drinking more alcohol in their own homes than they did on the streets, forcing the problem underground. Margaret Damer Dawson insisted the WPV only enforced these regulations to see how poorly they worked, so they could then protest against it. This sounded hugely unbelievable. The curfew was eventually lifted, but this was more due to protests against it from Nina Boyle and Sylvia Pankhurst than to any WPV action. However, Nina was now no longer part of the WPV and whatever moderating influence she had once had was now gone forever.

With Nina gone, Margaret and Mary's true feelings on prostitution became clear. Despite her suggestion that she felt sympathy for the girls around Belton Park, in reality Mary was hardened to their plight. Again she epitomised the attitude of 'them and us'. Margaret and Mary saw clamping down on prostitution as a means to ingratiate themselves with male authority, thereby increasing the likelihood of policewomen being retained after the war—it did not concern them that members of their own gender were suffering. Mary was hopeful that Grantham would be a proving ground for the women police, where they would be tested and 'acquire merit'. They changed the name of the service from Women Police Volunteers to the Women Police Service, which indicated that they now felt themselves to be semi-official.

Controversies aside, the women were still putting themselves into harm's way, with little in the way of back-up, on a regular basis. Mary was still morbidly fearful of white slavery, which weighed heavily on her mind since her time with Damer Dawson. Outside one house, which she and Ellen intended to search, she turned to her colleague and said:

'How do we know that we shall ever be permitted to come out again?'

Mary was referring to the possibility of abduction, which was rather an optimistic dread seeing as she was standing in full uniform, had mannishly cropped hair and, at age 36, was well beyond what was deemed 'young' in Edwardian society. However, her fear was real enough, even if it was mildly absurd. Beneath her uniform Mary was still a woman and therefore still vulnerable. It should not be forgotten that they were facing danger from both men and women; though in the early days the uniform had earned them a little respect, and most men would refrain from confronting them, over time familiarity grew and the outraged male—when caught in a delicate situation—became more inclined to take a swing at a lady. Even with their knowledge of ju-jitsu there was always the risk of knives being drawn against them, or of them simply being overwhelmed. The dangers did not just come from men; one morning, after a night shift of 12–14 hours, Ellen and Mary came upon a street fight between two factory girls. The women were big, fighting tooth and claw, with a crowd eagerly cheering them on. Ellen and Mary had to jump into the fray and calm the girls whilst avoiding injury to themselves.

The success at Grantham quickly created demand for the ladies of the WPS. In May 1915 Ellen and Mary travelled to Hull to set up a women's force there, and in Grantham they were replaced by Miss Teed and Mrs Edith Smith. The newcomers were formally sworn in to act under the orders of the chief constable. They dispensed with the WPS cap badge, wearing the arms of Grantham instead, and were paid out of the same fund as male police; the women had effectively been officially recognised. Shortly afterwards, Edith Smith would became the first officially recognised woman police officer when she was granted powers of arrest. Prior to this women police could only detain individuals under the civil procedure of citizens' arrest, so this was yet another significant step forward.

In Hull, Margaret was once again on hand to do the initial press talks and settle her officers. Hull already had women patrols, but the Bishop persuaded the council to formally employ two WPV women in order to organise the disparate groups. This, naturally, did not go down well with the existing patrols. As per usual, Mary was rather antagonistic towards the existing women patrols, and she perceived her new role as one of leadership. This was not always appreciated by the forty women patrols who already policed the town. While local papers enthusiastically applauded the arrival of women police from London, groups such as the Woman's Patrol Committee criticised the move.

The policewomen's role in Hull quickly moved beyond cautioning prostitutes, as the city became a target for German zeppelin raids. Mary Allen soon witnessed her first airship skirting the night sky and dropping bombs on unsuspecting civilians.

> The first I knew of the trouble was that a girl on the opposite pavement stopped, stared up into the grey sky and shouted: 'Look! There's an airship.' Far above us, like a silver cigar, stately and almost motionless, hovered the form of the Zeppelin. I recognised it from illustrations I had seen but strove to still the stab of terror the sight gave me. Surely it could not be a raider, here without opposition, just looking down on us like that? It *must* be a British airship![2]

The raid Mary describes occurred on 6 June 1915 and was the first to hit Hull. Gusting winds forced German airships off course, away from London. Unable to hit their intended target, they dropped their bombs over Hull instead. Eyewitness William Dugdall told part of the story:

> On Sunday night, June 6 1915, German zeppelin flew over Hull. Reported to have arrived at about 11.40, flew past Hawthorne Avenue at 12 exactly. Bombs dropped on various parts of the city. Considerable damage done.

Terraces wrecked in Market Road. Edwin Davis' shop burnt to the ground, absolutely destroyed by fire caused by incendiary bombs. Bombs gave terrific reports when exploding. About 50 bombs failed to explode. Death toll amounted to between 25–30 men, women and children.[3]

Mary must have been fairly close to Hawthorne Avenue when the raid began. She remembered her first raid vividly:

There came a muffled roar from a street a quarter of a mile away. The first bomb! It seemed that the town was instantly full of screaming people, running to and fro, pointing upwards and madly piling furniture and knick-knacks out of windows and doors into prams and trucks and handcarts. There came the whine and crash of another bomb. Already I was running towards the place where I judged that the first explosion had occurred, and soon I reached it. Some old houses had been blown down across the street; already, policemen had drawn a cordon to prevent people rushing in amongst the still smoking and collapsing ruins.

Outside the barrier of blue heaved a mass of struggling, screaming people, some in aimless terror, some feverishly trying to escape with their pitiful household goods. I was allowed because of my uniform to pass through the police cordon and assist in picking up the writhing or still figures among the dusty brickwork, and help in getting them to waiting cars. Overhead, the Zeppelin had already disappeared.[4]

Mary was alarmed by the horrific events of that night and unsurprisingly so. For many, rescuing the dead or wounded from the rubble of their homes left a lasting impression. Many of the casualties would have been crushed to death, or would have suffered gruesome injuries, and this brought home the carnage of warfare. This shocking raid, many miles away from the front, set the realities of war firmly and brutally at the forefront of the nation's minds.

The police later reported that the first bombs had dropped on Alexandra Dock. Special Constable Thomas Turner, a photographer who later took pictures of the damage to Hull, remembered:

On reaching the earth the explosive bomb causes an extremely instantaneous wink of light over the vault of the sky ... The incendiary bomb gives a peculiar metallic ping, perhaps the sound of crashing slates at a distance.[5]

The impact of the zeppelin raids was pure panic—no one had ever experienced the horrors of bombing raids carried out on non-combatants. Mary saw hysteria strip people of their rational senses:

The unfortunate inhabitants of the poorer districts would seize the first objects at hand—piling up their possessions in the family perambulator, from under which it was sometimes necessary to rescue half-smothered babies. As a consequence the parks were littered with large framed pictures, birds in cages, huge vases, sea-shells, bundles of clothing, bedding and the most incongruous and astonishing articles.

I saw one old lady start off down the street, half running, shoving a bumping pram filled with salvage, perched on top of which was a canary in a cage, shrilling wildly. The woman had left behind her, whimpering at the door of the house she had just left, a tiny girl of two or three years old. The canary was being saved, but her own grandchild was forgotten! [6]

This was police work at its most vital. Mary and her patrols aided all victims of the raids, from the injured to the traumatised. Patients had to be loaded into vehicles and driven to hospital, those made homeless had to be helped to shelter and the houses of the vulnerable had to be checked to ensure the occupants were safe. Once again, the policewomen had to intrude on the private lives of individuals:

In one house, the family was hiding pathetically under a double-bed. When they heard my boots on the stairs, someone screamed; I think they thought the German invaders had landed.[7]

All this had been caused by a single airship, the L9, a 600 ft long zeppelin captained by Heinrich Mathy. His fateful decision to avoid London because of strong winds resulted in the deaths of 24 people, the injury of 40 people, and the destruction of 40 homes and businesses. Just over a year later, in October 1916, Mathy and his airship would go down in flames over Potters Bar.

As the raids continued, increasing numbers of people took to sleeping outside, in fear of being crushed or trapped in their own homes. This was another problem for women patrols, who had to ensure some sort of order among the refugees and keep them and their possessions safe in the pitch-black night. The women were called upon to calm nervous civilians and see them home safely, and occasionally this provided opportunity to demonstrate their superiority over certain members of the male population. Mary enjoyed recounting her experience of when the WPS was trying to assure people the air raid was over: one irate soldier insisted he could see a zeppelin in the sky, obviously thinking this was a clear sign of the fallibility of women police. Those same women police pointed out to him that it was not a zeppelin in the sky but rather the planet Venus—rising.

During the day Mary and Ellen attended the police court in the Town Hall, were they were deeply unwelcome. On occasion, when the judge deemed a case particularly sordid—and not for the delicate ears of women—he would dismiss all women from the courtroom. Mary and Ellen ignored this order on every occasion, causing disruption to proceedings. Finally, after an appeal to the chief constable, it was agreed that they should be allowed to stay in their capacity as women police. Five members of the WPV served in Hull, and though they were not sworn in they had the unofficial authority to arrest any woman who was drunk and disorderly—however, they were still not granted the power to arrest men.

The antagonism between male and female police continued, despite the latter becoming more common. The extent of the challenges is difficult to judge. Mary Allen preferred to ignore any confrontation, soundly commending her male counterparts as helpful, friendly, and respectful. This was a far cry from what other policewomen encountered. Some male constables were very critical of the female police, not least because they felt threatened and undermined by their new colleagues. Tensions simmered, but mostly beneath the surface. In areas where the chief constable encouraged the idea of female police, discord was kept to a minimum and the ordinary policemen put up with the new situation as best they could. In areas where the WPV or other patrols had been thrust on the chief constable by his superiors, the tensions quickly became more apparent. However, the police were aware that they needed the help of the women to maintain order, despite their reservations. Complaints had to be swallowed and grudges placed to one side, at least for the duration of the war.

9

New Challenges

Because of the prestige the WPS achieved it becomes easy to forget that other female patrols were operating during the war, including the voluntary patrols of the National Union of Women Workers. Unlike the WPS, which had managed to obtain funding and effectively employ its constables on a full-time basis, the NUWW had to rely on unpaid volunteers who operated in their local area for only two or three hours a week. They had no uniform but wore dark and plain clothing, with an armband on their left wrist (including a numbered badge) which identified them as NUWW. As one of the leaders of the NUWW patrols, Mrs Louise Creighton spent much of her time attempting to have her ladies recognised in the same manner as those of the WPS. She contacted the commissioner and asked for advice, hoping that if he offered his support chief constables in other counties would be more inclined to use NUWW volunteers. After already accepting the WPS, the commissioner would have looked churlish to refuse what was a relatively minor request in comparison to those which Nina Boyle and Margaret Damer Dawson usually threw at him. He issued the NUWW women identification cards and instructed the ordinary police to render them assistance when required.

Mrs Creighton went on to have a meeting with Home Secretary Reginald McKenna, who promised to encourage chief constables to utilise women from the NUWW patrols. In many regards the NUWW volunteers were more agreeable than those from the WPS, as they were less militant and more accommodating. Margaret Damer Dawson and Mary Allen were highly political and not merely patriotic; the lack of wartime police resources simply aided their cause, and the commissioner was wise enough to see this. The NUWW, by contrast, was far more open in its intentions. As its women were purely volunteers, who worked for a few hours a week, there was little worry of them wanting a police career after the war.

There remained those who were outraged by the mere thought of women police and what their presence implied. For instance, the Bishop of London was furious that the women patrols were being employed for the sole purpose of keeping men's morals in check (via control of prostitution). At an NUWW meeting he told Mrs Creighton:

[I repudiate] with righteous indignation the idea that the men in training were behaving badly as a body. In many cases the troops had set a remarkable example of good behaviour to the people with whom they lived. During the 10 months of the war there had not been one crime in the three battalions of the London Rifle Brigade.[1]

The bishop was clearly mistaken as many men had committed offences in London, although they were mostly minor and not worth reporting. In addition to this, ordinary police and constables were reluctant to punish soldiers caught in compromising positions. What infuriated the bishop most, however, were the recent press stories of 'war babies.' The illegitimate children who resulted from short liaisons caused something of a scandal, epitomising the delinquent behaviour of men in uniform—men Mrs Creighton and the NUWW wanted to keep in check. The bishop continued:

The cry of 'war babies' raised by the Press had turned out a great delusion. It was a large bubble that now exploded. As a whole the women had behaved well, but there were a number of young, giddy girls excited by the presence of so many young men in khaki; they caused mischief at some of the camps, and at the beginning of the war the problem was serious.[2]

Yet again it was the women that were the problem and not the brave boys in uniform.

It was not just the bishop who was concerned. Chief Constable Farndale of Bradford was worried that these dogmatic women would end up 'in great danger of being insulted by indecent loafers, if not outraged'. He had a point, as even male police constables could be violently assaulted. The women were undeterred and, with the backing of McKenna, Farndale felt he had no option but to agree to women patrols. The Chief Constable of Manchester was another matter: he simply refused to recognise or endorse women patrols in his city, and this remained his position throughout the war. The Chief Constable of Reading followed suit, but was finally persuaded to allow women patrols with the caveat that on the identification cards of the ladies he could write this: 'I, the undersigned, am in no way responsible for the conduct of this patrol.' This allowed him to only superficially recognise the policewomen, as he had stripped them of any authority.

There was one matter that troubled everyone—how did the former military suffragette fit into this picture, having made it her objective to violently confront the police at every opportunity? It must be remembered that even Mary Allen had attacked the police; some members of the WSPU had gone out of their way to assault policemen and get themselves arrested. There was little love lost between the militants and the Metropolitan Police force, yet these same women now wanted to join forces with the police whom they had persecuted. The question of militant suffragettes was always going to be a tricky one; the NUWW central committee avoided responsibility by stating that 'the first responsibility of the selection of women patrols must rest with the local committee'. However, they did admit 'it would constitute a grave difficulty' to appoint women who had formerly been arrested by the police. Not all former suffragettes saw things this way—why should they be prevented from patrolling with men? Surely this was the goal that all that violence had been in aid of? However, the central committee decided that while the selection of less provocative former militants was allowed, no former militant suffragette would be eligible to be an organiser of women patrols.

By June 1915 Mrs Creighton was reporting, with understandable pride, that 'patrols in England numbered 2,014, and in Scotland they were some hundreds. In London there were 235.' But Mrs Creighton wanted more, keen to express to the public the official support her women had gained; even Lord Kitchener, that great icon of the early years of the war, gave them his approval.

What other women made of the patrols was another matter. The NUWW employed organisers and paid them £3 a week, sending them out across the country to help other branches set up women patrols. The first appointee was Mrs Hartwell, who went to Grantham—ahead of Margaret Damer Dawson and the WPV—on 27 October 1914. She hardly had a chance to begin before Mary Allen and Ellen Harburn waltzed onto the scene—the male authorities were yet again hedging their bets and casting the women against each other. With the 'official' WPV patrols settling into the area, the fledgling NUWW patrols were doomed. Mary Allen makes no mention of the clash, though for a time there must have been an overlap as the two organisations vied for control.

Grantham was lost, but the NUWW did not give in. Organisers were sent to Dublin and even as far away as Cape Town, ahead of the much-later attentions of Mary Allen and the WPV. Dublin proved problematic for an unexpected reason: locals were agitated when the women of the patrols were from protestant backgrounds. The NUWW quickly advised that all future Dublin patrols should be two-thirds Catholic.

Despite his concerns over the defamation of the British Tommy, the Bishop of London was on the side of the NUWW and added his spiritual authority to their campaign. But just as the war was dividing the Church over matters of religious belief and thought, so too it was divided over the function of women in this time of crisis. Reverend W. Hodgson, vicar of Southport, told the *Daily Express* his concerns about women patrols:

> Surely this is an unnecessary precaution, which is un-English and savours of German espionage, besides interfering unduly with the liberty of the subject.

Much better to appeal to mothers to guard their daughters against all possible dangers and temptation and to instil in them true ideals of modesty and self-restraint.[3]

Basically, the good reverend did not want women to tell him what to do. Needless to say, his opinion was ignored. The NUWW was making significant contributions to wartime society, not just in terms of policing but also in the organising of clubs and guilds, somewhere young people could go for an evening rather than wandering the streets. Mrs Creighton explained her thoughts on the subject:

[The NUWW] wanted to found clubs both for girls and men where girls could meet their men friends in the Army. They wanted to teach the girls greater self-control and greater modesty, and the men what the great majority of them showed—namely respect for women.[4]

Mrs Creighton knew they could not stop girls meeting with soldiers, but thought that if they had a respectable place to go and socialise then they might be restrained from worse temptations.

The Honorary Secretary of the NUWW's central committee, Mrs M. G. Carden, kept the Home Secretary well informed on the situation—a prudent move to keep the government aware of the women's useful contributions. One report on the women's patrols ran:

Two of our Patrols went on duty at 8 pm; they were walking on one of the paths when a military policeman came to them evidently very perturbed, he said he had been watching a couple (man a civilian) for some time, and would the lady patrols try to get the girl away?

The Patrols thought they must do what they could, so went to the place pointed out by the MP. They found the couple indicated partly screened by bushes but with other couples all around and in a disgraceful position. After a time they moved off, the patrols followed them, after a long tramp traced the girl to her home. The young man took her to the end of the street where a young sister met her, at 8.30, when the patrols passed this same place they noticed that all the couples, though lying on damp grass, were in decorous attitudes. The two patrols are high-minded women, fond of girls and anxious to help them. Some patrols might have caused a disturbance; I also fear that some of them are inclined to dwell too much on the seamy side, and unless they see evil, they imagine they are doing no good. The girl mentioned above will be looked after by a Rescue Worker.[5]

Was that last comment a pointed barb at the WPV patrols? Both the NUWW and WPV had found that time had made them more welcome among the public. They had stopped being the enemy, out to spoil the fun of young girls, and instead had soldiers and parents coming to them for advice. Their organisation of clubs boosted their popularity; for many young people it was the first time they had been involved in a recreational society, except perhaps for when they joined Church organisations as children. Activities varied from teaching dancing and singing (a popular hobby of Constance Lytton's before she became a suffragette), making letter-cases for soldiers, or holding bandage-rolling parties. Mixed clubs gave young men and women a place to go other than the streets, where poverty meant that most social activities were unavailable to them; even the homely comfort of tea in a Lyons shop was out of their reach. It was not so much that this problem was new, rather that someone was at last paying attention to it.

The natural disharmony generated by rival women patrols caused problems fairly quickly. Aside from the two already mentioned, numerous smaller societies and women's groups formed their own patrols, often only operating in a very limited area. For the ordinary man or woman on the street, the politics that defined and differentiated the various patrols were beyond them. Even the media—who had actively followed the rise of female police—struggled to keep track of who was who. This confusion was quite understandable considering the similarities of their names and functions. The Women's Patrol Committee of the VWP was very aware that although they had the support of the Metropolitan force the WPV had also gained funding and were semi-official, if perhaps not so welcome among certain sectors of the police. The Met still considers the VWP to be the first official Metropolitan policewomen, but Margaret Damer Dawson and her lady volunteers were hardly skulking in the shadows. They had support, they had a grant, and they were being asked to send women across the country to set up patrols.

Attempts had been made to co-ordinate the disparate groups, or at least to develop cooperation between them. In a quieter moment, when tensions had not reached their height, the Women's Patrol Committee floated the idea of inviting Damer Dawson to join them, thus uniting the two services. However, somewhere along the line Damer Dawson's invitation went astray. By the time this was realised matters had moved on and the VWP was less comfortable about the union, especially as they wanted to retain their identity amidst the already notable public confusion over the two female forces. The success of the WPV was blamed for the lack of response to VWP newspaper appeals, and jealousy and rivalry had replaced friendly tolerance.

Outside the two organisations no one was really sure what was going on, so Margaret Damer Dawson asked to have permission to speak to women and girls in Hyde Park. A police inspector rather petulantly said that on a prior visit the women had only been interested in talking to the girls: now they wanted to talk to women as well. The police inspector had his patrols wrong, as the 'prior visit' had been conducted by the VWP as part of their rescue work of young girls. Regardless, Margaret's request was denied.

The next problem to arise should have been expected; all this confronting of girls and women, and demanding to know what they doing out at night was going to ruffle feathers. One complainant said that the women patrols went about flashing torches in peoples' faces, and this was highly infuriating to respectable people who just happened to be sitting in Hyde Park after dark. One has to wonder, however, why someone respectable would be sitting in a pitch-black park all on their own. Another complaint was lodged by a woman who was stopped by two patrols while waiting for her husband, a member of the navy, outside Crystal Palace. The patrols wanted to know if she was meeting a sailor; of course she was, but they suspected her of being a prostitute. A damning complaint was lodged against the WPS for their heavy-handed puritanism: they allegedly stopped a 14-year-old girl, telling her not to crimp her hair and to put her hat on straight. She was also told off for dressing herself up and walking around in a manner which would attract men. As a result of the complaints, the patrols switched to lanterns rather than torches as these were deemed less offensive to members of the public.

However, the policewomen felt they had a just cause. For every dozen girls who met with a sailor without incident there was always liable to be one who came to grief, as the case of Alice Elizabeth Jarman demonstrated. In February 1915 Jarman vanished from her lodgings. Unmarried and not well-known locally, all that could be discovered about the 41-year-old was that she frequented Hyde Park and was suspected of being a prostitute. Jarman was found with a slit throat and cuts to her body and right arm in a ditch in Hyde Park; the weapon used was identified as a sword-bayonet, placing suspicion firmly on a soldier. Jarman was described as weak-minded, and a woman who enjoyed going to Hyde Park to chase men. Witnesses eventually came forward to state Jarman had last been seen with a soldier of the Argyll and Sutherland Regiment and a sword-bayonet was found in a sewer nearby, but no culprit was ever traced. This was just the sort of case that stirred the women patrols; girls could vanish overnight with no one ever being prosecuted for their disappearance. Women such as Jarman were outside the reach of most of the patrols, at an age deemed 'beyond help' in a moral sense, but young girls could equally be lured to their doom by a madman in uniform.

The women police were prepared to learn from the complaints thrown at them and began sending out notices containing advice about dealing with the public. VWP members were reminded that their aim was rescue work, not detective work—they did not have the official powers for the latter—and that they should look to befriend women. They were also advised to develop strong ties with the local clergy, no matter which denomination, as well as other officers of the council, rescue workers, Vigilance Associations and so on.

Not only could they help the women patrols, but they could also inform them of cases that required their attention. It was also advised that clubs be opened on a Sunday because this was often the only day young people had completely free, and they were desperate for somewhere to go other than home. From a spiritual perspective, small prayer meetings with singing could be organised, opening religion to many who had never been inside a church in their lives.

The successes of the women patrols encouraged expansion. Organisers wondered if there was now a possibility of providing railway police; women were beginning to play a larger role in the running of the railways, ranging from lady porters to a handful of female train drivers. Female railway police was a logical next step and so Dorothy Peto was asked to patrol the Bristol railways by the authorities. The work was very much in line with what the women were already doing, as Dorothy explained:

> On the station, we dealt with girls stranded for the night or loitering there for amusement; distressed women seeing their husbands, sons or sweethearts off to the front, and other similar predicaments. At the weekends, our tour of duty was extended to 1.30 am, so as to enable us to cope with the noisy throngs who came to see off the midnight leave-trains, and whose emotions found vent, as the time drew on, in last drinks from beer bottles, and in dancing 'Knees up, knees up Mrs Brown' in serried ranks across the platform.
>
> When the train itself drew in, the stalwart patrols picked for this duty took up strategic position at the edge of the platform ready, when the train moved out and hysterical women—and even men—leaped onto the footboards for a last farewell, to seize and drag them back by main force to safety … The only disaster we could neither foresee nor prevent was the shooting of a woman by her husband or sweetheart one night from a departing train; on which occasion the patrols on duty found themselves witnesses at his subsequent trial for murder.[6]

The case to which she refers is that of Private Albert John Cross of the Gloucester Regiment, who shot his wife Bessie. Albert killed his wife with a rifle while waiting for a train at Bristol Station, not actually from the train as Dorothy Peto had described. He had been home on a week's leave and was due back in France. Bessie had had an affair with a married man while Albert was away, and it seems she had fallen pregnant. Albert had written to her from the front, heartbroken by what she had done, stating he would take action to have his legitimate children removed from her. The tension at home during his leave can only be imagined, though the defence argued 'he had been on terms of unbroken affection with her' while in Bristol. It is doubtful this is true, as it is unlikely he shot her accidentally (as his defence claimed) while carelessly handling a weapon he did not realise was loaded. Would a soldier with experience at the front be really that clumsy and negligent? The prosecution didn't think so—they argued he had been standing 'stolidly' when he fired the rifle, 'and did not move to his wife's assistance'. When an officer approached him (presumably from one of the women patrols, though this is not explicitly stated) Albert said 'that he had shot his wife and that she had been misconducting herself'. The judge at the trial advised the jury 'that they could not judge a man who was accustomed to the grim side of war as they would an ordinary prisoner'. With war sacrifices and heroism very prominent in the minds of the public, it is hardly surprising that Albert found himself acquitted from an act of blatant public murder.

Women who were not part of the WPS patrols noticed that their lack of uniform could make it difficult to carry out their duties. They could appear as interfering busy-bodies; a uniform made them seem more official and garnered instant respect. This was becoming a real issue by 1916 and one organiser suggested that the ladies should adopt a black felt hat, with the letters WP on it, as a sort of uniform. Uniforms could make a big difference to policing. One patrolwoman described how, when she and her colleague spotted girls and servicemen cuddling in a doorway, they would not directly confront them but rather stand with their backs to the couple, their armbands highly visible. The couple would usually take the hint and leave, preventing any need to speak to them. With patrols becoming a familiar sight on the streets they had less of the novelty factor that had initially cowed troublemakers, and the women felt it was more important than ever to rely on what little official status they had. 'I would like to emphasise the importance that the Badge gives us,' another member of the women patrols noted, 'and its usefulness time after time. I notice that couples move on as soon as they see we are officials.'

10

Children at Risk

The willingness of the ordinary public to listen to women police was decreasing, and there was little respect for voluntary patrols who did not wear full uniform. One training tip for policewomen noted: 'If you tell a group of bystanders to move on, don't look back to see if you have been obeyed'. The honeymoon period was over, but although this was disheartening it also meant that, for many, women patrols had become a common sight. This in itself was significant. They were also making inroads into areas which had previously been neglected, and perhaps the most important of these was the welfare of children.

Concerns over the exploitation of children had grown during the Victorian period, coupled with a growing recognition (and even idealisation) of the concept of childhood. For centuries children had been considered miniature adults and put out to work at a young age. Better-off families might educate their sons but girls were little more than bargaining chips in marriage deals and could become a wife—in the fullest sense—at the young age of eleven or twelve. Increased prosperity and cultural changes had sparked the Victorian idea that children should be coddled rather than exploited, at least until they were around ten (or six or seven, in many working class families). This idea emerged alongside the growth of the middle classes who now had a surplus income with which they could indulge their children, but it also reflected the downsizing of many families. Vast numbers of children were starting to become less common in wealthy households, especially with child mortality rates gradually decreasing. However, the death of children was still a common enough problem that most families had the misfortune to experience it, if not directly then through the agonies of friends or relatives. Still, the world was changing; children were being perceived as something other than a bargaining chip or wage-earner. Educational reform saw to it that all children had the chance to go to school, even if enforcing the reforms was not always easy. Other new laws were also created to protect children. Concerns about young girls being forced into prostitution made the government create an age of consent, which was set originally at 13 before being eventually raised to 16.

Child labour laws meant limits were imposed on the age and hours of working children, and stated they had to receive some form of education. Despite these new laws, however, the truth remained that many children were still vulnerable to abuse during the Edwardian period.

The onset of war only made things worse; a lack of able-bodied men and income forced parents to send their younger children out to earn a living. A 1915 government report on child labour outlined the problem clearly:

> ...child labour was being exploited unduly, especially in agricultural districts ... advantage was taken of the concessions made by the Government on the outbreak of war, and ... there was nothing to prevent the exploitation of children from spreading to the industrial areas, and even to London.[1]

The 'concessions' had come from a speech made by Prime Minister Herbert Asquith during August 1914, which tried to appease farmers concerned over how they would bring in the harvest with so many labourers joining the army. The Prime Minister stated that the government would not look harshly on children who missed school to work on a farm; this concession had only been meant to last for the harvest season, but farmers had taken it to mean the whole farming year. The Prime Minister had not anticipated the long-term consequences of his words. He had been aiming to push up soldier recruitment, but instead inadvertently caused himself a child welfare problem. The issue of child welfare was already a pressing challenge in the cities, which the women patrols quickly saw. Groups of children were regularly seen wandering the streets at night, sometimes begging and sometimes getting into mischief. For many of them the lack of male authority at home—or a mother who was keen to entertain soldiers—meant that the streets were the only place for them. The most tragic cases were those where children had been orphaned, mothers perhaps dying in a zeppelin raid, or of illness, or even suicide, while fathers were dead or missing at the front. The women patrols found this sight hugely distressing; outside the factories crowds of starving children gathered at the end of the working day, begging for stale bread from the leaving workers.

Other children found themselves as the sole breadwinners of a family, with their mother and often younger children dependent on them. Children sold everything on the streets, from matches to newspapers, and could be found working as late as 11 p.m. Exhaustion and exposure to bad weather were only two of the perils they faced, because lone children were always extremely vulnerable to the predatory attentions of perverted adults. In addition to this, even when the children worked consistently it often did not result in much income for them or their family. One patrol noted, 'two small boys of eight and nine years were found selling papers outside a wine shop one bitterly cold night [it was January], very ragged and without shoes and stockings'.

Policewomen were appalled at such scenes, having come from the ranks of society that cherished the innocence and joyfulness of childhood. Attempts were made to educate parents and at least get the child into a Sunday school, where they might achieve some form of education (at least in a moral sense). In the worst cases the NSPCC would be informed.

The alarming number of over-tens found wandering the streets late at night caused an additional problem; in 1916 the papers were reporting an increase in juvenile crime. Many young people—homeless and alone for various reasons—were forming gangs to survive, and naturally turned to petty crime to sustain themselves. On 3 February *The Times* reported:

> A few days ago the Alderman sitting at the Guildhall was obliged to order a birching for the ringleaders of a gang of young window-breakers and thieves, who styled themselves 'The Black Hand' ... cases at the Tower Bridge Children's Court on Tuesday reached the unprecedented number of 55. At the Old Street Court 10 boys were charged, and at Tottenham, where the children's homes are stated to be full, the magistrates were also busy. Yesterday at Ashford, Kent, nine boys were charged with somewhat serious thefts in the darkened streets, and at Croydon, just over a week ago five magistrates were deputed specially to deal with juvenile prisoners. Boys are blamed for thefts of soldiers' parcels from the lorries from the Regents Park depot.
>
> Workers in the interests of child welfare, police-court missionaries, and others, regard the increase in the number of young offenders as a disturbing result of war conditions. To some extent they say the situation is due to a slackening of parental control. Many fathers are on active service, and often the unruly boy who roams the street and is open to all their temptations is not very amenable to a mother's discipline.[2]

Other causes for the rise in crime were suggested, such as the dimming of streetlights to hamper zeppelin raids leading to a greater opportunity for mugging or violence, the general atmosphere of excitement generated by war, the half-day closing of schools, and stories of violence from the front, which encouraged young boys to commit their own 'daring' acts. The article also suggested another problem: 'in addition there is, of course, the fact that the police are fewer in number, and the bad boy does not apparently stand in much dread of the special constable as of the regular uniformed police.' This was a parting shot at the women patrols.

There was even the strange suggestion by Miss Ashworth:

> Speaking at the British Dominions Woman Suffrage Union Conference yesterday Miss Mercy Ashworth (India) said that the fundamental cause of

the enormous increase of juvenile crime was not the absence of the father or the elder brother on active service, but the fact that many children for the first time in their lives were getting enough to eat. Their vitality, and consequently their power for good and evil, had increased....

Miss Damer Dawson (Commandant of Women Police) said that in the early days it had been assumed that women could do police work in 'pneumonia' blouses and velvet shoes. When they first applied for uniform they were told that it would look very severe, and that the idea of women doing severe work was unpopular. 'I have not had a stone thrown at me for at least two months,' she added. 'The children like us, and if you are accepted by the children you need not worry about the grown-ups.'[3]

If juvenile crime was up, it was also accompanied by an increase in the use of the term 'child welfare'; finally people were taking notice of children and considering them as victims, at least until they perpetrated a crime. Cases that would have caused little stir a few years ago were now attracting attention. For instance, there was the 1917 case of Augusta de Munck, a 36-year-old Belgian musician who lived in Edgware Road with her 14-year-old daughter Kathleen. In June of 1916 an army lieutenant was sitting in Hyde Park when he was approached by de Munck, who had been sitting with her daughter. Kathleen was well-dressed, and her face was painted. De Munck invited the soldier back to her home and, once there, left him alone in a room with Kathleen. The implication was apparent; de Munck was trying to pimp out her daughter. Embarrassed and uncomfortable, the lieutenant left the room before giving de Munck £2 (as she was in apparent need), telling her: 'It was an awful thing for a child of the girl's age to be leading such a life.'

De Munck was unfazed; she needed the money. There was no work for a musician during the war, and her daughter was being trained to go on the stage. The lieutenant tried to aid the family and save the girl, but it was clear de Munck was not interested—so he reported her to the Child Welfare Association. Police had followed Kathleen and seen her take a taxi to Piccadilly Circus, where she talked to officers; it was quite clear what was going on even if de Munck insisted on pleading her innocence. She was eventually sentenced to 15 months hard labour, while Kathleen was placed under the protection of the authorities.

It is more than likely that the police who followed Kathleen would have been women, chosen to avoid arousing suspicion, and this means that women would also have given evidence during the trial. The newspapers would fail to mention this. These were cases the women patrols had to face on a regular basis, but at least now they were being reported and taken to court. Not so long ago the authorities would have ignored the plight of children such as Kathleen de Munck, turning a blind eye to her suffering.

The VWP, meanwhile, continued to improve the lives of the young— they found their clubs to be particularly popular. In a publicity statement, circulated in the press to demonstrate their effectiveness, they stated:

> The club has proved a success and filled a great need ... The girls gave a splendid Xmas party to twenty-five wounded soldiers, they gave a very nice entertainment, collected and gave a gift of fruit and tobacco to every man, the whole tone was excellent.[4]

Talks were offered to older women, accompanied by patriotic sing-alongs and tips for being thrifty during the war. Mrs Carden was always at pains to emphasise how popular and well-received her ladies were; such comments as, 'the country cannot afford to do without women patrols now,' and 'they made an incalculable difference to the state of the streets,' were liberally dropped into the reports sent to the Home Secretary. On one occasion, she mentioned an unnamed chief constable who had wondered aloud what he would do without the women. Naturally the quotes were always from unspecified sources, but there was truth in them: women had made an impact.

There were those who were now keenly pushing for women police to become a truly official branch of the ordinary police force. There had been similar pressure pre-war, but the tests of the last three years had gone a long way to proving not only that women were capable of the work, but also that they were valuable assets to the police. MP Frank W. Perkins prepared a memorandum for the Home Secretary Sir Herbert Samuel, outlining at length several arguments for the official appointment of women police. Sir Herbert turned the recommendation down as, in his opinion, women already had considerable powers of arrest that were similar to those of the general public. He insisted that while this did not cover all offences, Mr Perkins was ill-advised to give women powers they could not physically enforce. He couldn't imagine society finding it acceptable for women to expose themselves to the same level of risk as male police. Despite it all, the same prejudices that had interfered with female police work from the start (that they were not strong enough, that they would put themselves in harm's way, and that it would be repugnant to the public to have women acting as police) were still being thrown at them— but this time the Home Office could not simply back away.

From a recent commissioner's report the Home Office were able to form a brief list of the significant patrols operating around the Metropolitan, which naturally contained both the WPS and VWP. The question was which, out of these two organisations, should the government support and officially recognise? The answer was relatively simple, as while the WPS and VWP performed very similar duties the WPS endeavoured to cover more ground— and were pushing the limits of their power with attempts to enforce their own interpretation of the law. The VWP operated with a lighter touch and were strictly preventative; it might be argued they were hardly policing their patch at all, since they did not attempt to catch criminals. This made the VWP rather attractive to the Home Office and the constabulary, as they were not treading on any toes nor insisting on full official powers of arrest. They were operating in areas the ordinary police were not really interested in. They were dabbling on the side-lines and represented no threat to the status quo. The WPS was another matter—staffed largely by militant suffragettes, they were not happy to pick up the discarded work male police thought was unimportant, nor to toe the line so as not to intimidate the regular policemen. They wanted to be recognised, they wanted to be equal to male police, and anything less would not be tolerated. When the commissioner suggested that the WPS should amalgamate with the VWP and restrict itself to the latter's limitations, the amusement and indignation caused to Margaret Damer Dawson and Mary Allen can be easily imagined.

Sir Leonard Dunning—His Majesty's Inspector of Constabulary—believed the women of the WPS to have overinflated ideas of the exact role and powers of policemen. Dunning supported the women police and would later be influential in getting them officially recognised. His career had begun in the Royal Irish Constabulary, and he had borne witness to the tides of change within that country before moving to become Head Constable of Liverpool. He would be remembered fondly after the war for his contribution to reforming and developing the police force, along with his integrity and high standards for discipline, efficiency, courage, honesty, and impartiality. For these reasons, Dunning may have felt a little aggrieved by the low opinion many in the WPS had of the police. Their viewpoint was nevertheless understandable: the suffragettes had been badly treated by some members of the police (though many others had protected them from mob violence) and the unlawful use of DORA during the war had incensed women in other patrol groups.

Dunning realised that forming a female police force based around the WPS would be impossible in face of the extreme opposition in government. The VWP, on the other hand, were a safer bet; less dogmatic, willing to be controlled by men, and not overambitious in their plans, they could be employed (and if necessary disbanded) with very little fuss compared to the WPS. However, there was a problem in that the NUWW was short of money—very soon there would be no VWP at all unless some sort of funding could be provided. Fortunately, the Police Act of 1916 was in the process of being passed and one of its clauses necessitated the involvement of women in police duties. Without hesitation, the commissioner announced he was employing women patrols to operate in the royal parks on a part-time basis, in order to prevent indecent behaviour and to try and have an impact on the growing cocaine trade among women and soldiers.

While the VWP were pleased with their recognition, their apparent mildness (which had so appealed to the Home Office) was not as simple as it seemed. The VWP were still as ambitious, just not as vocal as the WPS, and they *did* want policewomen to be accepted in the post-war force. In fact, they were slightly worried that male politicians might perceive the new Police Act clause as a sop for the women, thus negating any further discussion of creating a female police force. Nevertheless, the opportunity seemed worth the risk as it had the potential to open the door for women. At first glance the newly-employed patrols were not vastly different from the normal VWP units, except they now wore the armbands of the official police. There was one crucial difference, however: the women now had a police constable to escort them and do the messy business of arresting people. The Special Patrols, as they were now called, had just gained a new degree of power.

11

Cocaine Combatants

During this period one of the growing concerns among the police, the government, and the general public was the prevalence of drug use. Drugs had been an accepted part of British life for centuries, with tobacco use probably the most widespread; other drugs were also prolifically used during the eighteenth and nineteenth centuries, encouraged by the fact that the government was disinclined to do anything about it. Opium remained the most visible of these drugs since many poets, writers, and artists consumed it on a regular basis, and it was easy to obtain as it could be prescribed by a doctor or bought at the local pharmacy. The compound was also present in many home remedies, including laudanum, a soothing medicine for babies, which contained a mixture of alcohol and opium. It is not clear how many children were killed by this mixture; it was given to them either by over-stretched mothers who needed to go out to work or slap-dash nannies tired of a crying child. The children who did not die often suffered from the side-effects of opium, which can include acute constipation and a reduced appetite.

While the dangers of opium were still prevalent, cocaine was the new kid in the narcotics world. It was discovered by the Spanish when they conquered South America in the fifteenth century, but there had always been problems shipping the leaves to and from Europe because they did not survive the long journey. Therefore only occasional supplies of the drug reached the Old World and Britain. However, in 1863 an Italian chemist solved this problem and paved the way for a cocaine crisis; Angelo Mariani discovered that the ethanol in wine could extract the cocaine from the cocoa leaves and thus enhance the effects of both the cocaine and the alcohol. He tested his concoction on a depressed actress to great success and began marketing his product as Vin Mariani, endorsed even by Pope Leo XIII, whose portrait appeared on a gold medallion on the bottle. In the days before safety testing on new products there was no control over Mariani's super-drug and it was quickly being taken by anyone needing a boost—including Queen Victoria, Sir Arthur Conan Doyle, and Robert Louis Stevenson.

Unsurprisingly, there was soon a surplus of cocaine-laced products on the market. Ernest Shackleton took tablets containing the drug on his expedition to Antarctica, while cocaine was readily available over the counter at home to 'sustain and refresh body and mind'. It was marketed as a cure for toothache, and even for hay fever—the preparation for this consisted of 99.9 per cent pure cocaine. By 1916 Harrods was selling a gift set described as 'A Welcome Present for Friends at the Front'—this contained cocaine and morphine, along with syringes and needles.

There is something very tragic about the status of this box as a 'Welcome Present'—although, considering the extremes of horror and suffering that these men were about to face, it was perhaps apt. For many, the war would change the way these drugs were used; they were still taken recreationally, but now they were also used to dull horrific memories and ease the agony of wounds that would never truly heal. After the soldiers were first exposed to morphine and cocaine at the front—where it was doled out to comfort the injured—a new brand of addict was created, his habit supplemented by his army wages. Men who would never have thought about drug-taking were now hunting for dealers in back streets and parks.

By 1900 it had become apparent that cocaine was not the easy-going pick-me-up it had been marketed as. It had some quite serious side effects, including erratic behaviour, anxiety, insomnia, depression, dizziness, headaches, movement problems, and hallucinations—none of which were wanted in a soldier. It was also highly addictive and regular users needed increasingly large quantities to achieve a high. Cocaine had outstripped opium both in popularity and in its effects on society, but Britain was slow to act. The government was notoriously reluctant to pass legislation on drugs; it took decades of arsenic-related deaths for even the smallest regulations on the sale of poisonous substances to be introduced. At the 1912 International Opium Convention Britain reluctantly agreed to stop the trade in opium, morphine, and cocaine, which was occurring freely between countries. Britain was hardly making headway, as the 1916 Harrods advert demonstrates. In 1914 *The Times* reported that Britain was now making its own cocaine, effectively reducing the drug trade between countries, but hardly solving the issue.

The cocaine problem was complicated by the start of the war. A correspondent to the Times, J. Hill Guillermo, had encountered raw cocoa on his personal travels to South America. He advocated that the soldiers of the British Expeditionary Force of 1914 should be supplied with coca leaves for chewing; he suggested that 1 oz should be supplied to each soldier, at the minimal cost of two pence, to provide relief from hunger and fatigue for 48 hours. Guillermo's suggestion was soundly shot down by a former magistrate of India, C. Treatfeild, who in a rebuttal letter to the newspaper stated:

It is well that the public should be warned that cocaine is a most dangerous drug ... It is therefore most seriously to be hoped that no individual hearing of the marvellous effects of this drug will unwittingly allow himself to become a victim to this vice.[1]

However, cocaine was still widely seen as a beneficial drug; for example, famous Victorian and Edwardian actress Sarah Bernhardt was openly described as using cocaine injections to help her perform on stage while she was suffering from an injured leg. On the other hand, some were criticising cocaine and its popular use in restoring the nerves of soldiers suffering 'war-strain' (shell-shock). In *The Times,* a Mr Sandow, who ran a nerve clinic on St James' street, decried the taking of cocaine for temporary relief and informed the public that, due to the request 'of a high military personage', he was unable to tell them more about his own treatments.

While the public were arguing over the efficacy of cocaine, the police and the military were growing concerned at its widespread use among soldiers and the effect this could have on the war effort. Crackdowns on illegal drug-dealing were beginning to make the papers—in 1916 the chemists Savory and Moore Ltd were summoned before the Marlborough Street Police Court (home to Frederick Mead) and accused of selling cocaine and morphine to Mr Frederick William Branch, without a prescription and without recording his name and address. The restrictions on the sale of certain drugs meant that chemists were obliged to pay close attention to their customers, and to only supply these drugs to people they knew to be respectable and who would use the items for medical purposes. Savory and Moore had been following the example of Harrods by offering pocket-cases containing drugs for sale, advertised as gifts for soldiers on the front. Branch had purchased one of these which contained morphine and cocaine, and had used it for recreational purposes; the chemists were fined £1 for the lapse in protocol. Another case is recorded which describes Horace Kingsley and Rose Edwards of Folkestone, who were each sentenced to six months' hard labour for selling cocaine to Canadian soldiers. The disparity in the sentences of the two cases highlights the differing views on supplying drugs to civilians versus the views on supplying drugs to soldiers. The Canadian military camp in Folkestone was apparently suffering from an outbreak of cocaine addiction, with 40 cases already reported.

The Times medical correspondent gave his own view on the Folkestone case and the problems among the Canadians: '...cocaine is more deadly than bullets when a man yields to its influence,' he explained, before quoting a colleague as saying, '"If I wished to destroy a man so that he would be of no use to himself or the world, I should not incite him to the use of alcohol nor yet of morphia; I should recommend cocaine."' The medical correspondent added that Britain was woefully ill-prepared to deal with a cocaine epidemic:

In this country we know little ... of the disastrous effects of the drug. Most of us associate cocaine with the dental chair—a salutary association. It is probably true that many of the medical men who use it freely as a local anaesthetic are ignorant—from lack of experience—of its effects when it is taken for the pleasure it can afford.

In America they know better, because cocaine is an American drug ... How widespread is the evil in that country may be gathered from the fact noted by one observer that less than 4 per cent of the cocaine sold in Philadelphia in one year passed into the hands of doctors and dentists, and only from 3 per cent to 8 per cent of that sold in New York, Boston, Chicago and St. Louis was used professionally.

The drug has a most astonishing effect. Its victim is exalted to heaven and then cast down to hell. He is rendered intellectually bankrupt, yet often he remains brilliant in an inconsequent way. If he goes far enough his sanity may become dependent on his use of the drug; deprive him of cocaine and you make a lunatic of him.

[Crowther] speaks of the delusions of superior strength and perfect command which are produced, and then of the hallucinations and delusions of fear and terror which ensue. Most cocainomaniacs [*sic*] carry revolvers to protect themselves against imaginary enemies. They are terribly loquacious but their talk lacks proportion and propriety; it is involved. The downfall of many a clear intellect has been wrought by this drug, taken in the first instance to add lustre to intellectual expression. According to most authorities, the latter end of the cocaine eater is as terrible as his first entry into the forbidden country was joyous ... it will also, in the end; render him worthless as a soldier and man.[2]

No wonder the army was so worried about cocaine use among the troops. During 1916 the problem seemed to be coming to a head, with the papers full of stories about chemists being fined for not properly recording their sales, and people were caught using forged prescriptions to obtain the drug. However, these were small fry compared to the larger problem, particularly in the West End where gangs had formed to deal cocaine. In May 1916 26-year-old William Charles Johnson stood before a London police court, charged with the unlawful possession of cocaine, after being arrested trying to sell it to some women in Leicester Square. In typical criminal fashion Johnson was ludicrously over-charging for the drug, asking for 2 shillings 6 pence for a dose that had the commercial value of 1½ pence. It was known that he belonged to a gang who trafficked in cocaine, but despite this knowledge and the evidence of the arresting police the magistrate felt there was not enough evidence to prosecute Johnson. He was released regardless of the reminder from the prosecution that 'the use of cocaine was now largely on the increase among prostitutes and some soldiers, particularly those in the overseas contingents'. As far as the courts were concerned the prostitutes could take care of themselves, but the health of the fighting man was a real worry.

Action finally came in July 1916 with an extension of DORA, which banned the sale of certain drugs to British troops without a prescription. Cocaine could now only be imported to those who held a licence, and a person found holding the substance without good reason could be charged with a crime. This also marked the end of the days of the Harrods 'Welcome Gift'. The media optimistically assumed that this would stamp out the trade, failing to appreciate the ingenuity of those already making money from smuggling the drug.

One of the duties of women police was to watch suspected drug dealers and report them to a constable with arresting powers. They were invaluable for collecting evidence and acting as witnesses against these criminals, and they might also speak a gentle word in the ear of a soldier seeking the drug—or send him to an appropriate place for help. One notorious group of female cocaine dealers were kept under special watch, as they had a habit of visiting wounded soldiers in hospital, befriending them and then—when the men left the hospital—drugging them and stealing any money they had. They were closely observed and tailed at all times.

At the same time as the newspapers were widely reporting the successes of the new ban and the reduction in cocaine-related offences, they were also reporting court cases about drug possession where it was apparent the defendants had no problem finding the substance. One such defendant was John Reid Laird, who was found unconscious at the Imperial Hotel with 11 phials of powder cocaine and one bottle of liquid cocaine. Laird came close to dying from the overdose. He had been a cocaine addict for a considerable time; coming from a wealthy family, he had more than enough money to secure his drugs. Addicts like him remained common, and it quickly became clear that the ban was not stopping access to the drug as expected. By December the government had tightened the rules of the ban further, making it harder to obtain a prescription for the drug and making it an offence to prescribe it for anything other than the conditions stipulated by the order. The days when Mr Guillarmo could buy an ounce of coca leaves for 2 pence were at an end.

Despite these greater restrictions the cocaine evil did not disappear and now the papers began commonly reporting overdoses as well as charges of possession. In July 1917 a verdict of suicide was given in the case of Mark Ellis Berg (aged 31), who had been found dying in a lavatory at Cambridge Circus, a 1oz phial of cocaine and a syringe lying empty beside him. Berg was an ex-soldier who had legally obtained the cocaine from a doctor. He had told the physician that he had been wounded in March 1916 and then declared medically unfit, presumably asking the doctor for cocaine as pain-relief. The doctor, who did not know Berg, risked his reputation by prescribing cocaine without further questions. The coroner was astonished by the ease with which Berg had acquired cocaine. Whether Berg intended to commit suicide or merely accidentally overdosed, he had obtained the means to do so without any difficulty and fully within the parameters of the law.

Another former soldier overdosed only a month later. Cyril Hammond Elgee had been in the colonial service and started taking cocaine and morphine to alleviate the symptoms of the malaria which he had contracted in the Amazon. Elgee had gone from being a fit and healthy 11-stone man to an 8-stone shell and, by the time he retired from the military and came to London, his physical and mental health were in a bad state. By that point he was addicted to the two drugs he regularly used to ease his suffering, having to take increasingly large doses to achieve the same level of relief. His housekeeper, Mrs Mullins, was used to finding the captain fully-dressed and asleep on the floor, and had been advised not to disturb him when she found him this way. One Thursday afternoon, before she went home for the evening, she noticed him in this state but thought little of it. She returned the next morning to find him dead. The police searched his flat and found hundreds of hypodermic needles and bottles of medicine, many of which contained cocaine or morphine. They also found empty phials and a syringe concealed in a case in the captain's pockets. An examination of Elgee's body revealed it was covered in puncture marks, the hallmark of a long-term drug addict. He had died of an overdose, but the inquest jury returned the kindly verdict of 'death by misadventure'.

The most famous cocaine-related death of this period was that of the actress Billie Carleton, who made her name in musical comedies during the war. Billie (real name Florence Leonora Stewart) was the illegitimate daughter of a chorus girl, raised by an aunt, who took to the stage aged 15. It was remarked that Billie had a weak voice, but that her stage presence and delicate beauty encouraged directors to cast her in their main roles. Her first break came in 1914 after Charles Blake Cochran promoted her from the chorus in his revue *Watch your Step*. Billie was 18 at this point, and had fallen deeply into the darker side of show business; Cochran fired her when he learned she was attending opium parties. However, he chose to give her a second chance in 1917 with the lead role of 'Gertie Millar' in *Houp La!* Billie's weak voice still troubled the critics, and an appearance in *Some More Samples* failed to win her much acclaim, but she had something about her that won roles, and by August she secured the part of 'flapper' Joy Chatterton in the hit musical farce *The Boy* at the Adelphi Theatre. In May 1918 her career faltered and she was reduced to playing the role of a maid in *Fair and Warmer*, but this brief glitch was soon eradicated by successfully obtaining the lead role in *The Freedom of the Seas*. It was a triumph for a girl with a weak voice, not least because, at the age of 22, it made her the youngest leading lady in the West End.

Her success did not last long. In November Billie attended the Victory Ball at the Royal Albert Hall, dressed in a daring outfit designed by her friend and fashion costumier Reggie de Veulle. The Victory Ball, as might be imagined, was a long affair that lasted well into the next morning and when Billie finally returned to the Savoy Hotel it was late enough for her and her guests to eat breakfast. After bacon and eggs Billie got into bed, still talking to her guests and telling them all about her plans to go to America and Paris and continue her career. They left her, bright and cheerful, shortly after. Before long Billie's maid came in; her mistress was sound asleep, looking a little pale but snoring lightly, so the maid did not disturb her and tidied about the room quietly. She could still hear Billie snoring at 3.30pm. A short time later the maid thought it might be best to wake her, but Billie could not be roused. A doctor was summoned, but Billie was already dead.

When the police arrived they found a small gold box containing white powder (later identified as cocaine) next to Billie's bed. There were also various pills and sachets of a white substance scattered about the bedroom. Other drugs were also found in a box. Billie was lying on her bed with her eyes open and her pupils dilated, while something had trickled out of the side of her mouth and her fingernails were blue. It appeared she had died of asphyxia, caused by an overdose of cocaine. The case quickly turned into a scandal and exposed Billie's use of drugs—which was already widely known among her friends. De Veulle was charged with supplying the drug as he was widely known to be a drug dealer and user himself. He was eventually found guilty of Billie's manslaughter.

In the short span of four years cocaine had gone from being a harmless drug supplied to the troops to stave off hunger and fatigue, to a deadly killer that stripped men and women of their willpower, intellect, and ultimately their lives. It was a plague on society and slap-bang in the middle of it all were the women police, trying to put some sort of order into chaos. Tailing drug dealers, watching over soldiers and picking up the pieces of addiction was neither an easy nor a risk-free job. Criminal gangs would think nothing of assaulting a policeman if necessary, yet the women patrols were eager to throw themselves into this new battle. In their minds it was just another campaign against morality, another crusade against vice, and who better to stem this tide of evil than the women police, advising and shepherding the unfortunate soldier? Their existing duties brought them into contact not only with the most common victims of the drug—prostitutes—but also placed them in a position to observe women who were also commonly dealing. But—as our ongoing battle with illegal drugs demonstrates—the impact the women police were to have was limited, a drop in the ocean compared to the larger problem, despite the bans and the police's greater powers against drug dealers. They could not just chase cocaine off the streets; the problem would outlast the war and cost many lives. Mark Berg, Captain Elgee, and Billie Carleton were just the tip of the iceberg, and before long deaths from drug overdoses had become such a regular occurrence that it was no longer deemed newsworthy—unless it involved someone famous or something scandalous. The modern age of narcotics had come and there was very little anyone could do about it.

12

The 'Oscar Wilde' Syndrome

If drugs were an issue because they were increasingly visible, crimes of a homosexual nature caused consternation because no one wanted to know about them. Homosexuality has always been a complicated issue in Britain; while homosexual men were occasionally brought to trial, as long as their 'crime' happened behind closed doors then no one was interested. Indeed, some believed it was such a heinous sin against nature that it was inconceivable anyone could possibly commit it.

During the late Victorian period attitudes were changing; the old habit of 'brushing under the carpet' was being replaced by a hardened attitude towards what many still considered a mortal sin. In part this was because gay men were becoming more overt, and less prepared to hide themselves away. With the rise of famous figures such as Oscar Wilde, it was becoming harder to ignore the undercurrent of homosexuality filtering into Victorian society. Several scandals were about to make it much worse. The most famous of these is the Cleveland Street Scandal of 1889, which involved telegraph boys and notable members of respectable society; it was even suggested that Prince Albert Victor, eldest son of the Prince of Wales and second-in-line to the throne, was mixed up in the mess. The story had begun with a brothel manned by underpaid telegraph boys looking for extra money on the side. Their list of clients contained many notable people and this shocked decent society—or at least the part of decent society that was ignorant to such goings-on. The case ended up in the courts but light sentences were given to those involved and the absolution of many notable names from punishment aroused suspicion among those who sensed official conspiracy. Everyone wanted the Cleveland Street case to go away discreetly, but it instead created the idea that homosexuality was an aristocratic vice which, in turn, corrupted the working class man.

The Victorian period had been something of a watershed for the gay man, largely because of the aesthete movement in art and literature that encouraged effeminate behaviour in men. This was typified by Oscar Wilde who cultivated an image which today we could only describe as 'camp'. However, while some might have been offended by Wilde's foppishness few would have assumed he was sexually inclined towards men. In fact, there had been a growing trend for casual homosexuality among boys and young men of the middle and upper classes for some time, encouraged by the public school system. Enough evidence exists, in the form of writing during the period, to confirm that it was very common for young boys to develop crushes on each other while at school. This was often described as a 'pash'. These relationships were mostly between older and younger boys (the age differences could be as much as 17 and 12, which today would lead to a completely different scandal) and extended into confessions of love, affectionate hand holding or kissing and fondling, but rarely into full-blown sex. However, it did leave boys with rather a confused perspective of their own sexuality; Robert Graves has argued that the public school system created many 'heterosexual gays', where straight men thought they were gay because of a 'pash' at school. It also made the issue of homosexuality in adult life rather complicated—after all, having indulged at school, most of the upper and middle class men were far more familiar with the concept then they liked to admit and were quite keen to keep this a secret by denying that any such practice existed. For many it was comfortable to privately acknowledge that some of their friends were gay, as long as nothing occurred in public.

Things might have carried on in this state of secrecy had it not been for Oscar Wilde's trial, which he helped spawn by foolishly attempting to prosecute the Marquis of Queensberry for libel. Queensberry had left Wilde a note at his club, in which he called Wilde a sodomite. Wilde, who was having an affair with Queensberry's son, should have let the matter drop and attempted to be more discreet. Instead, he believed his fame and the public love for his effete behaviour would stand him in good stead in court. The opposite turned out to be the case—the libel charge raked up plenty of dirt on Wilde and he was subsequently arrested for gross indecency. The case generated a huge stir and Wilde ended up in prison; for a time British homosexuals felt deeply persecuted and afraid to reveal their sexuality. The aesthete movement fell out of favour as something unnatural and the public still held on strongly to the belief that homosexual behaviour was extremely rare. By the time of the war 75 per cent of cases of gross indecency between men brought before the Metropolitan Police courts were dismissed by the jury, who simply could not believe such things occurred in London's parks.

For police, there remained the problem of finding enough evidence to convict a man of indecency, no matter how serious his crime. So determined was the public to believe that such things did not occur the smallest discrepancy in evidence was jumped upon and used to acquit the accused. This was the case with James Welton, a 61-year-old professor of Education at Leeds University. In October 1915 he was brought before the Oxford courts accused of attempting to procure a boy for indecent purposes. This boy was named

Stanley King and he was a worker in a hosiery shop—he was 14. Welton had gone into the shop and invited him to come on a walk with him that evening. He added, when Stanley seemed reluctant, 'It would mean a little pocket-money.' Stanley refused, but Welton returned on another day and repeated the invitation. A disturbed Stanley reported the incident to the police, but there was a problem—they had no evidence. The police decided they would have to orchestrate a sting using the unfortunate Stanley as bait.

Stanley agreed to go out with Welton the next time he was asked. The police were informed, and they discreetly tailed Stanley and Welton as they walked to the outskirts of the city, before the pair sat on some scaffold poles and Welton 'acted improperly'. Stanley jumped away and the police swooped in for an arrest. Despite seeming a clear-cut crime by modern standards, Stanley King was quickly made to feel the real perpetrator in the crime. In *The Times* on 19 October 1915, it was noted that the boy never received any money, and it was implied that he had lied about the offer. It was also alleged that when Welton interfered with Stanley he was supposed to shout to the police, but he did not. These small inconsistencies were seized upon by those who refused to believe a respectable man could act in such a way. Welton was, after all, respectable; the vice chancellor of Leeds University, Michael Sadler, assured the jury Welton was a man with a 'good name for morality' which 'had never been clouded'.

The police's assertion that such crimes were almost impossible to successfully prosecute was proven by the report of the next day's proceedings in *The Times*:

> [The defendant] could give no definite reason, except impulse [for asking Stanley out] a second time to go for a walk after he had declined ... Mr Elliot, in addressing the jury for the defence, said he must admit that the defendant's conduct, was indiscret, (sic) stupid, and wanting in judgement, but there was nothing criminal in it. Mr Justice Bailhachie, in summing up said the case had given him more than usual anxiety on account of the seriousness of the charge, and the position of the defendant, who had borne an irreproachable character.
>
> The jury, after 20 minutes' deliberation, returned a verdict of not guilty.[1]

The jury simply could not resolve itself to impugn a respected professor, despite the evidence suggesting quite strongly he had indeed behaved improperly to poor Stanley King. It was yet another frustration for the police; we can only hope that Welton was so shaken by the case he never attempted to procure a boy again.

Most cases involving homosexual indecency never made the papers because it was frowned upon to report these matters. Those that did were often reported in a roundabout way, as in the case of Captain Huggett of the Royal Fusiliers. It seems—reading between the lines of the newspaper reports concerning the matter—Huggett may have been homosexual, as there is the suggestion a letter was found in his possession which could have seriously impeached his character in the army—a letter from a Captain Jebens.

The story began when Huggett was on leave and residing in a flat that Captain Jebens had rented. Jebens was away on military duty. One night in winter 1917 Huggett was returning home after dining at the Savoy, when he came across Private Robert Smith and Private Frederick Charles Carter, who asked him for directions to the nearest YMCA. Huggett couldn't help them, but instead invited them to his flat. What might have otherwise been deemed as an act of Christian kindness to fellow soldiers was eventually described by Huggett's counsel as 'to say the least … an act of grave impropriety'. Was this because Huggett was a captain or because there were rumours about his inclinations?

Huggett offered the men a drink, but within a quarter of an hour he was tiring of their company and suggested that they left. Smith and Carter stated that they were broke, hinting that they were not going anywhere. Huggett, getting a touch desperate, pulled all the money out of his pockets—a few shillings—and gave it to them. The privates were not impressed, became aggressive, and locked the door of the flat.

'What the devil are you doing?' exclaimed the captain.

The man at the door (it may have been Carter, but the press does not state this explicitly) stated he would not leave unless Huggett gave him more money and, if Huggett didn't, he would cause a row and accuse the captain of indecency. Huggett, panicking further, gave them a £1 note.

'That is not enough,' said Carter, 'I want £10.'

'Well, I have not got it,' said Huggett, pathetically.

The men argued a bit more before Huggett said he would go out and fetch the money for the men, leaving behind his sword belt as collateral. He went to his friend Mr Jones, who returned with him to the flat. The privates had spent the intervening time searching the flat and had found the incriminating letter from Jebens. They had locked themselves inside and when Jones and Huggett returned they refused to leave unless they had the money they wanted.

'Why do you want the money?' Jones asked.

'You go out to the front as we have been, and you would rather do five years than go back again.'

'Then it is a case of blackmail,' Jones said.

'Yes,' admitted Carter.

The men were finally calmed by a cheque, written by Jones under the fictitious name of Edgar Wallace. Jones, a boot maker, seems to have been well aware of Huggett's proclivities, though under cross-examination he denied saying to the captain, 'I suppose you have been up to your games again.' It is interesting to note that when the case came to court Huggett was also under arrest, presumably for indecency, a crime on which the army was notoriously strict.

Carter's side of the story was very different indeed. He had absented himself from his regiment and was staying in a YMCA, and while walking about London he came across Smith. After some careful talk they both discovered they were absentees and frequently met up. On the night of the misadventure Smith spoke with Huggett, and when he walked off Smith followed him. It is not clear why he did this; perhaps he recognised Huggett, or perhaps something he had said roused Smith's suspicions. In any case, Carter followed Smith in pursuing Huggett to Paddington tube station. Here the testimony becomes confused: Smith went up to Carter and said 'You have done a nice thing by following me.' What did he mean? Was it sarcastically said to imply Carter had hampered whatever he was about? Or was Smith really pleased Carter had followed? In any case, Huggett now approached the two men and said, 'I am sorry I have given you this run, but can you both come in with me and have a drink.'

No wonder the counsel stated Huggett had acted improperly; it almost seems that Carter and Smith had set up their own sting. Back in his flat, Huggett directed Carter into a room full of books and encouraged him to look at them. Meanwhile, Smith was alone with Huggett. Suddenly, Smith burst into the room and accused Huggett of indecent conduct, telling Carter to call the police. Huggett hurried in behind him and started offering money.

Though the reports are sparse, it seems Huggett had been set up, whether by chance or by deliberate intention, as Smith had baited him and Carter had acted as a witness. The language of the newspaper reports would have only hinted at what really happened; in cases of homosexuality very little was ever explicitly mentioned. Huggett's case shows how complicated matters involving homosexuality could become.

Women patrols were unlikely to be thinking about this while they patrolled the metropolitan streets. Their duty, as they interpreted it, was to try and retain some moral decency among the general public. The place that kept them busiest in this regard was the West End, that hub of entertainment, artists, and socialites. Not only did it attract the innocent reveller looking for a night of fun, but also whole range of criminals, from pimps to pickpockets. It was the haunt of the drug dealer, the place to get invited to opium parties, and the place to meet starlets such as the tragic Billie Carleton. Mingling amongst them all were the prostitutes, male and female, young and not so young, each looking for their next turn and chumming up with the soldiers. No wonder then that one prosecutor, Sir Archibald Bodkin, stated that 'the West End of London was a scandal to civilisation' (as quoted in Hansard).

He was referring to a case of gross indecency that took two years to come to court. The defendant in the matter was Christopher Sclater Millard, who was 'something to do with literature'—as the newspapers disdainfully reported. In December 1915 Millard had invited two officers and three boys to his flat in Marylebone; one of the boys later went to the police and accused the officers and Millard of gross indecency. We can only speculate on what happened in that flat on a dark December night—not to mention on the age of the boys, as back then papers used the word 'boys' to refer to youths of 18 and 19. In any case, the statement was enough for the military to arrest the two officers and court martial them, stripping them of their rank and returning them to the military as privates. The civilian police went to arrest Millard but he had vanished. Millard claimed he knew nothing of the warrant for his arrest (issued in March 1916), and he joined the army in September; what he had been doing in the intervening months was a mystery.

The law finally caught up with Millard in 1917, after he had become ill in the trenches and been declared unfit for active service. He was now working as a clerk at the Home Office. Millard's past quickly caught up with him in court; he had been convicted of a similar offence of gross indecency in 1906, and had been sentenced to three months of hard labour as a result. His defence counsel argued that Millard had 'rehabilitated' himself after 1906 (as though homosexuality was an addiction, like drink or drugs) and had only acted the way he did in December 1915 because he was under the influence of alcohol. The court was unconvinced, and sentenced him to twelve months in prison. Summing up, the recorder stated:

> In 1915 such conduct was rife in London, and a great number of cases were brought into that Court, several of which he had to try. The condition of things at the time was truly appalling, and in many cases the persons involved were educated men.[2]

For many of the women on patrol, such cases of indecency were beyond their scope of understanding. They had lived in a shielded world and sex between men was alien to them. Lesbianism was equally misunderstood even though, as we will later discover, they potentially had the chance to witness it.

The women police soon discovered that their role in policing such crimes was far from easy. As stated in *The British Policewoman*, not long after the initiation of the special patrols Mrs Bagster and Mrs Summerton were taking a turn around Hyde Park—the scene of many illegal activities—with their police constable escort, when they came across a stunning sight. A young man was lying on the ground while an older man straddled him, engaging in 'an act of gross indecency.' Mrs Bagster and Mrs Summerton's initial response is not recorded, but the women police were a hardy bunch and swiftly moved into action, assisting with the arrest of the two men and assuring the constable they would act as witnesses in court. For once there was a hope that there might be a conviction—until the police realised their case was going before Frederick Mead.

Mead was still not particularly enamoured with the women police and was certainly not happy about women being present in his courtroom during cases of an indecent nature. He was of the firm opinion that women were too delicate to be exposed to the unpleasant side of human nature, and any who really wished to stay must be very odd. When the arresting constable finished his evidence against the two culprits from Hyde Park and told Mead that two further witnesses from the women patrol were prepared to give evidence, the magistrate point-blank refused to let the women in. The men had hardly offered a defence anyway, he argued, and had practically pleaded guilty. Mead's foolishness and determination to adhere to his own concept of propriety was to swiftly come against him: the men actually did intend to offer a defence, and had certainly not plead guilty.

Mrs Hartwell, who was now the organiser of the London Women Patrols, was indignant about Mead's attitude. She promptly wrote to Sir Edward Henry and asked for his advice on the matter. Henry, unsure himself, referred the matter to a chief constable, who in turn asked for the opinions of senior police officers operating in the areas where crimes of indecency commonly occurred. Through this cascade of inquiries strong views slowly arose: the sub-divisional inspector of Hyde Park was emphatic that the women should be allowed to give evidence, because it might have been the only way to obtain a conviction. He argued that the women were of mature years, doubtless hard to offend, and their testimony may have a stronger impact on the jury—which was naturally all-male. His views were shared by his superintendent, who agreed that the evidence of the women was necessary despite the unsavoury nature of the case. The sub-divisional inspector of Gipsy Hill added that these cases were extremely difficult to prosecute without overwhelming evidence— evidence in the possession of policewomen. Sub-Divisional Inspector Jackson of Richmond, commented that although he had no special patrols in his district, he did have policewomen from the WPS who would be willing to give evidence in such a case, no matter how unpleasant the scenes they had witnessed. His superintendent agreed, although he tainted his support by adding the caveat that it was a sign of the times that men's work was having to be performed by women, even if it was 'often with satisfactory results'.

Not everyone was so open minded: the divisional detective inspector of Harrow Road felt that it was up to a magistrate to decide whether or not there was enough evidence to commit the case to trial. He did admit that it was usual for police witnesses to be heard, but this was rare in cases where the witness was a woman and the crime was inappropriate in nature. He added

Emmeline Pankhurst was a driving force behind the militant suffragette movement. This famous photo illustrates the manhandling many of her cause suffered. (*IWM*)

The smiling policeman suggests this photo was rather staged. It shows one of the earlier tactics of the suffragettes—delivering petitions demanding change. When these women were ignored, they chose more direct action. (*Mabel Capper and Suffragettes with petition, Johnny Cyprus*)

A suffragette meeting with Emmeline, Christabel, and Sylvia Pankhurst on the platform. Behind them handmade banners proclaim 'Deeds not Words' and other strident slogans. (*Suffragettes, England 1908*)

Suffragists are often confused with suffragettes—even in contemporary sources. However, the suffragists disliked the violence of the militant suffragettes, and this became significant when they created rival police groups.

Suffragettes demonstrate outside a police court in 1911. The suffragettes deemed the police courts unfair and biased against women; this brought them into conflict with the police force. (*Johnny Cyprus*)

Suffragettes with police. The relationship between suffragettes and police could often be cordial. In this photograph, campaigning suffragettes talk to police officers in a peaceful way.

A suffragette being arrested in London, 1914. By this time the trouble between suffragettes and police had peaked, and both were engaged in violent struggle. It was common for the ladies involved to be arrested. (*Mu*)

Margaret Damer-Dawson and Mary Allen pose for a photograph in their women police uniform. There is no denying their masculine appearance, which raised questions about the nature of their relationship; however, the suggestion that they are holding hands in this image is clearly false. (*Damer-Dawson and Allen, IWM*)

Above left: David Lloyd George. Lloyd George was one of a number of MPs who dragged their feet over the emancipation of women, incurring the wrath of the suffragettes.

Above right: Edith Smith. Often considered the first true policewoman, she operated in Grantham. Very little is known about her life other than that she committed suicide a few years after leaving the police. (*Victualler*)

The Women's Reserve Ambulance. Until women police began serving, the only other uniformed roles for women were in nursing services such as this. Mary Allen, in particular, found this unacceptable.

Policemen in 1919. The police had a bad reputation before and during the Great War. Corruption was thought to be rife and a faulty legal system lead to general mistrust towards them; it was hoped that bringing women onto the force would improve their image. (*Edward*)

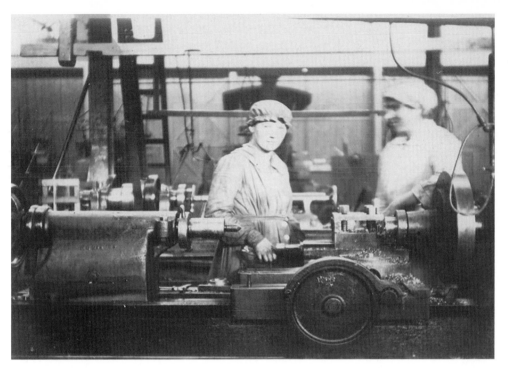

Female munition workers. Perhaps the most significant role undertaken by the WPS was the supervision of munitions factories. These were dangerous places, and not for the faint of heart.

Postwoman, First World War. Women soon found themselves fulfilling previously male-dominated roles. Here, a postwoman feeds her horses.

Shell workers. Despite their dangerous occupation, munitionettes were often looked on with scorn by their supervisors.

Men and women worked side-by-side, raising concerns about 'immoral' behaviour.

Women workers with shells in Chilwell Filling Factory, 1917. As the war progressed various measures were put in place to lessen the danger to munition workers, but it remained a perilous profession. (*IWM*)

Women railway porters. The railways were heavily male-dominated environments, but the war meant that women became employed as porters, with special divisions of female police introduced to help them keep order.

Women police, 1917. This is a 'before and after' shot, with recruits lining up to receive their uniform. Throughout the war increasing numbers of women were recruited to satisfy demand.

Police on strike. A strike right at the end of the war caused a reassessment of how the force operated, also demonstrating the worth of the voluntary police women.

Policewomen in 1931. During the interwar period women police became increasingly accepted, and were a more familiar sight, but it would be decades before true equality was achieved.

A newspaper advert appeals for women to come forward and join the police patrols, 1916.

WOMEN IN EVERY POLICE FORCE.

SIR L. DUNNING'S HOPE.

In 1919, Sir Leonard Dunning is prepared to publicly announce his support for the women police, though many areas are still reluctant to employ them.

Emily Walker. While it is unclear which service Walker belonged to, she appears to have been a policewoman during the war—one of many who would have joined the small patrols set up across the country. (*Greater Manchester Archives/ Public Domain*)

Jujitsu. Women volunteers learned martial arts as part of their training; this made many uncomfortable, as women were not expected to be violent.

This picture, probably taken for publicity purposes, shows a small division of policewomen.

Women formed the backbone of industry during the First World War. Women workers prepare clothing for soldiers.

Traditionally male roles were carried out by females: here we see women cobblers, an unprecedented sight before the war.

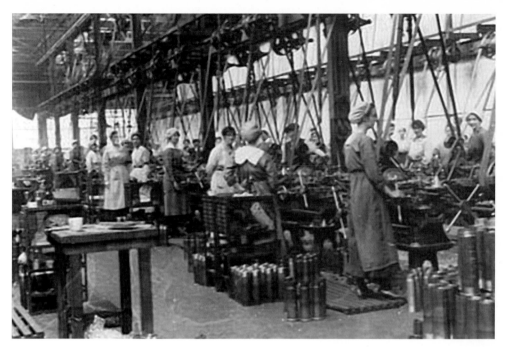

Women shell workers. Shell factories were the most dangerous places to work, where safety standards were not high and many women were badly injured while preparing explosives.

MEN OF BRITAIN !
WILL YOU STAND THIS ?

Nº 2 Wykeham Street, SCARBOROUGH, after the German bombardment on Decr 16th. It was the Home of a Working Man. Four People were killed in this House including the Wife,aged 58, and Two Children, the youngest aged 5.

78 Women & Children were killed and 228 Women & Children were wounded by the German Raiders
ENLIST NOW

An emotive poster calls for men to answer the call to arms and protect their women; when the men left, only the women remained to protect those left behind.

Though largely forgotten, a few places still recall the controversial name of Margaret Damer-Dawson. She may have been difficult, but she still provided the spark which began the revolution of female police.

Mary Allen. As the war came to a close, Mary chose to immortalise the activities of the women's police force in writing. Her first effort was titled '*The Pioneer Policewoman*'.

that convincing a jury that men had been performing such acts in public was notoriously difficult, making the extra evidence vital. Perhaps, he suggested, statements could be taken from the women rather than calling them to the witness box. His superintendent was of the opinion that the women patrols were determined to get themselves up before the magistrates, no matter what the case, as it gained them a level of fame and promoted their cause; he thought women should not be encouraged to get involved in such 'filthy cases'. The superintendent blithely ignored the fact the women were already firmly involved, having witnessed the 'filthy' acts first-hand. It was ironic that the women were very likely to encounter lewd behaviour in the course of their duties, but not allowed to hear about it or comment on it in court.

Having listened to all the views, Sir Henry told Mrs Hartwell that her ladies would be allowed to give evidence at the Old Bailey. Police solicitors would also be placed at the Magistrates Court so that, in future cases, the women could give statements to them. Mead was upset by this turn of events and felt his judgement had been questioned. He blustered and puffed himself up over the insult he perceived this to be—but Mead was very much a man of hot air. He had his clerk write to Chief Constable Major M. H. Tomlin outlining his grievances; he felt he was operating under a cloud of disapproval, and his sense of propriety was being inverted by Sir Henry's insistence on placing police solicitors at the Court. He rumbled about working under an 'atmosphere' of disregard—he was an old dinosaur facing up against the modern age, and suddenly he was very alone.

Tomlin paid him a visit to try and resolve the matter. His conversation with Mead did not generate warm feelings towards the women police, but the magistrate finally agreed that women could appear in the witness box if they felt it was necessary to justify their employment. 'I think Mr Mead felt a little hurt,' Major Tomlin reported, 'as he considered that his discretion was in some way questioned, and his dignity ruffled' (The British Policewoman).

Shortly after this scandal, a Mrs Salisbury and a Miss Peebles proved that Mead's attitude was not unanimously disliked within the women patrols. When reporting for duty in Hyde Park, they asked if they would then have to give evidence in court if they stumbled upon a crime of indecency. They were informed that, after the machinations of recent weeks, this was now to be the case. Neither woman was impressed and they informed their superiors that they could neither appear in court nor become involved in any case of indecency; in fact, had they known before that evening that they would have to be witnesses in the future, they would not have reported for duty that night. However, as they were already on duty, they felt that they ought to do one final patrol and therefore they went out to Hyde Park with a constable.

It was unfortunate (or perhaps ironic) that on the final patrol of these prudish ladies, ten minutes before they were due to go off-duty, they happened across a soldier having sex with a female Harrods clerk. The constable arrested the couple, but back at the station Mrs Salisbury and Miss Peebles caused consternation by refusing to have their names written down on the charge sheet as witnesses. They simply refused to appear in court. This infuriated the police, who were just trying to go about their duty, and caused the acting superintendent to question the function of the women patrols. However, the prudishness of Mrs Salisbury and Miss Peebles did not characterise the entire women police force, and with their resignation the problem was solved. It seems they were not really cut out for police work.

Politics continued to interfere with policing, while dissidents within the women police were making life harder for their comrades. It was fortunate that, in the midst of this conflict, Sir Herbert Samuel wrote a letter to the commissioner of Hyde Park, full of optimism for the influence of the female patrols. The special patrols sorely needed the support.

> Lady Minto saw me last week at the Queen's request about the question of prostitution. You may like to see a copy of the statement I have sent her for the Queen's information. From what Lady Minto told me and from what I have heard from other quarters, I gather this question is being very much discussed at the present time, and there is a strong feeling that the police ought to be able to do more to check the evil. There was a proposal to hold a large meeting in the Albert Hall to call public attention to the matter, and no doubt the police would have come in for unmerited blame. Fortunately, this proposal has been dropped. One must not attach too much importance to unreasoning and unreasonable criticism, but I think public feeling would be reassured if some steps could be taken. I should be disposed to try the effect of employing a much larger number of women patrols in London, as, even if the experiment were not entirely successful, it would at least give women the opportunity of helping to cope with an evil which concerns their own sex as much as men. I notice you recently obtained sanction to pay a few women patrols, but I understand that you do not propose to employ more than about six. This seems to me far too small a number for a large area like London, and I should be disposed to try the experiment on a much bolder scale, by employing fifty of even a hundred women if you could find so many with suitable qualifications. Will you think this over and let me have your views as soon as you come back? [3]

Mead, however, was another matter. Having recovered his composure from the earlier debacle, he resumed his stern stance that no women should be allowed in his courtroom during cases of indecency. In a barbed comment he explained that this was not because he feared the effect the cases might have on them: 'they [had] already, in taking up this peculiar work, sterilised any maiden modesty they may have had'. He just found it distasteful and embarrassing to have women in court when these matters were discussed; like many men, he preferred for women to have no knowledge of the indecencies of some of his gender. As far as enemies go, Mead could not have been more caricatured or ludicrous—he needs no artistic exaggeration to be portrayed as a chauvinistic relic of the previous century, a man losing pace with the modern world. The only problem was that he still had a fair amount of authority within the police courts and would continue to do so for another decade. He was determined to make life difficult for the women police, and every victory they scored against him only made his stance more resolute in the next instance.

In September 1916 a group of trainees from the VWP were sitting in Marlborough Street Police Court, listening to proceedings as part of their standard training, when a case of indecency came up. The women had been making a point of attending such cases after their value as witnesses had been recognised. Mead was uncooperative. When the case came up he asked all women to leave the courtroom, but the VWP trainees refused to budge. Infuriated, Mead called them to the witness box and demanded to know why they thought they could ignore his orders. The ladies produced their signed police ID cards, explaining that they were in training. This agitated Mead, especially as he found the women's uniform offensive—he made the error of thinking that the women were from the WPS and would therefore subsequently go about the streets in the round felt hats and military costume that Margaret Damer Dawson had commissioned.

What really annoyed Mrs Carden and the VWP was that Mead, either deliberately or out of ignorance, could not recognise the difference between the Women Patrols and the WPS. When the matter was reported in the papers it was the WPS who were given the credit for standing up to Mead. The VWP were rightly enraged and began a short publicity campaign to try and clear up the matter, but Mead refused to acknowledge the difference between the groups and now deliberately sought to cause insult. In November he wrote to the commissioner, complaining about women in uniform being in his court and stating that their dress imitated that of real police officers—he was clearly referring to the WPS as the special patrols wore ordinary dress and armbands. Not only did he again refuse to acknowledge the existence of the VWP, but he added that being female not only disqualified women from being constables, but also probably made their appearance in court illegal.

As usual Sir Edward Henry acted as peacemaker, and suggested to Mead that while he may have had a point, in times of war what was normal had to be reassessed and that the magistrate should refrain from being too hasty in his judgement of the women. Irritated, Mead responded that Sir Henry was being deliberately vague to avoid a direct answer and was trying to keep militant suffragettes distracted by employing them as policewomen. Again these suggestions were directed at the WPS, where the majority of the militant suffragettes had ended up. Perhaps Mead really couldn't differentiate between the two groups of women, or simply found it impossible to overcome his fury at the WPS long enough to notice how different the VWP was.

As time moved on it became clear that Mead would not be mollified, and he used many of the cases brought before him to justify his stance. Just ten days after he rebuffed Sir Henry's attempts to appease him, he was presented with the case of a prostitute who had told a police officer to 'fuck off'. The language was enough to shock the delicate Mead and he was appalled to realise there were trainees from the Women's Patrol in his courtroom when the police constable reiterated the insult. Summoning the female officer in charge of the trainees, he asked her how she could possibly justify having the young women in court: the officer simply stated that her ladies were there to learn about giving evidence.

'I don't know what position you represent,' Mead blustered, 'you represent to the public by your armlet that you are a constable, but you are not.'

In this instance Mead had recognised these were members of the VWP, making later errors seem deliberate on his part. The women were unmoved.

'We work with the police,' their superior informed Mead.

'I should have thought you would not have these young folk here to listen to this filth. How old are they?' demanded Mead, referring to the trainees.

'One of them is thirty,' was the slightly smug reply.

Mead had to contradict himself, as quite clearly the women were not as 'young' as he had initially thought and this ruined his argument.

'Whatever the age, I should have thought your natural instinct would have revolted against a matter of this kind,' he muttered.

'Shall I remove them?'

'Please yourself about that. You can stay in court or leave.'

'I am only obeying orders in coming here,' answered the female superior, before she decided to remove her 'young girls' from the courtroom.

Mead took every opportunity to ridicule the women patrols and demonstrate that they weren't cut out for police work, as in the case of the unfortunate Miss Freda Mackenzie. She must have missed the courtroom training session which informed officers that witnesses had to wait outside the court until they were called in. Miss Mackenzie waited *inside* the court; when she was called to give testimony, Mead was astonished to see she had already been watching the proceedings. 'This witness has been sitting in the court!' he declared, outraged but also delighted at the breach—it was yet another thing he could throw at the women police.

Miss Mackenzie was allowed to testify and then cross-examined about her role as a policewoman. It seems Miss Mackenzie's partner, Mrs Frazer, was equally inexperienced—though she had obeyed the rules and waited outside the court to give evidence, she took her duties as a witness very seriously and therefore lacked a certain degree of discretion. She was called to give evidence against the defendants, a couple who had been found having sexual intercourse in public. Her constable escort had provided the initial details with official prudence, explaining that it was the disarray of the couples' clothing that led him to suspect criminality. Mrs Frazer decided to be more explicit and described the movement of the couple, telling the court that they were moving backwards and forwards. As a married woman, Mrs Frazer knew precisely what they were up to and was keen to bluntly express her knowledge of the situation. She was unaware of the discomfort this would cause Mead.

Horrified, Mead condemned Mrs Frazer for her brash behaviour, describing her and her policewomen kin as abnormal and as clearly suffering from a lack of moral propriety. Prudery finally got the better of him, as he was so furious with the policewomen that he dismissed the case against the couple—even though three eyewitnesses had testified to their crime.

Mead has to come across as one of the most incompetent magistrates of the era. His own prejudices often made a farce of the cases brought before him and he would sometimes dismiss cases on a whim. Mead should have been retired, but he continued to carry out his idiosyncratic form of justice for several years. Who knows how many criminals slipped through his fingers or how many innocent people he condemned?

13

The Sensible Smith and the Factory Girls

Edith Smith was a stocky woman with a round almost motherly-looking face. Adorned in her police uniform and her thick circular spectacles, she didn't look like a typical policewoman—possibly a schoolteacher or a country-house cook, but not a policewoman. Edith's appearance belied her true potential. Dorothy Peto considered her a woman of outstanding personality—fearless, kind, and adaptable. Yet, considering the importance Mrs Smith had to the history of policewomen, very little is known about her. She has passed in and out of history with hardly a murmur.

Edith was born around 1880, she was married and she had at least one son, who was called Jim. Edith has the honour of being regarded as the first official policewoman of the British Isles: she was sworn in and given powers of arrest at Grantham Police Station in August 1915. Edith's role was to control the high levels of prostitution within the town and apparently she did this with a light touch. When finding courting couples in a state of excitement, she would quietly speak to them and remind them of the very real risks of pregnancy and sexually transmitted diseases. She would be frank with the girl and appeal for chivalry from her partner, and very often this approach was taken without rebuke, with the couple even thanking Mrs Smith for her tactful manner.

Edith was a native of Grantham, Lincolnshire and lived on Rutland Street. Her motives for joining the early patrols around the town seem to have been based on a genuine desire to help, and less to do with the power it could give women. Unlike many of her colleagues, she had no real ties to the suffragette movement and her motives were probably not political.

Edith is such a shadow that defining her is nearly impossible. There remain only a few stark facts about the remarkable woman. She spent three weeks training with the WPS in London (where she met Dorothy Peto in training) and then spent three years with the Grantham police, working seven days a week. She perhaps saw her role as war work as she retired in 1918, not interested in pursuing a career in the force once the conflict ceased. Many women felt the same, only play-acting as 'men' for the duration of the war. One last fact tells us that Edith was a sensitive woman, who was vulnerable beneath her exterior of calm: in 1924 she committed suicide by overdosing on morphine.

Edith has left us a few words about her time as a policewoman in Grantham. During her first year she felt it necessary to befriend the 'bad girls' in the town, a tactic used by many of the women police. She also visited theatres and cinemas to prevent prostitutes from trading there:

> I received nothing but courtesy and co-operation from the managements as soon as I made my methods known and they realised I was there to act as a deterrent to their houses being used by prostitutes as a hunting ground and to look after frivolous girls likely to get into mischief.[1]

Over the span of twelve months Edith cautioned 100 wayward girls, handled fifteen cases of theft involving women or girls, took care of sixteen female drunks, helped convict ten prostitutes, placed eight in institutions, and handed ten over to the care of their parents. She had one fortune teller charged and convicted, helped eighteen respectable lost girls find their way home and handled five cases of assault on women and girls. When she was not patrolling Edith visited the parents of 'frivolous' girls and suggested they supervise the girls better, talked with wives gone astray from absent husbands and gave advice to those who needed it. This was all in a day's duty, but the emotional and physical toll must have been exhausting. It is rather tragic that Edith's death did not warrant a mention in *The Times* despite her significant contribution to policing and her exemplary work during the war. In contrast, Frederick Mead got a lengthy column simply for retiring—such is the fallacy of the media.

Edith might be largely forgotten outside of Grantham, but her contribution to policewomen was far greater than merely being a good worker. Her appointment as a fully official police constable had opened doors. In February 1915 the work of the Grantham women police had generally earned the female patrols high praise:

> In Grantham, a town of about 20,000 inhabitants, with a camp of over 18,000 troops lying just outside, two policewomen have been stationed for many weeks past. They work under both the civil and military police authorities, and have been able to render valuable assistance to women and children. The General commanding the 11th Division has expressed the opinion that had they been installed six months earlier a great deal of the trouble which has been occasioned by the coming of so large a body of troops into the town would have been prevented.[2]

A few months later the Bishop of Grantham declared that the women police should have national support. This was brilliant, considering the dislike and hostility that had initially greeted the women's arrival.

However, Edith's official recognition was very much a local matter. The chief constable had gained permission from the town council and watch committee, but this did not mean that other towns would immediately follow suit. HM Inspector of Constabularies Leonard Dunning pointed out that this 'swearing in' of a woman was not precisely legal, but as constabularies were independent there was a certain flexibility in the rules. In fact Dunning was not pleased at all with events in the town, and this is shown by a private Home Office memo in which he stated that the Chief Constable of Grantham had apparently fallen into 'the hands of some strong ladies'. Even nastier was his comment that the chief constable's 'senior woman police is perhaps a better man than he is'.

For the WPS, however, Edith Smith was a boon. After all, she had been trained by them—and it was Mary Allen and Ellen Harburn of the WPS who had begun the good work of the policewomen in Grantham. This success was sorely needed for the organisation as they felt increasingly under threat from the VWP, which now had semi-official standing in the form of special patrols. By 1916 it was apparent that the WPS had lost ground and was operating on the periphery of events, even if Frederick Mead kept mistaking the actions of the VWP for that of their rivals. Sir Edward Henry found himself confronted by an agitated Margaret Damer Dawson, who wanted to know why her women were seemingly so excluded. Any talk of the difficulty of employing former militant suffragettes would be inappropriate—Damer Dawson had never been a suffragette.

At the same time there was a growing problem, beyond soldiers and prostitutes, which Minister of Munitions David Lloyd George was becoming increasingly concerned about. For a number of months Britain had been replacing the male workers in its munitions factories with women and often young girls from working class families. The scheme was designed to free up men to join the army, but it had rapidly become clear that Britain's output of shells was dangerously lagging behind what was required. British forces were finding themselves running out of ammunition—this was an undesirable situation for those in the trenches, particularly when the Germans appeared to have no issue with their supply. The answer was to increase production and thus employ more girls, who became known as munitionettes. The numbers soon became unwieldy. Many of the new workers were young and away from home for the first time, living near the factories where they worked. A heady mix of their newfound freedom and the ample amounts of money they earned created a carefree atmosphere and this inevitably led to affairs with soldiers, late-night parties, and drinking. Out of all the girls in the factories only a few succumbed to temptation so much that they became unproductive or dangerous in their handling of explosives, yet this remained a significant problem. The ordinary police were unable to do anything about it.

Lloyd George raised the possibility with Sir Henry that trained women police could be employed at the factories. Firstly, they would supervise the girls, ensure they were at work on time, monitor their health and wellbeing, and help them evacuate during zeppelin raids. Secondly, they could keep an eye open for troublemakers and naïve girls falling into bad habits. Another reason for the usefulness of having ladies supervise the munitionettes—which Lloyd George did not consider—was that they could prevent any male employees or foremen from taking advantage of the girls.

Sir Henry saw this as an ideal opportunity to distract the WPS and simultaneously solve Lloyd George's problem. He asked Damer Dawson if she could supply the women and, with more confidence than wisdom, she agreed. She stated she would supply 140 women, trained and in uniform, with no financial assistance for the first six months. Why did Damer Dawson take on such an extraordinary challenge? Part of it was wanting to show up the VWP and their special patrols, but it was also that if the women were successful in the munitions factories she would have proven both herself and her organisation. Damer Dawson was full of bravado, but largely only because she needed her women to demonstrate their worth without any initial disquiet over official funding. Her 140 officers would be funded out of her own pocket, since the means of the WPS were limited, and after six months—if her ladies had proved themselves trustworthy—the Ministry of Munitions would begin to pay them. The money was unimportant to Damer Dawson, as long as it meant having the WPS recognised and respected.

The Ministry of Munitions of War came into being in March 1915, headed by Lloyd George. Britain was short of the shells for the big guns they were using to bombard the Germans, but ordinary guns were also in regular danger of running empty. Everyone had their own thoughts on who to blame for this crisis: some turned on Herbert Kitchener, who had been the icon of the British war effort ever since his face had appeared on those famous army recruitment posters. It was suggested that he had lied about the amount of available ammunition, or at the very least had misinterpreted it, and had kept the British government blind to the shortage until it was almost too late.

In reality, the blame for the disaster did not fall on just one person. Many factors were behind the calamity, not least the way in which the war had dragged on beyond the original estimate of a few weeks and the unprecedented heavy expenditure of ammunition used during combat. If the war could not be ended quickly, nor the guns forced to go silent, then the only option left was to make more shells.

Much of the munitions labour force had been depleted by factory workers joining the army. Additional manpower was required, of which there was only one source—women—and this was an uncomfortable matter. Munitions work was not only dangerous but could also involve heavy labour that women had previously been seen as unfit to do. Opening the factories to women was yet another watershed moment in the progress of the women's movement, even if it was just out of necessity. It proved that women could do a man's job with equal skill and competency, something that would have been inconceivable just a few years before.

The women employed by the factories were mostly young and single, which created a naturally lively workforce with little to spend their wages on but drinking and frivolities. Unsupervised, the sheer number of the women was unmanageable, especially as most were young and keen for a little adventure. On the other hand women were vulnerable in this male-dominated environment, and they could not turn to ordinary police for help. Before long it was recognised that the women patrols were needed to keep everything running smoothly.

Mary Allen suggests that she was personally approached by Lloyd George over the use of women patrols. Since Lloyd George had acted against the suffragettes throughout his political career and was only changing his mind on female suffrage due to pragmatism, rather than genuine feeling, this seems highly unlikely. Mary Allen told a second version of the story, where it was instead Sir Edward Henry who approached the WPS and suggested they might supervise the munitions girls: this is probably what actually happened. The result of the government approach—whoever it came from—was that the WPS responded by putting their entire organisation at the disposal of the ministry.

This move almost destroyed the organisation. In 1916, when the ministry asked to train and equip ten women on an unpaid six month trial basis, they were almost financially ruined. The WPS relied on donations and the generosity of its wealthier members and Margaret Damer Dawson in particular sunk most of her fortune into the women police. The strain of the additional ten unfunded women was a heavy burden and before the year was out they had appealed to the ministry for a grant of salaries and office expenses. Agreement was reached on funding in January of the following year.

The WPS were providing policewomen for HM Queensferry Factory, HM Factory Gretna, and also for factories at Waltham Abbey and Pembrey. They were swiftly spread thin and in need of new recruits. On January 26, the same day the finance agreement was settled with the ministry, a notice appeared in *The Times*:

> The Ministry of Munitions has need of several hundred policewomen to take up police posts in his Majesty's factories…. The Women Police Service offers the necessary training…. An allowance is granted during training and good salaries are offered on appointment. Three hundred women are wanted immediately.[3]

The allowance was 24 shillings a week, but on full pay a policewoman could expect £2, a sergeant £2 5s, an inspector £2 10s, and a chief inspector £3. These were not vast sums in comparison to a male chief inspector's salary, which was the modern equivalent of £176 a week, while the lowly policewoman was on around £117. Recruits also had to buy and maintain uniforms out of their own wages, which stretched their small funds even further. However, the fact that they were being paid at all meant that, for the first time, the ranks of the women police were being opened up to women who did not come from wealthy backgrounds.

At the munitions factories the policewomen's duties included anything from supervision to evacuating the entire building during an air raid. There had been calls for women to take on some sort of role over the factory girls for a while, spurred by complaints that women workers were being indecently approached by foremen and male workers within the factories. Some felt threatened by the behaviour of their male superiors and the policewomen were designed to be a counteracting force against this sexual harassment. Problems also arose between the women workers when the girls' backgrounds sometimes made their behaviour difficult. Mary Allen noted that it was to be one of their duties to remonstrate with the girls when they were heard to use profane language or be coarse in their conversation. She saw this as the expected blight of women brought up in a working class home and thought that it was the duty of her and her colleagues—as moral superiors—to improve the girls. They also monitored petty crime and regularly searched the girls for cigarettes and hairpins which could cause a fatal accident in the vicinity of temperamental explosives. Despite the hazards a lit cigarette or a hairpin could cause, the women persisted in trying to smuggle them inside the factories.

The canteen and factory buildings had to be regularly patrolled, contact between male and female workers had to be supervised, and the health of the munitions girls surveyed at all times. The chemicals and components used in the making of shells caused various reactions in the body, including jaundice and damage to internal organs. The policewomen grew accustomed to the signs of a girl being poisoned by her work, and would get her removed from the factory to be put on rest. Just as much as they were there to prevent crime, the policewomen were also there to save lives. Checking the girls for sickness was one thing, but when a German raid came over (which it frequently did) it was the job of the policewomen to ensure hundreds of workers secured their stations and fled—in an orderly manner—to the nearest shelters. If the worst was to occur, and a factory was bombed while girls were inside, it would be the policewoman who was first on the scene to bring aid.

However, this was not all philanthropic—Mary Allen soon realised the political value of the work that she and her colleagues were doing. Once again, lower class women were pawns in this game; to promote their own importance Mary accentuated the defects of the lower class girls and made them out to be an example of the need for female police. Now that the munitionettes had money of their own, Mary wrote that it:

Drove them to feverish excitement or extravagances and, coupled with their anxiety and loneliness, often to drink; so that some of them sank, during the four years of their freedom from all supervision, to a terrible and often scarcely human condition.[4]

Mary condemned members of her own gender to promote her own work, but that was hardly surprising as, along with the suffrage movement, the WPS was formed largely of middle and upper class women with independent means, with very staunch views on how the lower classes acted and behaved. The women police claimed, and most of their equals agreed, that the factory workers were less well-educated and therefore lacked the restraint of the upper classes. Using the DORA provisions against these women—who had little means of protest and were not well-read on the subject—was deemed absolutely appropriate and not contrary to the women's suffrage movement. It was alarming how many suffragettes firmly believed that the vote should only be given to a woman of a certain class.

Mary Allen made her bias against working women plain, often spouting half-truths and urban myths concerning the poor. To Mary's mind, only educated women (who were naturally from the middle and upper classes) made effective policewomen. As appalling as her views were, by 1918 the WPS had recruited and trained over 1,000 'educated women' and deployed them across the country. Policewomen were becoming an accepted part of British life and, though still rare in many areas, in cities and military hubs they were a familiar sight. It was natural to assume that this popularity would continue after the war.

The factory policewomen were divided between the Queensferry factory in Chester and a new development on the Scottish border near Gretna, which was comprised of munitions factories and accompanying accommodation for the workers. The latter would absorb 100 women from the force, and they would have the task of supervising 3,500 workers at the new site when it was completed—1,300 of those workers were women. The site would also include male construction workers, and wherever there were men and women mixing freely there was always opportunity for lewd behaviour; the WPS would be expected to keep things respectable. By October 1918 they were being asked for more recruits:

With the continuation of the war the work of the Women Police Service obtains more recognition and appreciation. The second report of the service, which has just been issued, shows that, whereas in July 1915, the number of training women in the corps was on 50, in July this year the total reached 612, and is still increasing.

The growth has been chiefly due to the demands made by the Ministry of Munitions for trained and uniformed policewomen, but the work which the women are able to carry out in the various metropolitan and provincial districts is said to be proving to magistrates and other authorities that there is a sphere of activity for a permanent force of policewomen. Twelve cities, towns and boroughs, the report states, are at present employing policewomen; and of these six are employing members of the Women Police Service. In the munition factories the women police act as guards, and their work includes the checking of the entry of women into the factory, the examination of passes, searching for contraband, such as matches, cigarettes and alcohol, and patrolling the neighbourhood for the protection of women going home from work. At one factory the military and male police guard have been withdrawn. The factory employed several thousand women in the manufacture and disposal of some of the most dangerous explosives demanded by the war. When an air raid is in progress the operatives are cleared from the factory, and the sheds and magazines are left to the sole charge of the firemen and policewomen, who take up the stations allotted to them. Not a woman has failed at her post or shirked her duty in the hour of danger. At another factory the force of policewomen now number 160, all of whom have been sworn in and take entire charge of all police cases dealing with women.

Referring to the present status of policewomen, the report says that this, whether the women are employed in special police areas or factories, or attached to provincial police forces, can only be described as anomalous and unsatisfactory. The present conditions, it is added, need not cause despair of an improvement in the future. It is stated that there is a difference between women police and women patrols. It is the duty of the patrols to talk to girls, to act towards them as preventive agents, and to help them when in trouble, but not to undertake such cases as those which only trained policemen and policewomen could handle. Policewomen desire to be recognised and salaried as servants of the State. A criticism that they are too ambitious is answered by a request to look at the work already accomplished, and it is urged that it is work which the male police gladly handed over their keeping. [5]

Factory life was a dangerous business. Factory accidents had long become a fact of life for those who worked or lived in industrial towns, where the factories and mills ground on every day. Exhausted workers faced exposed machinery, often resulting in the loss of fingers, hands, and even lives. After toxic explosives were added to the mix, the perils the girls faced every single day were considerable—and there were would be no medals for them at the end of it. The girls did not always help themselves, with the women police having to forever search them for items that might cause disaster. They smuggled in cigarettes, which were so obviously dangerous that it is hard to believe any girl took the chance. They also smuggled in pen-knives and hairpins that—to the girls—were less overtly dangerous, but which could cause a fatal spark and send the whole factory heavenwards.

Girls had to be searched again on the way out of the factory, this time for smuggling out souvenirs such as unexploded shells or cordite. The light-hearted way in which the girls took such materials demonstrates how naïve most of the population was about explosives. Cordite was actually notoriously volatile, so much so that when it was stored aboard ships anyone operating nearby had to wear felt slippers to prevent sparks. It could even spontaneously combust, especially if it was older material or allowed to get too hot. More than one ship in the First World War exploded in harbour, not from enemy fire but from its own volatile cordite, as reported in *The Technical History and Index*, Vol. 2 (1919). However, the women workers still attempted to smuggle it home, with one rumour even suggesting that they were eating it.

Cordite was also a major cause of illness among the factory workers. The various acids in the explosive seeped into the skin and caused toxic jaundice—the first sign of which was usually yellowing of the skin. Fortunately, a few hours away from the factory usually resolved the problem. However, the munitionettes were not alone in their suffering. A lesser-known branch of World War One female workers, who doped the wings of planes, were known to suffer severe nausea and headaches caused by the fumes of the varnish they used. Sylvia Pankhurst was disgusted to find that it was common for six out of every thirty workers to be lying outside a factory suffering from the effects of the fumes. Fatigue was another issue, with long hours in the factory interspersed by zeppelin raid warnings and mass evacuations, which wore down the nerves and stamina of the employees. While not a killer in its own right, exhaustion can easily become dangerous when operating around volatile material. Accidents due to fatigue were all too real.

Other problems were unique to women workers. In *Lady in Blue*, one of Mary Allen's autobiographical works, she recorded the constant issues caused by the long hair of the girls. Persuading girls to cover or tie back their hair was difficult, as some perceived the instruction as a petty reproach against their perceived vanity. Few understood the motive behind the regulation until an incident occurred. Mary described one such event in a factory, where a girl had allowed her long hair to slip out from under her mob-cap. It was too late when she realised that her hair had become caught in the machinery:

> Before the scream of her neighbour at the bench had ended, before the victim had been dragged completely off her feet and while her head was still several inches from the pitiless whirring wheels, a policewoman had gripped the hair and cut it free with a slash from her clasp knife. Rescuer and rescued fell in a head on the floor, while the machinery, giving a disappointed grind and grate, hungrily dragged the fair hair among its wheels and tore it tress from

tress. But for the intervention that might have cost the policewoman her hands, or her life, had things gone wrong, those wheels would by that time had been cutting flesh and tissues into bits instead of hair.[6]

There were plenty of tales, from the Victorian and Edwardian factories, of similar accidents which lead to horrific injuries, including the scalping of victims. It should be remembered that many of the workers were quite young and therefore less conscious of the hazards than the older workers. Girls under 16 were often employed (as they had been for decades) and paid just 3*d* an hour for such deadly work.

Sylvia Pankhurst was indignant, but Mary Allen (with her usual attitude of superiority) was more concerned with girls shirking work than with their health. Both she and Margaret Damer Dawson visited prisons to persuade women offenders, many of whom were prostitutes, to accept work at the factories. There was little sympathy for them once they were there; exhausted girls found hiding, trying to rest, or perhaps sickened by the toxic explosives were accused of 'habitual loitering' in Mary Allen's later works. While some girls were doubtless attempting to do the minimum amount of work possible, Mary felt no need to make a distinction between these girls and those who simply could not go on.

If all this wasn't bad enough, the ever-present risk of explosions made it remarkable that the girls returned. It was partly the fact that so few of them really knew the risks—or believed in them—that kept them going. Besides, this was an age where many industries carried the danger of life-changing accidents; Mabel Lethbridge, for example, was to discover the very real dangers she faced during a tragic accident in 1917.

Mabel had gone to work at a factory in Hayes where 397 buildings were housed on a site of 200 acres. The factory floor space covered 14 acres alone, and the walk around the boundary fence was estimated to be 5 miles long. The spaciousness of the site enabled several workshops to be built, spaced at least 75 feet apart—this was to ensure that if one workshop blew up the others would not follow suit. The factory and its workers were watched over by a colonel, his captain, three subalterns, and 190 other men; at night forty watchmen patrolled the buildings and there was a female fire brigade consisting of sixty women. Surrounded by a 10-foot corrugated iron fence, the factory looked fairly impregnable and rather intimidating. When Mabel went to work, coming through one of the four entrances to the factory, she had to pass through a barrier and be given a pass by a 'recogniser'. This had to be shown to police before Mabel could enter the shifting house. Here, women changed out of their ordinary clothes and into 'magazine' clothing, designed to limit the production of sparks that could cause an accidental explosion. The shifting house could accommodate the clothing of 7,500 people. With 10,000 women and over 2,000 men present on the site as ammunition workers—there were also many others who operated as cleaners and general maintenance workers—it was an enormous undertaking to monitor everyone, yet as few as forty policewomen would be patrolling the site at any given time.

Mabel enjoyed the work despite the long hours and she made a number of close friends around her 'bench', the table where girls would work in sets. Towards the end of 1917 Mabel's bench volunteered for some of the most dangerous work in the factory. A sign had gone up: 'Volunteers urgently wanted for The Danger Zone'. Perhaps too young and reckless to realise what this meant, Mabel and her friends instantly volunteered. Three hundred girls marched off to the Amatol Section, the cheers of their fellow workers ringing in their ears.

The Danger Zone was so-called because it was here that, in various sheds and workshops, the dangerous business of filling shells with amatol soda and TNT took place. The buildings stood on raised concrete pillars—the idea being to avoid contact with the ground, where even the smallest piece of metal could be picked up and cause a spark. The buildings were connected by a miniature railway that also ran above-ground. Workers had to change into magazine shoes before entering the buildings, but had to change out of them before stepping back onto the ground. Under no circumstances were the magazine shoes allowed to come into contact with the earth, and the girls were not even allowed to cut across the grassland outside the workshops to reach the canteen - just doing so was cause for instant dismissal. The danger of picking up grit on shoes was very high.

Mabel went to shed 22 and was shown to a raised platform, where four huge cauldrons stood full of the filling mixture. Twelve girls sat on a bench before it, four of them using ladles to tip the mixture into scoops; the scoops were then weighed and the correct amount of mixture was poured into empty shell cases. Hundreds of these empty cases—18-pounders—sat on the floor at their feet. Mabel was given the job of carrying the filled shells to a machine where they were then 'stemmed'—the amatol mixture firmly tamped down to make room for the fuse. The stemming machine was also known as the 'monkey machine' and it represented another hazard to the munitionettes. It operated automatically to bring down a heavy weight on the contents of the shell and thump it down tightly. The 'monkeys' were eventually condemned by the Ministry of Munitions, but it would take time for new machines to be installed in the busy factories—in the meantime many accidents would occur in their use. Mabel was installed on the 'monkey' on her second day in the Danger Zone. It was an overcomplicated contraption: one girl set a shell in a clamp and fitted in the 'stemmer' while, behind an improvised shield of wooden boxes, four girls on a rope raised a massive weight which they called the 'beater'. When the beater was at the top of the machine they released the rope, causing the weight to slam down on the stemmer. Each shell had to be stemmed up to twenty times to tamp the powder down sufficiently; twenty was the maximum amount of stems that was considered safe. Between each fall of the beater the brave girl at the front would swiftly twist the stemmer a fractional amount, to ensure the beater did not become wedged inside. This girl also had the task of checking the fill level; there was a mark on the stemmer that indicated when it was far enough down, at which point the girl at the front would call on her colleagues to hold the rope. She would then engage a brake for the beater to rest on. It was a primitive system and easy to mishandle.

On her first afternoon Mabel witnessed both a near miss and a real accident. There was something wrong with the amatol mix being placed in the shells and because of this it refused to tamp down sufficiently. Mabel was placed on the front of a machine to install the shell and watch the stemmer, but every time she put in a new shell and called for her pullers to haul, she would quickly reach twenty tamps without the stemmer sinking sufficiently. Each time this happened the shell had to be put on the reject pile. The pullers quickly became agitated because they earned a bonus for every shell successfully filled. Mabel started to become the target for griping and grumbling, until at last the overlooker—a woman—came to see what was happening. Mabel had achieved 79 rejects by this point, much too high a number and the overlooker was determined to improve the rate. She tamped her shell twenty times but the stemmer remained too high, and so she called again to her pullers and added two more blows. Everyone held their breath, as this was against the rules. One of Mabel's colleagues refused to follow the overlooker's instructions and was subsequently removed from her machine.

The new girl had barely started on the machine when Mabel, trying to figure out why her shells were not filling properly, heard a scream. The new girl had fainted onto her machine as the beater was coming down. The weight hit her on the head and she was carried away, covered in blood. It was plain to see why the monkey had been condemned. A new machine, which screw-filled the shells inside a concrete chamber, had already arrived at Hayes that morning to replace the monkey, but there had been no time to set it up.

Mabel went back to work and a male overlooker advised her to try and reduce the number of rejects by removing some of the mixture. This made a difference and soon she was producing good shells. Mabel saw no problem in removing small amounts of amatol to make the shells work, but her more experienced co-workers were worried.

'Shells are peculiar,' one told her, 'You can't muck about with them.'

At the end of the day the workers would be given milk in an attempt to minimise the effects of toxic exposure. Mabel looked forward to this as she finished her last shell, but this is when the worst happened:

The last shell! The last shell! A dull flash; a sharp, deafening roar, and I felt myself being hurled through the air, falling down, down, down into darkness … I lay quietly on my side. Now a blinding flash and I felt my body being torn asunder. Darkness, that terrifying darkness, and the agonised cries of the workers pierced my consciousness. I struggled to rise, turning and twisting my body. 'Help! Help! Mother of God, have mercy.'

The cries were drowned in a dull roar … but now the screams held a new note of terror … fire, fire … there was a crazy rush for the doors; the shed became a blazing furnace. In the glare I saw girls rise and fall shrieking with terror, their clothing alight, blood pouring from their wounds. I made a last effort to get to the doors … huge sliding doors of steel. I crawled through the pile of blazing boxes which had surrounded my machine … the agony was indescribable. I made an almighty effort to rise, catching at some machinery with my hands. The sickening stench of burning flesh met my nostrils … cries of anguish escaped my lips. I saw my hands; they were blackened and seared. The machinery I was holding was red-hot. 'God help me,' I cried, sinking down among the flames, unable to stand the torment any longer.

'Mabel, crawl; for God's sake try!' came a voice. Slowly, slowly, inch by inch, I crept free of the flames. 'Jesus save us … save us …' they screamed. 'Oh God … let us die …'

Burnt, bleeding and tortured, I reached the doors and tried to force them open, but the metals were twisted by the intense heat and I was weak. Swiftly, surely the flames crept nearer … was something lying across my legs that I could not raise? I tried desperately to free them, tugging at the left one, which appeared buried in a wet mass of blood and earth. It lifted easily in my hands, so easily, so light. Can anyone imagine the anguish and terror I experienced when I realised that my leg had been blown off, and I held in my tortured hands the dripping thigh and knee?

'Mother, Mother … Mother!' I shrieked in my childish terror, and tearing the string from my 'magazine' cap, I applied it as a tourniquet. 'Mother!! Mother!' the others took up the poignant cry. Another explosion, and I fell over on to my side, a rush of warm blood flowing down my face. Still no one came to rescue us … Where were the ambulances … the doctors … had the whole factory blown up? Suddenly we became aware of a great noise outside and renewed our cries for help.

'Save us! Save us!' we screamed, 'Come over the top … The doors are jammed … We are burning to death … Save us … Save us!'

Streams of water came over, gushing from the hoses of the fire-fighters outside, falling heavily on our tortured bodies, taking our breath and well-nigh drowning us. 'Jesus! Save us, save us!' The cries were growing weaker. We had been trapped in a blazing furnaces, a crucible of death, and now in our agony we were to be drowned. The pitiful cries of the others reached me.

'Steady girls! Someone's sure to come,' I shouted. The wounds on my face and head were pouring blood, and now I tried desperately to wipe my eyes. In the light of the flames I saw a long row of ladders show over the top of the walls where the roof had been. Up came the fire-girls, flinging themselves bravely into the furnace, dragging their hose-pipes ... the sound of cheering reached me faintly ... faintly, through the tortured cries of the wounded ... the flames came nearer, nearer; water poured over my mutilated body ... then a long silence as I passed into a blessed oblivion.[7]

Mabel Lethbridge survived that horrific day in October 1917, though she was permanently mutilated. The bravery and courage of the women who rushed to her aid cannot be forgotten. The 'fire-girls' would have been joined by other munitions workers and possibly women police, who had a duty to deal with the aftermath of such tragedies. There was little in the WPS training that could prepare the women for dealing with such terrible accidents. They were faced by screaming, burned, and wounded girls, some missing body parts, who had to be calmed and brought to safety. It was a scene that could have been found in the trenches, and it reiterated how dangerous the munition factories were. Every day that a policewoman walked into a factory she was faced with the possibility of disaster for herself and her charges.

Inspector Guthrie at Pembrey, personally had to deal with the after effects of three explosions. On two occasions her landlady was informed that the inspector had been blown to bits. Meanwhile, at a Halifax factory, Sergeant Williams and Constable Rainbird received praise for being cool-headed in a crisis when they rescued a fireman who was overcome by fumes from a burst shell.

Accidental explosions were one thing, but air raids were another. The WPS ladies had to be on hand in an instant when the Germans came over in their silver zeppelins:

When an air raid is in progress the operatives are cleared from the factory, and the sheds and magazines are left to the sole charge of the firemen and policewomen, who take up the stations allotted to them. Not a woman has failed at her post or shirked her duty in the hour of danger.[8]

When the courage of the women was reported it caused a surprise to some, the *Police Chronicle* stating that 'subjected to any such horrible danger before the war, one would have expected to find the women concerned all huddled together, crouching in corners, or in a half-fainting condition'. Clearly this reporter had a very dim view of the female character. In fact the ladies quickly demonstrated their courage under fire, with even Mary Allen a little taken aback by their bravery when the zeppelins came across.

Skirting the Borders

When not watching over the girls, or dealing with the inevitable tragedies in making explosives, the women patrols were tasked with keeping an eye on the towns that had been specially created for the workers. These largely consisted of wooden barrack-style huts and the townships endeavoured to be self-contained, but when an existing town was nearby it was tempting for workers to stray there for a change of scenery.

Patrolling the perimeters of the township kept the policewomen busy at night, when they scanned the blacked out buildings with big bulldog lanterns, guiding lost waifs such as drunken navvies, who were still working on the construction of the township when the first WPS women arrived. The women happily helped the men find the darkened canteen and left them with friends, as drunken navvies were preferable to the other creatures they found as they patrolled. Opportunistic burglars saw potential in the wooden buildings and over-loaded purses of the workers, not to mention the stacked building supplies. Peeping toms—or just curious men—were a nuisance around the women's quarters and had to be deterred before they caused trouble.

Then there was the matter of spies. They were a complicated subject, as their threat was disproportional to their number. Identifying a spy was no easy task for the women police—a voyeur could actually be an agent disguising his actions, but they could only be charged if they were caught obtaining secret information or found in an off-limits area. Even then, they could protest that they were just adventurous burglars. Many of the spy cases relied on verbal evidence from witnesses, who claimed the suspect had been asking unusual questions—such as in the case of a woman who asked one of her servants too many questions about her work as a munitionette. The woman was of German origin; most charged spies were, or at least had, German relatives abroad. This didn't exactly make it easier to spot them. The WPS patrols do not appear to have unearthed any spies during their sojourns at the munitions factories.

Half-built townships, hastily constructed in what had previously been fields or open land and with no roads or paths, were not the easiest places to live in. Matters were made worse when the winter came and thousands of weary feet churned sodden grass up into mud; it was not just in Flanders that rain brought an extra level of misery. The women police soon discovered that regularly patrolling in ordinary dress boots was impossible. Mud sloshed up legs, ruined stockings, and made walking uncomfortable. In busy places the township became a miniature quagmire, and this was hardly helped when the heavy snows of the north melted and added to the abundance of water. The WPS quickly started to wear shooting boots with leggings, which provided better protection. Even so, patrolling on cold Northern nights was tough, as Margaret Damer Dawson told the Commissioner in November 1916:

> The weather conditions are very severe for patrolling work in the north, and we find it difficult to provide our women with rainproof clothes and boots. The things usually made for women are quite useless in such incessant rain.[1]

It was just another small irony of pre-war life that women were not expected to be outside in bad weather for long—this was little comfort to the women police. Shifts varied, but were often 6 a.m. to 4 p.m., 10 a.m. to 7 p.m., or 3 p.m. to 10.30 p.m. When they could be spared, women were sometimes handed over to Carlisle to patrol or to assist with the women's work at the police station there. More difficulties were caused by the foolish agreement Damer Dawson had made with the Ministry of Munitions—suggesting the WPS could support the new recruits financially for the first six months had been reckless. Damer Dawson was forced to dip into her own ever-decreasing coffers to sustain the new force. The large number of new recruits she required meant waiving the limitation of only employing women with a private income, as this was simply no longer feasible.

Administration of the women patrols started to dominate the lives of the three leaders of the WPS, and there was little time left over for delivering stirring fundraising speeches. The WPS was something of a black hole when it came to money—Damer Dawson would exhaust most of her considerable fortune keeping it alive during the war. Publicity was deemed the key not only to receiving official recognition, but also to attracting financial support. Sometimes, however, the women's bluster did more to irritate the ordinary public than it did to aid the cause. This was the case of the *Times* article of 26 November 1916, which was entitled 'Women's West End Night Patrols':

> Every night at eight o'clock a small procession starts out from the headquarters of the Women's Police Service in Little George Street, London. It is a quiet, unobtrusive procession, two or three women in neat, dark blue uniforms and a dozen or so girls plainly dressed and bearing on their arms a band marked WPS.
>
> The procession disperses as the various omnibuses come rumbling along in the gloom, one group going up Piccadilly, another to Paddington, another

to come part of darkest London. These are the women police sergeants and the new recruits who are being enrolled daily.

'I think you had better go with sergeant P to Leicester Square,' said the Superintendent when I told her I wanted to join a policewoman who was patrolling the streets. So, with Sergeant P and two tall young recruits, I started out from the headquarters. Sergeant P's hair is turning grey, but her eyes are childlike in their clear blueness. They are keen eyes too, and they look unflinchingly at life in Leicester Square—and unflinchingly into the eyes of those poor girls who only come out into the streets at night and walk up and down, up and down, watching, waiting, ready to seize opportunity, quick to evade detection ...

These are young girls of seventeen and women over thirty. Some are well-dressed, some much over-dressed, some poorly clad, yet with pitiful efforts at coquetry in their gay hats and the vivid flowers which fasten the little fur pieces round their necks.

It is woman's wit against woman's wit in Leicester Square now. There is the pale, shadowy little street-walker and the resolute little sergeant. Let a gay young soldiers or a rollicking sailor boy speak to one of the shadows, and the sergeant is there, motionless, but sternly chaperoning—and over and over again the soldier and sailor walk away. The presence of that other woman I more than they can face.

'Don't these women ever resent your presence here? Don't they ever insult you?' I asked.

'No,' said the little sergeant cheerfully, 'some of them tell us we have ruined their chances on this beat, but I know most all of them now and they know me. I have got work for several of them who used to come, and they are doing well, I'm glad to say. And there are others I have taken to the Church Army shelter, when they had not the price of a night's lodgings, and others I have taken home when they were intoxicated and helpless. Many of them have children, you know, and I go to see them occasionally. Oh, we are on good terms, though we do not speak to each other here at night.

'Those who wear nurses' uniforms are the worst of all,' said the sergeant, and pointed out two tall, handsome girls in dark blue capes and floating veils. 'Those are well-known women in Leicester Square, but when they speak to a young officer he takes them for two pretty nurses out for a lark. It is such a shocking thing that nurses are not registered and that many of the women of the street can masquerade in a costume which should be respected.'

It was a kaleidoscopic four hours from eight to twelve. Never did the sergeant rest or pause except when she stood by some girl who was talking to a soldier until he or she walked away, or when she spoke quietly to some boy, warning him as he hesitated as to whether or not he should follow one of the pathetic painted phantoms in the square.

Now we paced Leicester Square, now Piccadilly Circus; now we walked through the tube station, now lingered outside it. Now we watched a restaurant, from which came loud laughter; now we went up a gloomy sides street where the houses seemed to send forth from their darkened windows an atmosphere of evil. Several of these houses where young soldiers and sailors were drugged and robbed, have been closed, thanks to the watchfulness of the policewomen, but there are still streets which could be cleaned up to the advantage of London.[2]

The article heavily emphasised the value of the women police and their impact on London's society. The sentimental style of the writing and its jolly tale of hapless criminals—only too glad to be pointed in the right direction—were rather far-fetched, but it raised more than just a disbelieving eyebrow at the Home Office. Metropolitan Police stations had just submitted reports on the work of women police and according to the Vine Street police station no policewomen were working in the West End. Flustered, the superintendent looked into the matter, and two days after the article was published he was able to ascertain that six women *had* been seen patrolling in the West End. However, they did not all wear uniform and they wore detachable badges. As far as he was aware, they were not part of his patrols and had never approached policemen for assistance or acknowledgement. With Damer Dawson's influence, it would be unsurprising if some WPS women had decided to do some unauthorised extra patrol work.

What really infuriated the superintendent and his colleagues were the article's claims, which rather blatantly implied that the WPS had single-handedly cleaned up London's streets. Common sense alone dictates that this would have been impossible. The side-street backhouses mentioned had been closed by the hard work of the ordinary police, and it would have been beyond the powers of the WPS to do it themselves. In terms of combating prostitution, many felt the women patrols had done little more than drive it underground—where it was harder to manage. The article was full of exaggeration, making the women appear as crusading angels able to deal with problems that had confounded the male authorities for decades. This was obviously inaccurate, and it did little to ingratiate the WPS with the police force.

Unlike their counterparts in the NUWW, and Mrs Carden in particular, the heads of the WPS failed to be politically astute. There can be little doubt the WPS was the most efficient organisation in terms of training and outfitting their women, and in fact most other patrol forces sent their women to be trained by the WPS, but in terms of winning over regular police they failed all too often. This was disappointing because the WPS was the most progressive of the organisations and was in many ways the keenest to see women police recognised at the same level as men. To add to their problems, the WPS now found itself strapped for cash—fortunately, a mysterious donor appeared on the scene just in the nick of time.

At this point the success of WPS women around the munitions factories convinced Lloyd George that more should be recruited, and he even agreed to release them from their prior agreement and begin to pay the women. It was a huge boost; by 1917 the WPS women were allowed 25 shillings per week while training, and £2 per week when out on patrol. They also gave the organisation a grant of £750 a year. The WPS could hardly keep pace with the demand for women police and in January of the same year appealed for 300 new recruits—*The Daily Telegraph* assured readers that they received hundreds of responses to this advertisement. The *Ladies' Pictorial* ran a double-page spread of a new recruit before and after receiving her uniform, and the *Daily News* quoted Damer Dawson on the need for more patrols:

> The girls [they protected] are young, high spirited and careless. Fortunately for them, in many cases, they had little imagination, and the sense of danger is an unknown quantity; but in some cases their love of fun and mischief leads them to run serious risks, both to themselves and co-workers.[3]

No doubt Damer Dawson had the munitionettes in mind when she made this statement. The WPS had proved highly beneficial in watching over the girls in the factories, but they were certainly not alone. At Gretna five separate police forces (including the WPS and a force provided by the factory) were operating. The position of the factory, on the border of Scotland and England, meant two systems of law were in use. Co-operation was commonly needed to avoid utter confusion, but despite this there were often problems. The WPS came off best in this situation due to not being truly affiliated with anyone, so they could work in the way that best suited the other various police forces. In February 1917 they were even praised by the HM Inspector of Constabulary for their 'excellent work'. Considering the difficult conditions the women were working under, this praise was much appreciated. One paper recorded that women patrols could walk for as many as 17 miles while on duty, and in bad weather this was torturous. One constable who worked at a factory in Kent reported:

> We of this unit are very happy in our work, although we have practically no comfort. The weather has been bitterly cold, and from seven in the morning until six in the afternoon we have had nowhere to go to get warm. The little place we call 'office' is only heated by one tiny lamp, and in the bad weather the snow comes through the cracks in the roof and sides of the hut, and we have to wear our heavy coats and hats all day long, and we still shiver. Though the cold has been so intense, we are kept warm, however, by the thought that we are working for our King and Country.[4]

This quote appears in one of Mary Allen's books, and therefore we may wonder if a little editing or encouragement was used to give the constable's words the right level of patriotism. Mary Allen still felt the need to justify and promote the work of the WPS even years after the war, perhaps part of her idolisation of the deceased Damer Dawson. Avoiding the messy details was just part of her enthusiastic whitewashing of history. She failed to report some less-impressive incidents, such as one reported by *The Times* in 1917:

WOMEN CONSTABLES AT VARIANCE

In a Government Munitions factory yesterday a difference of opinion arose between a woman constable and her inspector. In her anger the constable, a powerfully-built woman, suddenly caught up the inspector in her arms, and threw her into an adjacent stream, which contained more mud than water. When extricated the inspector was uninjured. Officers of the regular police staff escorted the woman constable from the factory.[5]

Frederick Mead would surely have been delighted to read this story.

The WPS made such a name for itself through its work at the munitions factories that the chief constable of Reading, who had previously been firmly against women police, requested that the WPS send him two constables. The NUWW was irked—they claimed that it was the fine example of their VWP patrols that had changed the chief constable's mind, and that he had confused them with the WPS. This wrangling was standard between the two organisations, and when one received praise the other instantly claimed it for themselves. The early triumphs of the VWP were now in danger, as the WPS soared ahead in public support. It helped that they now had a government grant, and Damer Dawson did not waste any time investing the money in the latest technology—four brand new motorcycles. This was quite radical in an age when Metropolitan Police Superintendents still travelled to stations by horse and trap. Buoyed by the publicity, the WPS received requests from all over the country for officers: Nottingham asked for eight constables and an officer, while Oxford asked for one constable. However, not everyone appreciated the value of the women, as shown by one town in Northumberland which was only prepared to pay twenty-five shillings a week for a constable. Other towns had unrealistic expectations, such as Folkestone, Kent, which took on Sub-Inspector Fife from the WPS and expected her to be a cure for all the town's problems.

Folkestone had suffered in many ways during the first years of the war. Aside from increasing problems with the prostitution encouraged by military camps, the Kent coast was also a prime target for German air raids. In 1915 a debate in the House of Commons raised the issue of the town's vulnerability. Should the Germans succeed in the Western Front, ran one argument, then 'they would rush for Calais, and when they brought down their heavy guns and seized Dunkirk there would be no difficulty from Calais in bombarding Dover and Folkestone, and even, under cover of that bombardment, of attempting a raid or invasion of this country' (as quoted in *Magazine of The Friends of The National Archives*, April 2012, vol. 23 no. 1). For the ordinary folk of Kent it was a terrifying thought that the Germans could attack them from the safe distance of France.

In 1916 things became even worse when Folkestone was one of the towns hit in the 'first great aeroplane raid made by Germans on England.' Around seventy-eight people perished when seventeen German planes flew over the southeast coast and dropped sixty bombs. There was no form of counterattack and, as the raid occurred at 6 p.m. on a pleasant May evening, there were numerous people in the streets to witness it. The horror of the attack was magnified by the number of young victims:

> Mothers had brought out their children and the little ones, with no thought of danger, stayed on the pavement while the women went into the shops. Marketing was most actively in progress, perhaps, at a greengrocery store with an open front, and here a bomb, or more probably an aerial torpedo, burst and caused an appalling loss of life. The victims had practically no warning of the peril which threatened them. Before any explosion occurred the droning of aeroplane engines had been heard, but as our own machines often circle over the town the noise had not aroused misgivings. When a bomb dropped half a mile away and gave the alarm not even a majority of the people in the street could seek shelter. Shop assistants crouched behind counters, a few fled into cellars, but the terrific explosions which came within a few seconds mowed down nearly 70 defenceless children and adults.
>
> Thirteen women, six men, and seven children were killed instantaneously, and 42 others were injured. The street was like a shambles. Little ones left without their mothers were blown to pieces, a butcher's shop collapsed and customers and assistants were buried in the ruins.
>
> Around a police constable who escaped unhurt eight women fell dead or dying. Every window and part of the front of the drapery establishment had been blown in and when rescue work began many victims were found among the customers in the shop. In front of the greengrocery store a crater had opened, and some of the women and children caught there by the explosion had disappeared.[6]

This devastation occurred over the span of just ten minutes, but Sub-Inspector Fife was expected to somehow step in and immediately bring order back to Folkestone. The town was anxious for its future, divided by prostitution and the drug trade, and had a constantly fluctuating population of soldiers. Fife was expected to resolve problems that had built up over many years, largely due to mismanagement by the town authorities. Unsurprisingly, Fife struggled and was eventually fired. Her appointment had been contentious from the start—the Archbishop of Canterbury had pushed for it with the encouragement of Damer Dawson, whose own home was in Lympne, Kent. The authorities were annoyed to have this woman thrust upon them, and also to have Damer Dawson point out their inadequacies (particularly in relation to prostitution). Folkestone had severe problems with VD and had instituted stern measures under DORA; any woman with even a single conviction for prostitution could be ejected from the town. Damer Dawson was unimpressed, feeling that this just cast the women to London, ashamed to return home because of what they had done. From Folkestone's perspective, however, this was perfectly logical. Sub-Inspector Fife did her best to persuade girls to leave before they were ejected, and warned London when the girls were heading their way. In the end, however, Sub-Inspector Fife was never going to succeed against the antagonism of the Folkestone authorities.

They may have been part of the police force, but women constables were still expected to behave in a feminine manner. It was a regular criticism levelled at policewomen and suffragettes that their ranks were comprised of butch women who were unnaturally manly. Taking a quick glance at photos of some early recruits, this criticism can at least be understood (if not endorsed). Many of the ladies were robust and tall, but that was a standard prerequisite for the work as it gave them more presence in the street. Their stature also meant that, if needed, they could defend themselves against attackers. It is fair to say that they cast a stern appearance in their unflattering WPS uniforms, with their hair tied back in tight buns. Any hint of femininity was concealed beneath a mask of authority.

From a policewoman's perspective this was logical. Overt femininity drew flak from magistrates, ordinary police, and criminals, and it diminished the authority of the female officers. It was better for the policewoman to appear androgynous, with a visibly powerful presence, than be accused of feminine foibles. However, these women still risked being deemed abnormal for casting aside their womanly appearance. Their marital status was another bone of contention—some of the authorities envisioned all policewomen as vinegary spinsters, the leftovers of society looking for a way to fit in. A number of the constables were indeed single—and past what was considered a marriageable age—but many others were married and had children. The constant stereotyping of policewomen was never going to represent the true breadth and diversity of ladies who patrolled the streets. This didn't stop popular papers such as *John Bull* from lampooning them and identifying them as aggressive, ugly women who lacked charm.

The trouble was that no matter what the women did, someone was there to throw mud at them. Under the guise of patriarchal concern, women were told not to go on the streets because they could not defend themselves. When they proved otherwise they were treated with even greater disdain. Mrs Annie Morgan-Scott and Mrs Bagster (who had previously fallen foul of Frederick Mead) discovered this while out patrolling in Hyde Park in 1917. Recent changes in police protocol meant that while a male constable still went out with the women from the special patrols, he was not expected to be a constant escort but rather always near enough to rush to their aid if they required him. On this night it was one PC Silverson who was accompanying the ladies, and he was soon to discover that it was not just women police who benefited from travelling in threes.

Silverson walked ahead of the women that night, his eyes scanning the paths for miscreants. Were they to come across a couple behaving improperly, it was decided that he would deal with the man while the ladies spoke with the woman. If he had to make arrests, the women were mainly there to act as witnesses and to supervise the female half of the captured couple. Silverson marched ahead, gazing into the darkness among the trees and bushes until he saw a man behaving 'in an apparently indecent manner'. Silverson approached the man but the culprit, who was not native to Britain and went by the name 'Kung', took umbrage at the constable's interest and shouted abuse before striking him. Silverson stood his ground and put Kung under arrest, but in the commotion Kung called out to a friend—'another alien named Badertscher'—who rushed to his aid and grabbed Silverson from behind. Struggling in the dark with the two men, Silverson lost his balance and ended up on the ground. We will never know what might have become of Silverson in this struggle as, against all protocol, Mrs Bagster ran to help him. She grabbed Badertscher in the same manner that he had grabbed Silverson, and held on to him firmly while Morgan-Scott launched herself at Kung and held him too. Silverson eventually righted himself and performed an arrest. It tells us something of the nature and build of these ladies that they so easily subdued two irate men, though of course there is always the possibility the men restrained themselves upon being confronted by women.

Mrs Carden received a letter of thanks from the commissioner, who was impressed by 'the ladies' pluck and determination'. They had come to Silverson's aid despite one of the attackers 'using his walking-stick as a weapon', uncaring of the risk. Shortly after this incident it was decided that single women could now patrol with an escorting constable. For three years the ladies had strived to make an impact on policing. They had fought hardships, ridicule, and antagonism, but at last they were being noticed and recognised for the good they provided.

The Oldest Profession

The key problem for policewomen remained the rife prostitution on London's streets. Could women police have any more of an impact than men, aside from being able to talk to the girls with the benefit of their shared gender? The war had generated easier opportunities for the working girls to find clients, especially as fresh-faced soldiers from all over the world passed through London. Yet why had this caused an increase in prostitution, rather than just aiding those already involved in the trade? Part of the problem was the sudden sense of freedom many young girls felt, and the natural pull of a number of men dressed in their handsome uniforms. Some girls were so enamoured by the swarms of young men, about to risk their lives, that they were unconcerned by the prospect of a life in prostitution. This girls were innocent to begin with, but once they fell they found themselves trapped—they were sullied, and so they could not return home.

That was one type of the wartime prostitute, but many others were more calculating and simply took advantage of the situation. Some would not have gone into the life had it not been for the war, which stole away their husbands and fathers and them alone, desperate for money. With mouths to feed, and a stricken wartime economy, women found themselves having to take to the streets. Once entrenched in this world there was little way to escape. The women police could advise the girls, and perhaps even send the lucky ones somewhere they could be helped, but the resources for aiding these women were extremely limited. They were fire-fighting, moving the girls on with little way to change their lives; the problem was not being solved but rather being shuffled around. The women police were astute enough to recognise this and felt guilt for failing their fellow women, but what else could they do? Prostitution—with its associated problems of VD, drugs, and theft—had to be managed in order to protect the soldiers, who seemed to fall into the arms of a prostitute at the drop of a hat. If the men could not be controlled then the women had to be.

It was a sign of the policewomen's continuing success that *The Times*, a patriarchal paper which had previously maintained neutrality over the women's cause, was in 1917 arguing that the patrols were the only way to clear up the prevalent vice still on Britain's streets. The problem of widespread prostitution had certainly not diminished in the intervening years, as an article entitled 'Bad Conditions in Westminster' made abundantly clear:

The flaunting display of vice in the Waterloo-Road, to which attention has been drawn in *The Times* during the last two days, has its counterpart in more than one district on the north side of the river. In at least one of these districts, that which has its centre in Horseferry Road, between Victoria Station and Westminster, the evil is to a large extent foreign to the locality, and has sprung up there since the beginning of the war.

Unlike the Waterloo-Road area, this district was not of particularly bad repute in pre-war days. A woman who has been engaged in social work in the vicinity of Horseferry Road for some years, and who knows the place and its inhabitants thoroughly, stated ... yesterday, that one or two streets were 'very low'. She recalled the remark made to her by an old lady connected with her church that she must not go visiting in a certain street, because 'it is not a proper place for you to go alone'. But subject to one or two such exceptions, the district at that time was in no way comparable with any of the other plague spots of London.

Today by the evidence of everybody who takes part in religious or social effort in this area, the Horseferry-Road and the streets adjacent to it are a hot-bed of immorality, undisguised and unchecked. All the odious sights and practices which have already been described as prevailing in the vicinity of Waterloo Station are reproduced here. Prostitutes of all types and ages, but noticeably in most cases young and rather showily dressed, parade the streets and loiter at the corners with the same effrontery. They solicit the soldiers who are about the district with the same boldness. The same dark back streets and courts and out-of-the-way places serve the purpose of the more degraded of them, and the same convenient 'lodgings' abound in every direction. Public houses which once were tolerably 'respectable' have gone down the scale as they have been more and more used by depraved women and the men who consort with them, and reports of thefts from soldiers who have been encouraged to drink—occasionally drugging is alleged—are constantly being received by those who are trying to look after the comfort of the men. Only yesterday an Australian soldier complained bitterly that he had been robbed of £13 by a woman with whom he had gone the night before while in liquor. No fewer than nine Australian soldiers were seen one evening recently coming out of a public house in this neighbourhood, all of them more or less intoxicated, and each of them with a woman hanging on his arm.

The most distressing feature of the evil as it exists here, however, is the number of quite young girls between the ages of 15 and 18, who haunt the streets near the Australian Military Headquarters, and thrust themselves on men who, it must be confessed, are not always displeased by their attentions. Hundreds of these girls are to be seen about the district every night, and the arrival of a thousand men or more from time to time invariably brings them flocking towards the Horseferry-Road in even greater numbers. While it may be that many of them are able to play with fire and not be burned, those who have watched them night after night and tried at every favourable opportunity to warn them, will tell an inquirer that many of them to not escape the fate which their wanton conduct invites....

The work of the women patrols who have voluntarily undertaken the thankless task of protecting these girls from themselves, only touches the fringes of the evil. They have no real police powers, and if a girl with whom they remonstrated in a kind and friendly way, chooses to ignore their advice, they must stand aside. Their efforts, however, even in this limited way, have been valuable, by the consent of all who know the work and its difficulties, and many who have a keen interest in the problem believe that the experiment justifies the demand for a recognised force of official women police to assist in the moral cleansing of the streets. Policewomen armed with the same powers as policemen have been tried with success in several parts of the world. They have also been employed in some parts of this country [this possibly refers to Grantham], and high tributes have been paid to the value of their participation in the maintenance of public order and decency. Though the Metropolitan Police Authorities have not yet seen their way to extend the experiment to London, efforts are still being made to induce them to enlist the aid of women in dealing with prostitution, not only from the punitive point of view, but also from the point of view of prevention.[1]

This was just the sort of publicity the women needed; if a male-dominated paper could see the potential benefit of employing women police then there was still hope that the police authorities could be similarly persuaded.

However, the admittedly mild criticism of the Met had provoked more than just enthusiastic support of the women- some within the patrols wished to defend their new friends within the police force. The Chairman of the London Patrols Committee, Lady Codrington, quickly pointed out that women had actually been given some degree of power by their police employers, and were actually already operating in the areas of Horseferry-Road and Waterloo Station. She responded with a letter, which outlined some of the reasons for the numerous problems:

One aspect of the problem of vice in the London streets, which has been too long overlooked, is the absence from some of the worst districts of any provision for the comfort of young girls whose homes or places of employment are in those districts. In Waterloo-Road and Horseferry-Road, the soldier who has time on his hands can find rest, refreshment and recreation in a YMCA hut, and to that extent he had an inducement to escape the temptations of the streets. But there are no obvious corresponding facilities for girls and women who, for purely innocent reasons, may have to spend an hour or two about the district—perhaps their luncheon hour, or in the case of those living in the neighbourhood, their ordinary hours of leisure. Much has been done in the case of munition centres of the country to provide for the idle hours of the girl and women workers, and it may be worth consideration whether there is not need for a similar provision in the vicious centres of London.

Lady Codrington, chairman of the London Women's Patrol Committee writes—'The article in *The Times* on Saturday on the 'Bad Conditions in Westminster' gives a terrible picture, which I fear is not exaggerated, but by your courtesy I hope I may be allowed to correct the statement that Women Patrols are voluntary preventative worker, who have no police powers. Their works was certainly started as a voluntary organisation, recognised by the authorities, e.g. War Office, Home Office, etc. and the Commissioner of Police, who signed their licences to work; but since July 6, 1916 special patrols have been employed officially by the authorities of Scotland Yard, working under their orders, and paid by them. Their work has been of the greatest value, the police testifying to the fact that owing to their assistance a largely increased number of convictions has been obtained. The need for more work of this sort is palpable, and the numbers of the Special Women Patrols must be largely increased. No body of women has ever before, or since, received the same official recognition as the Women Patrols.[2]

The last line was a little parting snub at the WPS. *The Times* chose to couple this article, either by choice or unintentionally, with two snippets of news from the Waterloo Road area, both of which dampened Lady Codrington's praise of the Women Patrols. One was the story of the sentencing of Annie Young to twelve months of hard labour for keeping a house of disorderly conduct, while the other was a depressing story of the death of a 15-year-old girl who had contracted VD. Her distressed mother could not understand how it had happened because the girl was a good child who went to Sunday school. Considering the area she was from, the obvious assumption is that she was one of those 15 to 18-year-old girls *The Times* had described hanging around the soldiers.

While the war was far from over, interest in women's politics had been revived. While Emmeline and Christabel Pankhurst were avoiding such things other women had reinitiated the suffrage movement. Women were now proving themselves on a daily basis, so all those old, tiresome arguments against female empowerment now seemed laughable. They did the work of men, risked their lives the same as men did, and on occasion suffered horrendous injuries just like the soldiers at the front. It was inevitable that the female police service would become a hot political topic.

Mr Thomas Ferens, MP for Kingston on Hull, had long supported the work of the women, and he now wanted to bring it to higher attention in the House of Commons. On 1 March 1917, addressing Home Secretary Sir George Cave, he asked, 'In view of the scandals in connection with certain districts, such as Waterloo Road, [will you] appoint women police for street work of this kind, with powers of arrest?'

It was a loaded question when considered alongside the current political climate. At that moment the home secretary was completely against offering women the power of arrest, responding, 'I doubt whether the course suggested would be effective in attaining the desired result. Work of this kind requires a long experience of police duties and considerable physical strength in addition to special training and instruction. The commissioner of police, however, is employing women patrols for certain auxiliary work connected with these matters and speaks highly of them.'

By 'auxiliary work' the home secretary presumably meant speaking with prostitutes and trying to move them on. The women patrols would no doubt have wondered just how far removed their current work was from that requiring 'physical strength' or 'long experience'. The women had already proven that they could defend themselves and make the arrest of a struggling suspect. The home secretary's argument was unsound, and Thomas Ferens knew it. On 20 March he pushed the matter again, asking:

If [the home secretary] is aware that the Women Police Service has already trained a considerable number of policewomen, who are working a full eight hours a day in provincial towns, paid by the rates; that they have been exercising the power of arrest; and that they work in rough and crowded districts, managing their own cases with no disability of physical strength; if he is aware that the Ministry of Munitions is employing a force of about 250 policewomen, who live in barracks under their own officers and who are sworn in as constables in Dumfriesshire and Cumberland, use the full powers of constables, and deal with large crowds of men and women operatives, and that excellent reports have been received of their efficiency and service: and if the Home Office can make arrangements to provide the special training and instruction which is required for producing efficient women police?[3]

The home secretary responded:

I am aware that in some provincial towns as in the Metropolitan Police district women are being employed in aid of the police upon work of a preventative nature, but I cannot say that they perform their duties under no disadvantage as regards physical strength. I am also aware that a large number of women police (about two hundred) are employed by the Ministry of Munitions and rendering efficient service at munition factories, where many of the workers are women, and that in Cumberland and Dumfriesshire they have been sworn in, but not that they have the full powers of a constable or deal with large crowds of men and women.

I understand that courses of instruction for women are provided by the National Union of Women Workers and by the Women Police Service, but the Commissioner is unable to provide official instruction for them at the present time. The training classes for the Metropolitan Police have for some time been discontinued owing to there being no recruiting for that force, the teaching staff are engaged on other duties, and the training school building has been lent as a club for overseas soldiers.[4]

Women could do the work, but they would not be given the training necessary nor provided the same degree of power as men, despite facing the exact same risks. Another MP, Mr Harris, wanted to know how many female police were employed in the Metropolitan area, and how effective they had been. Cave told him:

Two members of the Women Police Service and fifty-eight members of the National Union of Women Workers are employed, most of the latter for part-time only, by the Commissioner of Police on work which is mainly preventive in character. If more are available they will be employed from time to time when their services can be employed with advantage.[5]

Harris now took up the baton dropped by Ferens, raking the home secretary over the matter of women police. On 2 July he raised the question of:

...whether two police women have been employed in Paddington since 25th May 1916, with advantage to the public at the cost of funds raised locally; and whether, as these funds are no longer available, the employment of these police women can be continued by the Commissioner of the Metropolitan Police?[6]

Cave had a quick answer for him:

I understand that two members of the Women's Police Service have been employed in Paddington at the cost of funds raised locally. The Commissioner of Police has, in any area where the circumstances justify this course, supplemented the regular police by employing patrols of the National Union of Women Workers, and, pending further experience, he does not propose to make changes which might lead to overlapping of agencies.[7]

The WPS would have been disconcerted that, after the good work they had done, they were now to be replaced by women of the VWP. It was a pattern that was becoming all too common: Damer Dawson had proved too efficient at getting under the skin of MPs and police officials, her recent publicity schemes making her appear determined to undermine the police. This was not the way to win friends in the force, and the subtle approach of the NUWW was rapidly eclipsing the undeniably good work of the WPS. It seems a shame that the two organisations could not find a way to work together, despite the similarity of their goals. There was too deep a clash of personalities at the top, and Mrs Carden was smart enough to know that the position of her own patrols would be diminished if she united with the WPS. Keeping her distance, in fact, was proving highly beneficial; in 1917 the VWP was given a grant of £400 to provide extra patrols around Leicester Square and Hampstead Heath. They were also asked to appoint two women as munitions police at the Woolwich Arsenal, stepping directly on the toes of the WPS.

The debates in the House of Commons would slowly quiet down, being replaced by discussions on enemy aliens, women tram drivers, and the ever contentious DORA. In the background the VWP was working to improve their own patrols. In March Mrs Sofia Stanley—formerly a patrol leader at Portsmouth—was appointed Supervisor of the Special Patrols. She would prove to be a significant asset to the NUWW. She began with thirty-seven special patrols in central London and twenty-nine in the suburbs, working one or two nights a week. Before the year was out she had increased the number in central London to fifty-five, and they all worked full-time. Mrs Stanley was clever and politically astute, and she also had tactful manner that enabled her to get what she wanted without the bulldog tactics of Damer Dawson or Mary Allen. She persuaded police inspectors to allow her women to work seven hours, instead of four, by explaining how this would bring them into line with other patrols in London. Her subtlety paid substantial dividends.

Stanley was more sympathetic to men than her rivals in the WPS. Damer Dawson and Mary Allen both held a slightly dim view of mankind; this was partly because of their family backgrounds, and, in Allen's case, because of her time in the suffragette movement. They had a tendency to unfairly expect the worst of men, and treated them accordingly. This could mean they were abrupt or uncooperative with their male colleagues. However, it might also be argued that, at least in Damer Dawson's case, this was her typical attitude to those people who failed to agree with her.

Considering the WPS consisted of a number of militant suffragettes—Allen included—this should hardly be surprising. Men had been the enemy for a considerable time, at least in the view of those women at the forefront of suffrage. It had become the norm to use aggressive tactics to get their point across, and to view men as inferior, dogmatic, and unapproachable. Mrs Stanley viewed things differently; she was a natural diplomat, and her gentle touch proved increasingly effective. Before long she had won a small victory in the Horseferry Road area—that place where Sir Cave had said women police with powers of arrest were not needed—when the special patrols were asked if they could start work a little later and be available until 11.30 p.m. or midnight, as it was being noticed problems of indecency frequently occurred after 11 p.m. She also won the approval of the commissioner, who asked her to arrange a special investigation at Blackheath after he had received numerous complaints of indecent conduct there.

Blackheath was one of those areas of London where the trouble was caused by a lack of activity for the young and a heavy influx of soldiers. The Bishop of Southwark commented, 'If I had been one of those [14 to 16-year-old boys seen wandering the district] and there had been withheld from my life all the securities and all the help necessary for my leisure moments, I should at this time, I have not the slightest doubt, have been doing seven years.'

Mrs Stanley sent in the veterans of indecency scandals, Mrs Bagster and Mrs Kate Summerton, and instructed them to patrol for seven days. She also patrolled for two days herself, after which she was satisfied that there was no further need of women patrols in the area—presumably the complaints had been of a milder nature than those in other districts.

One of Mrs Stanley's talents was knowing how and when to praise the work of her male colleagues. In October 1917 she paid tribute to the kindness and support of the Metropolitan Police Force to her special patrol ladies. Stanley also recognised the benefit of clubs to soldiers, women, and young boys. Various organisations (perhaps most notably the YMCA) had been opening such clubs throughout the war in an attempt to keep young people off the streets, and to provide entertainment for idle soldiers on leave. Lectures and instructional classes were offered, and one girls-only club even had its own bathing facilities. Mixed clubs were seen as a safe place for men and girls to meet; few romances had been spawned in such huts and were better situated here than being taken onto the streets and dark alleys, where misbehaviour might be encouraged.

Aside from the usual patrols, the women had also recently taken on duties to supervise tube stations during air raids, as the stations had become the best shelter against zeppelin attacks. Hundreds of people would gather underground for protection—vast numbers of them from slums, where there was no other form of shelter. However, mass panic tended to influence these slum refugees, and their confusion was intermingled with fraught tempers, chaos, and general havoc. The police had to monitor mass evacuations and even rope off side streets to try and prevent the panic spilling out. One can only imagine the fear that fuelled those people, and the dangerous stampedes that could therefore result.

Meanwhile the WPS was keeping an eye on train stations, where problems could be caused by drunks, drug users, and the traumatised men of war. Mary Allen recorded one shocking event which must have been very common in the latter years of war:

A boy among the first leave draft from the front, his nerves still at breaking point, discovered at the station that he had lost the train ticket to his home, or thought he had. It was the last straw. Flinging his kit down, he whipped out a razor. The policewoman closed with him and, after a desperate struggle, managed to knock the razor from his hand, and to persuade him to go with her to the Rest Room. There, after swallowing a hot drink, he instantly fell asleep, and slept for hours. During this interval she was able to find his address and telegraph to his people, so that when he awoke, comparatively quiet and in his right mind, she could conduct him to his train for the North, and was informed later of his safe arrival.[8]

Shell-shock became one of the main legacies of WWI, and opened up a totally new understanding of the effects of extreme trauma on the human mind. However, in those dark years of 1914–1918 the ones who were left to pick up the pieces of shattered nerves and broken minds were mainly women.

Another returning soldier was so disordered that while he was going down the stairs into the tube station, becoming suddenly aware of the crowd of people coming up, he looked haggardly about, and evidently mistaking the hollow space below for the trenches, and the ascending crowd for Germans, fixed his bayonet and charged. But for the women constable on duty at the turn of the staircase, who was quick enough to divine his trouble and, hanging on to him with all her strength, to prevent his forward advance, he would have wounded many and caused a dangerous panic.[9]

Many soldiers felt the need to dampen their nerves with alcohol, and drunken servicemen became commonplace. The police found them difficult to deal with as the general public had developed a staunch protectiveness towards theses sorrowful soldiers, and often refused to let an ordinary constable arrest a drunk serviceman. It was up to the special patrols or WPS to collect such men and escort them to a safe place where they could sleep off their over-indulgence. This was the idea behind the famous 'drunk man' publicity photograph over which Damer Dawson would get in trouble. Dorothy Peto, who was now serving with the special patrols, recalled the nightly saga of rescuing drunk soldiers:

I used to get out with the Special Patrols most often on a tour of night duty in and around a railway station (they patrolled without any PC here since it was private property); and of those nights I still have vivid memories, particularly of those at Euston. In those days there were several public houses near the entrance in Euston Road, much frequented by street women on the look-out for servicemen on their way to catch a night train to the North. If one such man could be enticed into a public house, the woman plied him with drink and relieved him of his cash, after which he emerged drunk and sometimes penniless. The special patrols developed their own technique. When they saw a soldier or sailor being picked up by such a woman, or staggering drunkenly out of licensed premises, they got him away and, if reasonably sober, saw him into the railway station and into safe company. If he was too far gone for this, they led him instead to the gate of the central enclosure in Euston Square, within which the YMCA ran a Service Canteen. Having rung the bell for the man on the gate, we pushed our charge inside as soon as it opened and then went back to the beat.

Within the station itself, a women's organisation ran another canteen for servicemen and women, and welcomed the co-operation of the patrols in dealing with customers either obstreperous or collapsed. It has to be remembered that most service men—or women—were generally tired enough to knock under to a comparatively small amount of drink, taken in all probability on an empty stomach. Patrols became skilled in 'sobering up' their patients by means of cups of black coffee laced with bicarbonate of soda which, after making them violently sick, left them sober enough to be entrained in due course.[10]

In 1915, in Richmond, Mrs Hampton—sister to Mary Allen—had proved rather more diplomatic than her sister and had secured herself a semi-official position, initially funded by the area branch of the Women's Local Government Association. Such associations had a mixed remit for trying to improve the conditions of their borough and support the war effort as much as possible. These associations enabled women to make decisions on behalf of their local area, and so Mrs Hampton was employed to take watch over the streets of Richmond, deal with unruly children, and attend the local Magistrates and Petty Sessional Courts when a woman was on trial. Often she was the only other female in the building, and could provide invaluable support to the frightened defendant. Unlike her sister—who had very little sympathy for women who got themselves into trouble—Mrs Hampton was compassionate and viewed watching over female prisoners as one of her key duties.

However, local funding soon ran out and at this point the Criminal Law Amendment Committee (CLAC) stepped in. A long-term supporter of female police, and the WPS in particular, the CLAC was able to find a member who was prepared to indefinitely support Mrs Hampton and pay her wages. Fortunately this was not for as long as might have been feared, as the Commissioner was then persuaded to pay Mrs Hampton a wage of 30s a week—making her the only member of the WPS to be paid by the Metropolitan Police. This says much for her reputation, and her tact.

At the same time, the CLAC were trying to push forward the old issue of the official inclusion of women into the police force. In March 1916 a public meeting took place:

A public meeting organised by the Criminal Law Amendment Committee and the Women Police Service was held at the Mansion House yesterday in support of a resolution urging the inclusion of women in the Police Force and the provisions of suitable training for them ...

The Lord Mayor said that though in the City they had not arrived at the stage of appointing women to the Police there had been for some time a system of patrol by women, and he was glad to acknowledge the efficient work of the patrols.

The Bishop of Kensington moved the resolution.

Sir F. Lloyd said that he was whole-heartedly in accord with the idea of having women patrols, and had given the military police orders to help them in every possible way. How far women should be accorded a police status must be determined by qualified authority. Certainly, women as police could be of great service in certain cases in which women and children were concerned, and could release men, if only a few, for the Army.

Lady Nott-Bower said that criminal statistics showed how many were the offences against young women and children that men could not and ought not to investigate. It was a crime and a blunder to put a young child in a Court with only men to ask her questions. This was work for women to undertake, and they were prepared to do so.

Lord Sydenham said it was natural to shrink from exposing women to the liability to perform those duties of the police which required the exercise of physical force. But there were many other duties which were of more importance and occupied more of the time of the police than the exercise of physical force. There were inquiries and investigations, some of them such as only women could make, and such duties had been performed by women police with marked success in America.

Mrs Creighton represented the view of 2,000 women patrols doing voluntary work. Their experience, she said, proved the value of their service, imperfectly trained though they had been for emergency work.

Miss Damer Dawson, chief officer of the Women Police, mentioned a case in which an inspector took a charge against a drunken woman whom a woman policeman had arrested, and upon the evidence of the woman policeman the offender was convicted. The whole proceeding was illegal, and what was wanted was that such actions should be made legal. They had received the greatest courtesy and cooperation from the police—she might almost say had been received with open arms...[11]

Damer Dawson's comments were ironic, especially when considering the consternation the WPS had caused the Commissioner and the constant antagonism directed back at them. The discussion went around in circles, but by the end a resolution was unanimously adopted that women should be incorporated into the main police force; if only persuading the real authorities was that easy.

Helping the Helpless

Mrs Hampton was kept extremely busy with her court work, almost to the point of being unable to go on patrol. She was a vital advocate for those lost souls who came into the courtroom and found themselves completely alone among men, many of whom could never begin to understand the perspective of a woman. She did her best to advise them and stayed with them until a matron could be found to replace her. The regular police were also keen to unload some of their more difficult work on to her—as Lady Nott-Bower had said, in certain cases 'men could not and ought not to investigate'. These cases included incidents of missing girls or those where the girl needed a quiet word about their behaviour. It was also seen as prudent to have a woman interview female victims of rape, as the police were highly aware that women found it hard to talk to men about their assault. In one particularly trying case, Mrs Hampton had to visit a woman who accused a man of rape:

> A solder in France applied to come home on leave to arrange matters with his wife, who was in great trouble. She wrote alleging that she had been criminally assaulted by an unknown soldier while in a lonely part. He had made her unconscious, and she had a child coming in consequence. The military authorities communicated with the police asking them to verify the wife's statement. For this the police had to obtain a detailed written statement of all that had happened from the woman herself, and [Mrs Hampton] was sent with the police officer to do this. In these cases it is most important that a woman should take these statements, for it is almost impossible for a respectable woman to give all the intimate details necessary to a man.[1]

Another of Mrs Hampton's cases revolved around the growing anti-German sentiment in Britain. A father and daughter had gone to the magistrates asking for protection from a neighbour's servant, who insulted them by criticising their nationality. As Jews they were genuinely unnerved at being perceived as German. Mrs Hampton wrote: 'As the abuse took place in the neighbour's garden, a summons could not be granted and I was asked by the magistrate if

I could do anything. Both parties were interviewed and everything arranged satisfactorily.'

One of the main areas the WPS focused on was the protection of children. For decades children had been the most vulnerable group in society, often to be found wandering the streets alone, especially in poorer regions, and they were regular victims of abuse. The women police had a keen awareness and concern for children. For a long time the abuse of children, and particularly of young girls, had been used by suffragettes as evidence for the brutality of men and the necessity of female empowerment, as it was argued that this could stem the tide of male abuse. In a 1912 edition of *The Suffragette*, Flora Drummond wrote:

> Even under the new Bill [the White Slave Act] which is now being carried a man can get less punishment for trapping an innocent girl and forcing her to a life of shame than for stealing a loaf of bread ... The outrages committed upon little girls, some of them only babies ... is a growing evil, which working-class mothers are determined to stamp out.[2]

As mothers or potential mothers themselves, the suffragettes held strong sympathy for the plight of the many street children they encountered as police volunteers. They were also appalled at the callous attitude many men had towards these victims. The same year that Mrs Drummond voiced her concerns about child abuse, a case came up in Sandwich, Kent, which epitomised the problem. A man who was found guilty of abusing a child was given only a nominal sentence, because the court decided he had succumbed to a normal, momentary temptation. This stunned women across the country, and the suffragettes saw this case as yet another example of the perfidy and unreliability of men.

Just a year before the first female police volunteers emerged, another case shook Edwardian England. A flat in Piccadilly was discovered to be operating as a brothel, with girls barely above the age of consent servicing a number of upper-class men. The issue was raised in the House of Commons, but Christabel Pankhurst later claimed that the WSPU offices had been raided to confiscate evidence which would have revealed the full extent of the government's role in the affair. This was a little far-fetched, but the case did further fuel the women's drive for votes. How was it that men who frequented such debauched surroundings, and then committed obscene acts with young girls, could not only go home unchallenged by law but then actively obstruct female suffrage? Their righteous fury was fuelled by maternal concern and the hideous idea that such activities were potentially being carried out in far more areas than just in Piccadilly.

Particular concerns were shown for children in the Paddington area, and the WPS made a special effort to watch over children in this region. The WPS ladies acted as guardians to the young, seeing them across roads, preventing them getting into trouble, and patrolling near a notorious canal and public house where mothers would leave their children unattended while they went to drink. The sale of alcohol to under-age people was yet another problem to be stamped out.

Why was Paddington perceived as such a high-risk area, when vice was rife in several London boroughs? Perhaps one answer might come from the horrific case of Margaret Ellen Nally. Seven-year-old Ellen lived on Amberley Road, Paddington, where her father was a night porter. He was working on the Sunday night, in 1915, on which Ellen was found murdered in Aldersgate Street station. She was found just before midnight, in one of the compartments of the ladies waiting room; she had been suffocated by a piece of cloth and 'terribly assaulted'—by which we can infer that she had been the victim of a sexual predator.

Ellen had last been seen alive at eight o'clock the same night, when she had been visiting an aunt about a half-an-hour walk away from her home, where she had spent time playing with her younger cousin. The two girls had just gone to buy some sweets, a present from the aunt for running an errand, when Ellen told her cousin she was heading home—which her cousin and aunt believed to mean Ellen's grandfather's house nearby, rather than the home she shared with her parents.

> ...his little daughter went to her aunt and grandfather in Carlisle Street on a birthday visit—she was seven years old on Saturday ... the girl knew the neighbourhood well, and had been there unaccompanied many times before. She had always come back long before it was dark, and as she was a particularly bright and intelligent child, and her relatives in Carlisle Street were very fond of her, they were pleased enough that she should go. When Margaret failed to return at her usual time his wife and he began to get anxious. At 8 o'clock he left for Carlisle Street. Thinking he might meet her, he walked the way his daughter usually took when going to her grandfather's house.[3]

When Mr Nally reached Carlisle Street he was told that Ellen had headed home around eight o'clock—he was satisfied that he had just happened to miss her and went on to work.

> Just after ten o'clock his wife came to see him and told him that Margaret had not returned. The John Street and Paddington Green police were informed of the girl's absence a little later and local infirmaries telephoned too. At half-past 2 a message came through saying that the body of a little girl answering the description of his daughter had been found at Aldersgate

Street station. The mother added that her daughter, a tall girl for her age and good looking, was not the sort of girl who would speak to strangers or appreciate any advances made by them.[4]

The grimness of the crime against Margaret, and the little hope she had of salvation, was made apparent by the evidence of Inspector Groves, the railway official who found Margaret's body.

> ...In accordance with his usual custom, after the last train had left at 11.50 on Sunday night [he inspected the cloakroom]. There are two compartments there, and when he went to open the door of that on the right-hand side with his private key, he found that there was an obstruction of some kind. He forced the door open and inside he found the body of the murdered child.
>
> Discussing the possibilities of a person entering the cloakroom from a train unobserved, Inspector Groves said that the only official who would be likely to observe anything was the porter, and it was quite possible that he was not on the platform at the time. There were generally very few passengers at that time on Sunday night, and once inside the cloakroom a person would be free from observation. Had the child screamed it is improbable that with the roar and rattle of the trains, she would have been heard by anyone at the station.[5]

So what had happened to poor Margaret? The police assumed that her murderer had arrived by train at Aldersgate Street, and that somewhere between Carlisle Street and the station he had picked up Margaret and persuaded her to accompany him. The police hoped someone might have seen a man with a young girl boarding or leaving the train. Their only other lead was a description of a dark-haired, clean-shaven man, who had was reported to have attempted to induce an eleven-year-old to accompany him shortly before Margaret's disappearance. What clues they had were minor. A post-mortem found that Margaret had been dead around two hours, so her murder had taken place before ten o'clock. The material that was used to gag Margaret seemed to be a dead end, though there was evidence she had bitten her attacker.

Eventually evidence emerged that indicated Margaret had been given a meal before she was killed. However, as the meal was identical to the one she had earlier eaten with her family, the experts were divided as to whether it was the remains of lunch or whether her attacker had fed her again. The assailant's identity remained a mystery, further confused by the confession of a mentally unwell soldier (who had not even been in London at the time) and a scrawled message on a railway ticket that said 'I intend to kill a child tonight'. Margaret's murder would become one of many to remain unsolved.

Her murder made the papers but other attacks or aborted attempts did not, and the WPS and the ordinary police knew this. Paddington was probably no worse in that regard than many of the darker regions of London, but this case drew attention there—not least because Margaret's killer remained at large. The WPS would have been drawn to Paddington's streets after seeing the story, keen to help. Damer Dawson had a fondness for saving children, even if it was in the slightly patronising and philanthropic style of the Victorians. She would eventually open a children's home, so it was natural for her to want to send her ladies into what appeared to be a cesspit of crimes against children.

There were other child-related problems that needed regulating, even if they were not as headline-grabbing as murder. Child labour, as mentioned before, had become quite the issue. It was causing consternation because it was seen as necessary to hire children, from a practical perspective, in order to free men up to join the army. The effect on child welfare was appalling, with children expected to work long hours, often in hazardous conditions, and then to attend school. Teachers were alarmed by the number of their pupils who fell asleep at their desks through sheer exhaustion. However, not everyone was particularly concerned that the education of the lower classes was suffering. The Earl of Selborne explained his opinion to the House of Lords in 1915:

> As to child labour he was quite clear that it was more important that all the children who were physically strong enough to do so should be allowed to go out and work on the land than that they should continue in the school.[6]

It was the primary concern of many to free up manpower for the army, and everything else could wait; after all, the only alternative could be recruiting older men, who were often not fit enough to go to the front. Employers naturally favoured children over the aged or the unhealthy, seeing as they were more productive. It sometimes seemed that very few were actually worried that children were being exploited. Inspector Harburn—a stalwart of the WPS—took time to assess the problem and reported back that the enforcement of the 1908 Children Act, which had made some effort to regulate child labour and to prevent children working in dangerous trades, was now impossible to enforce. In at least one London borough there were no by-laws controlling the employment of children under fourteen. The employers were bending the law without actually breaking it, aided by the tacit support of the government. In desperation the WPS turned to teachers and parents, asking them to keep a closer watch on their children.

Unfortunately parents often found their child's extra income vital, and schools were often closed or only operating short hours throughout the war—many male teachers had found their way into the army—so teachers were almost out of the loop. All the WPS could do was to manage the situation. They monitored children going into and coming away from work, tried their best to spot exploitation and stop it, and acted as escorting guards when a daylight raid on the city forced hordes of children from their factories to the nearest shelter. It was a thankless task, unaided by another piece of obvious propaganda that appeared in December 1916:

The policewoman has become a sort of mother of the mean streets, where unkempt and uncared-for youngsters spend much of their time. Her duty is to look after their welfare and behaviour day after day, in wet weather and in fine. It is not particularly exhilarating or exciting war work, but it is none the less necessary, and the women chosen for duty among the children are carefully selected. They are those who had a love for little children and an understanding of the difficulties of tired, over-worked mothers.

'Don't you get tired of the work?' I asked the children's sergeant, who took me on her rounds the other day, and she laughed at the very idea. She had spent her morning in court, but at twelve she led me to a school in one of the most crowded parts of London. Out of the school doors poured hundreds of boys and girls like a troop of little wild things. They were dirty and ragged, but they shouted and danced and ran into the middle of the road—unless they caught the policewoman's eye; they then became models of deportment.

'It is quite evident that in the family circles in that neighbourhood a mention of the policewoman is a thing to conjure with. Yet she is such a pleasant, cheerful, kind 'bogey-woman' that the smallest tiny-tot places his hand in hers and smiles up at her as she lead him safely across the road.

The London child of four is a model of self-reliance. He brings himself to school and takes himself home, but the policewoman sees him across the road nowadays, and she sees that no larger boys tease him to take his apple or his penny. Those larger boys are the difficulty today. They need the paternal authority, and the dinner hour must be a trial for the harassed mother as she chances to be there, and generally she is not, since she is off at work—or elsewhere—leaving a slice of bread and some cold carrots for her offspring's midday meal.

When the children are safely out of school, the children's sergeant patrols the neighbouring streets crowded with women gossiping and children playing games or eating bits of bread on the steps of the little houses, each of which shelters several families. She stops fights in their infancy, checks boys who wish to turn handsprings in front of carts, picks up the small girls who fall down, speaks a kindly word to the weeping child who has a grief she cannot express but which is noisily poignant, and keeps an eagle eye unhooded for the would-be truant.

And her reward is the confidence of those forlorn little mites who grasp her hand with their small grimy fingers, and the bright, grateful smile of those tired, bedraggled women the little ones call mother.[7]

Such sickly sweet sentimentality puts the tragedy of Margaret Nally into context, and explains why places such as Paddington were a delight to the predatory criminal. Children were running wild; in some regards employing the older ones at least kept them off the streets, easing the burden on mothers who also had to work. With their fathers either deceased or absent, many children had to fend for themselves and spent their days under very little parental supervision. Pockets of street-kids formed gangs to survive, and they quickly turned over to mischief and even crime. Hunger, loneliness, and fear all added to the tension of life on the streets, and without a secure home to retreat to many children were left floundering. The police were struggling to keep such strife under control; there were far too many children and not enough eyes to watch over them. It was inevitable that some were to disappear into the seething depths of London, but few such disappearances ever made the news unless they shared Margaret Nally's tragic conclusion, and even then it was noticeable from the reports that she was from a respectable working class family. She went out well-dressed and would not have been one of the street-kids the WPS had to deal with; this in itself made her a figure of pity, much more so than the urchins who many had simply washed their hands of.

Propaganda

After the split between Nina Boyle and Damer Dawson the Women Police Volunteers made a valiant effort to soldier on. While Damer Dawson's WPS made inroads into policing, Boyle's WPV was struggling. This was partly due to Nina Boyle herself, whose ties with suffrage were always a bugbear to the regular police, and she refused to set aside her beliefs to earn favours. She would not support DORA and she would not stop her push for greater female empowerment. In some ways this was a very valiant stance, but her stoicism severely hampered the work of the WPV and made them a pariah for the anti-women-police lobby. A prime example of the failures of the WPV's diplomacy came in Brighton, in March 1915, where troubles brewed due to a rivalry between the town's branches of the WPV and the NUWW:

> Brighton suffragists who have been parading the town as women police volunteers have been warned by the Chief Constable to desist. In answer to inquiries yesterday, Mr Gentle Chief of the Brighton Police said there were a number of local women attached to the National Union of Women Workers whom he had authorised to act as women patrols in the interest of young girls and others, and they were very helpful; but he had warned the local suffragists who were calling themselves police volunteers to stop parading the streets and representing themselves as police officers.[1]

Boyle's ladies had tried to take advantage of the favour shown to the NUWW patrols but the only consequence was further damage to their reputation. Throughout 1915 the WPV were still determined to achieve their goal of having trained women in every Metropolitan Police force and Assize Court, but they were a group in decline. Exactly when they ceased to function is debatable, as for a time the press continued to use their name when discussing women police—without necessarily being correct in referring to them. Presumably they were no more by December 1916, when Nina Boyle decided to become a nurse and to head for Macedonia where she helped wounded Serbian soldiers. She said her sudden departure was necessary because she was 'falling into a groove' and needed something to revitalise her ideas. She wrote:

Also, this Great War is the biggest thing the world has yet known; and I think it becomes me, who talk politics and finds fault with politicians, to see something of it for myself at first hand, and not be dependent in other people's impressions. I feel sure I shall get a better perspective and sense of proportion as the result.[2]

Nina was certainly a person who needed change to keep her stimulated, but one can't help but wonder if part of the reason for her departure was the disintegration of the WPV—at a time when the WPS, under Damer Dawson, were making a name for themselves.

In fact the WPS found themselves being offered a position in Brighton by the Mayor, who asked for one of their women patrols to attend the local court whenever a women or a child was the defendant. It was slowly becoming recognised that female offenders, victims, and witnesses needed support from other women in the male-dominated courtrooms.

The WPS was also making progress with its 'Baby Home', which was founded to look after illegitimate and orphaned babies, or those whose mothers could no longer care for them. Orphanages were becoming rather overloaded at this stage in the war, due to the high numbers of children being abandoned or losing both parents, so the Baby Home was a logical move and would have been encouraged by the sight of so many waifs and strays on the streets. Damer Dawson gave speeches to raise donations and WPS members paid regular subscriptions to keep the home operational. Unsurprisingly it was easier to persuade people to fund a home for orphans, a politically neutral act, than it was to garner donations for the WPS directly. The women police were also slowly changing their views on topics such as DORA; once firm advocates (Mary Allen never lost her determination to support the measures), after they were on the streets for a while the WPS realised that things were not as black and white as DORA implied. Venereal disease was nonetheless a big issue during the war years, and the number of debates in the House of Commons and the column inches dedicated to the subject enough proof of this.

However, it could be that debates on VD were more prevalent than the diseases themselves. A report from the Royal Commission on Venereal Disease in 1916 had found that current statistics indicated a decline in VD; for instance, the number of recruits who were refused enlistment due to having syphilis in 1873 was 16.5 per 1,000, but by 1911 this had fallen to 1.4. The commissioners of the report were rather keen to explain away this decline, which was inarguably significant. The government was determined that VD was on the rise, that it was a scandal, and that they should base stringent, vindictive policies upon this trend. There was a great desire to condemn statistics that suggested things were not as bad as they seemed, which could give fuel to the anti-DORA campaigners. 'This does not mean that the evil is not very great,' argued *The Times* when reviewing the Commission's report, 'and still less that there is no need to combat it; but it does weaken the plea of urgency. The real grounds of urgency are the revelations of recent medical research in regard to the numerous and varied secondary effects of venereal disease.'

Others used the report (statistics suggesting decline aside) to reinforce their arguments for the need for reforms. 'Venereal disease is another of the "baby-killers"—and all the weapons of the enemy are feeble when compared with it,' argued, rather over-dramatically, one medical correspondent, when commenting on a falling birth-rate and rising infant mortality.

Throughout the war various means for controlling VD—from education to licencing prostitution—were recommended and then mooted. DORA, heavy-handed though it was, solved the problem with little need for extra measures, at least from a government perspective; it also gave the appearance of 'doing something'. However, even the ladies of the WPS were becoming antagonistic towards the act. In 1917 it was noted that in one city the WPS had refused to put any woman in the dock for indecency unless the man she had committed the action with was also arrested. This was tricky because people were not keen to condemn soldiers, and much of the evidence would have to rely on fellow servicemen—who were even less keen to rat out their comrades. The WPS had finally realised that women were not the sole culprits in this sexual war, and now they were on the streets they actually began to feel women were being unduly persecuted. They stated that one specific case, involving an inebriated man who had lewdly approached and insulted eight girls, was 'typical of the impossibility under the present state of the law of obtaining any correction or punishment for men who persistently insult women'. The girls were all appalled, and a WPS sergeant finally convinced a PC to arrest the man. He did so, but only charged him with drunkenness as there was no law against men soliciting women. The man went to court and was found not guilty, claiming that illness had affected his behaviour rather than drink. Cases like this were beginning to infuriate the women police, and were reinforcing the long-held suffrage belief that men in authority allowed double standards in the treatment of male and female offenders.

Despite this, Edith Smith was still required to behave in a manner specific to her gender in Grantham. In her report for 1916–17, she conducted numerous interviews in the cases of 'husbands placing their wives under observation during their absence [and] husbands enquiring into the reported misconduct of their wives'. There was little sense of equality in these matters, but the adultery of a wife was still taken more seriously and considered to be more scandalous than the adultery of a husband. It might be argued that Smith's duty was to alleviate one of the many anxieties facing a man at the front; he had enough to worry about without concerning himself with the activities of his wife, and perhaps visiting and monitoring suspect wives was justified in that it helped the man survive his ordeal at the front. However, this was a flimsy excuse that demonstrates how the female police were forced to demean their own gender. Barely two years had passed since the *Sussex Daily News* wrote:

London has not yet grown accustomed to its policewomen. I saw one today at the corner of Whitehall, and she appeared very conscious of the attention she was attracting. There is nothing very distinctive about the neat blue costume that the women wear, and their hats rather suggest that they had just returned from a morning ride in the Row. It is only when you notice the WP on their shoulders that you recognise the work on which they are occupied. Physically the women are not of the type you would expect, and they seem little fitted to face the hurly-burly of a street row. Most of them are slight and fragile in build, and their hands are of the small, delicate type generally associated with the artistic temperament. If the women police act with tact and discretion, there is useful work for them to do in the West End of London, but the average Cockney seems at present to resent their presence in the streets. The suffragettes are to blame for this in large measure, for in the public mind the 'Copperettes', as the girls are called, have come to be associated, quite erroneously no doubt, with the women who used to break windows, and shout 'Votes for women' in Parliament Square.[3]

This writer clearly had very staunch views on both the rights of women and suffragettes. His article described a lady of the WPS in her 'riding hat' (which, of course, had been designed in a similar way to the hats worn by female horse riders), and his tone implies he thought very little of the exercise of bringing uniformed women onto the street. Subtly, he suggested they are not sturdy enough for such work with their 'small, delicate' hands and fragile build. In the next breath he links them with the troublesome suffragettes, making a point the government and Metropolitan Police often were at pains to call attention to—that early policewomen had been part of those suffrage movements, on the wrong side of the law, for many years. He also gives a very different picture of the public's reaction: Damer Dawson and Mary Allen were both keen to express how well-received the women police were, claiming that they were treated with respect and soon won over even the most hardened of hearts, despite the public's initial suspicion. Even a casual observer must wonder at the truth of this rather Disneyesque tale; perhaps there was a hint of truth in the resentment that the 'average Cockney' held against the policewomen's presence, and that the derogatory name 'Copperettes' was a pun on 'suffragettes'. However, two years later, in 1917, a very different story was being presented in *The Times*:

Women in uniform are so frequent nowadays that the passer-by scarcely spares a glance for a hard 'bowler' kind of hat, plain blue clothes, and a blue armlet with white letters on it. And the wearers of this uniform seem to be peculiarly unobtrusive people, anxious to avoid, not attract, attention. For all that, among the innumerable women who are picking up the work which men have had to drop, or tackling the new work which the times have brought to be done, these women police are by no means the least valuable, brave, and steadfast.

They are very carefully chosen and trained for their difficult task. Recruits must be well educated, physically sound, and provided with unexceptionable references. During the training a small percentage is weeded out; some proving not strong enough to face all weathers, others lacking initiative and resource, and few finding the discipline irksome ...

When the recruit is trained she finds to her hand more than enough work of a kind that is especially suited to women. It is commonly believed that great physical strength is essential to police work; and to some parts of it no doubt it is. But there is much also in which moral force and tactful supervision are of more value than muscle. In matters concerning women and children especially, the policewoman has powers sometimes denied to the man. Take, for example, the visitation of common lodging-houses. In this class of dwelling live girls so poor that many of them have but one set of underclothing, which has to be washed, partially dried, and put on before the owner can go out. Women alone ought to have *entrée* to the rooms inhabited by such as these. A child, again, turns instinctively to a woman. Every police court is familiar with the spectacle of a child so frightened that it cannot tell the truth, much less give a clear and detailed statement. The policewoman—very likely herself a mother—knows how to approach the child, allay its fears, calm its mind, and in time, as if by accident, win from it what the Court wants to know. And a policewoman will tell you that women have a much quicker eye for detail than men, and a passionate desire for justice, which makes them spare no time or trouble to get at the truth. So successfully has this work been done by women police that at Richmond the policewoman of that borough holds the rank of probation officer in addition to her own.

There is another field in which the policewoman has a special task—on streets at night. Without any authority to control the women or girls who, for their own ends of for fear of some threatening brute in the background, prey upon the sons of English mothers and of mothers overseas, the policewomen have already done much to cleanse the public thoroughfares. The blue armlet is well known not only in the Waterloo Road or in Horseferry Road, but in streets and squares much 'smarter', but no less shameful. The method employed is the exertion of an unobtrusive vigilance, a steady pressure of observation. 'Here I am!' says the blue armlet, passing quietly by at the very moment when secrecy is most desired. When it appears groups disperse, loiterers discover urgent business elsewhere. Time is given for that second thought, which is often the salvation of the tempted; the consciousness that decent, well-bred women are out in all weathers taking thought for his welfare may well check a young man's reckless impulse. There remains, of course, the drunkard; and the drunkard if he is too far gone for persuasion, is delivered by the blue armlet—for once exerting physical force—at the nearest YMCA hut, to be properly ashamed of himself, it may be hoped, when he learns who brought him there.

It is good work, well done. Perhaps, when the war is over, we shall find the women police officially recognised and established as a permanent force.[4]

This article has to be the work of a WPS supporter. The women in the article are clearly WPS, as shown by the description of their bowler hats and blue uniforms, and the lady in Richmond who was both probation officer and policewoman is very probably Mrs Hampton. However, this article appeared in *The Times*, a newspaper that had been previously ambivalent to women police and had mostly ignored them. In that sense alone it shows how the women had earned the respect of sections of this male-dominated world. Looking deeper into the article, it can be seen that the same qualities which the *Sussex* correspondent had derided are now presented as the main assets of women police, and as those which set them apart, in a good sense, from men. The statement, 'women have a much quicker eye for detail than men, and a passionate desire for justice, which makes them spare no time or trouble to get at the truth', definitely raises a wry smile. This somewhat implies that male police do not have similar attributes, but this is perhaps poor wording rather than a deliberate dig. Even more interesting is the end comment which, in black and white, raised the possibility of women police remaining after the war.

Of course it wasn't all to be harmonious, with the woman police's increasing confidence in their roles leading to resentment among those who fell afoul of them. *The Times* was soon reporting the flipside of police work:

WOMAN'S ASSAULT ON POLICEWOMAN—At Lambeth Police Court on Saturday, before Mr Chester Jones, Kitty Ivy, 24, was charged with being drunk and disorderly and assaulting Annie Wilson, a woman police patrol. The prosecutrix was on a tramway-car when the prisoner and another woman made some disparaging remarks about policewomen. Afterwards Ivy followed the prosecutrix, who told her she must have been drunk to say what she had said. The prisoner thereupon slapped her face. Ivy was ordered to pay 40s for being drunk and disorderly and a fine of 20s and 20s costs for the assault.[5]

Ironic that Ivy was fined more for being drunk than for her assault on a policewoman, showing the priorities of the court. No doubt this was only one of many minor incidents in which the policewomen found themselves involved.

The Bristol Training School and the Mersey Beat

Training women to cope with the various events they would have to contend with, not to mention how best to deal with drunken and abusive men and women, quickly became an essential part of policing. A training school was set up, in part, by Dorothy Peto. She had joined an NUWW patrol in Bath at the start of the war, and as a robust country girl her initiation into the world of policing urban streets was a little bumpy:

> I well remember starting out for my first tour of street duty, an umbrella hooked over one arm, and my skirt held up behind me—for the skirts, in those days, came almost down to the ground, and the hills of Bath were steep. Town life was new to me. As we passed through the darkened streets (all lamps have been broken by the special constables on the day that War was declared, for lack of any means of turning them off at source) I felt— nay, I hoped—that each group of persons whom we passed might turn out to be plotting some nefarious deed! In one of the poorer streets down by the river, we came on a long, low van like a baker's cart with doors at the back; whereupon I ingenuously remarked, 'How late the beagles are out tonight', only to learn from my convulsed companion that the vehicle in question was an undertaker's van delivering a coffin for an impending funeral! [1]

Peto might have been a little naïve but she soon found herself in the swing of things, and her clerical experience enabled her to be taken on as secretary to Flora Joseph, the newly appointed organiser for Somerset. It was Joseph who realised the great need for at least patrol leaders to receive some formal training before hitting the streets. Peto's stories of her early days on the beat may have crystallised this idea. Joseph contacted the Bristol Women Patrols Committee, who in turn approached the central committee and advised it that they wished to set up a school for policewomen. The committee in London gave its approval, with the caveat that the school should be available for all forces, but that instructors and students must remember the WVP and WPS were separate organisations—thus a WVP lady would not be expected to bow down to a

WPS superior or vice versa. Previously the WPS had conducted training for any policewoman who wanted it, and the Bristol Committee realised that tact was essential to ensure no one was upset; the Bristol Training School (BTS) would aim to be as neutral as possible in the politics of the women patrols. Damer Dawson was approached through friends and invited to join the committee. She hesitated, as she preferred to keep all training centralised and under the full auspices of the WPS, but eventually she agreed that the BTS was a worthwhile project and joined. Meanwhile, Flora Joseph had been appointed Chairman of the training school sub-committee, with Dorothy Peto becoming assistant director. *The Times* reported on the school in October 1916:

> The Bristol Training School for Women Patrols and Women Police has now been in existence for a year. Miss D. O. G. Peto, the director [Peto became director after the departure of her predecessor Mrs Gent], is assisted by a committee of ladies representing various women's organisations in Bristol and Somerset, including the local branch of the National Union of Women Workers. The object of the school is to increase the supply of educated women suited for employment in country police forces, for police duty in munition works, and for appointment as patrol leaders. It is recognised that the practical training in police work can be given only by police officers, but the school can give much useful preliminary training in its three months' course.[2]

Unfortunately the school's aspiration to neutrality was soon thwarted. Damer Dawson placed the blame firmly on the part of the NUWW ladies; she argued that they were not prepared to accept the unrelenting discipline her organisation required, especially when it came to the officers. She dismissed the endeavours of the BTS, snidely implying that it had only been set up for Peto and Joseph so that they could come to London and view the training methods of the WPS, before copying them in Bristol. Peto's version of the split inferred that Damer Dawson expected all women sent to the school to eventually come under the control of the WPS. This might be expected of women she had purposefully sent, but she soon expected other recruits to come under her control. The BTS committee didn't like this because it had intended to train women who could then go work for a variety of forces, integrating with these numerous organisations and not necessarily the WPS. It seemed Damer Dawson was trying to take control of the WVP via the back door, and that simply wasn't going to work. The differences between the two organisations effectively ended the collaboration, though the BTS did supply the WPS with thirteen trained munitions policewomen.

Flora Joseph also founded the Somerset Nursing Association, so it is unsurprising that some of the best write-ups on the school came via nursing journals. *The British Journal of Nursing*, a keen supporter of female police, published a feature on the BTS in January 1918:

The object of the school is to find promising women and to test their fitness for patrol and police work before passing them to such posts as Patrol Leaders, Paid or Super Patrols, Munition (sic) Police and Patrols, Railway Police and police-women in borough forces.[3]

Just from this list it is apparent how commonplace the women police had become and how they were widely utilised by various public bodies. The school offered a three-month-long training course which was designed to be both rigorous and thorough. The women were expected to go on to perform diverse roles after the course, and needed a range of knowledge to equip them for the challenges ahead. The *BJN* continued:

It is interesting to know that the women in training included nurses and midwives. It is found that about ten per cent of those who apply are suitable for training. During the process of transforming them into policewomen or patrols they are not put into uniform, but wear a plain blue or black coat, skirt, hat and white gloves, and the squad of recruits on the drill ground soon puts on an air of smartness and efficiency.[4]

The first month of training involved visits to a Police Court under the supervision of an officer, evening patrolling, report writing, study of first aid and criminal law, and of course lots of drill practice. In the second month the ladies undertook volunteer work in the Offices of the Civic League, which included gaining experience of 'case-investigations', learning about the social conditions of the working classes, and understanding the duties and powers of public authorities and other voluntary groups. In the final month the women gained practical experience in a different town under the supervision of a patrol leader. The aim was to give them as varied a range of work as possible to ensure they were fit for any future role they received. After all this, the policewoman proudly received her training certificate and awaited her first posting.

The *BJN* wanted to emphasise how vital this work was, and how appreciated it was by the public now that they had overcome their initial wariness. It recorded a case involving women patrols at Brandon Hill, Bristol:

The Patrols on duty heard a scream and found a woman on the ground with a man belabouring her. When the Patrols came into sight the group about them raised a cry of 'Here are the Police' and the man took to his heels, as did all the rest, except the woman on the ground who was too severely hurt to get up until the Patrols—one of whom was a trained nurse—had attended to various cuts and brought her to herself.[5]

No doubt this was a fairly common occurrence for the women patrols, who often dealt with vulnerable people too drunk to take care of themselves.

The Times added its own report concerning the school from a 'correspondent', who may or may not have been the same sympathetic supporter who had previously written gushing articles about the women police. Certainly their tone was one of exaggerated praise:

> The world moves so quickly nowadays that there may be by now more than a dozen schools in England for the training of policewomen; but with Bristol rests the honour of having the first. It was started as soon as women began to undertake patrol and police work; and its influence is felt and its advice and help are asked far and wide over provincial England.[6]

The writer had some of their information wrong—the school had not be set up 'as soon as women began to undertake' police work—but it was true that its influence was felt far and wide, since most policewomen had at some point come through its doors. At the same time, Flora Joseph was working on a new scheme she had devised for 'super patrols':

> Another organisation which is proving itself to be of great value is the Somerset super-patrols, with whom ... the police recruits are associated during the third month of their training. The super-patrols are paid by voluntary funds and have no official powers; but they wear a uniform with the NUWW armlet, and carry a card signed by the Deputy Chief Constable, authorising the police to give them every assistance in their power. Thus they have the prestige of the police force behind them, and, being at once official and unattached, inspire confidence in people who might be shy of taking their troubles to the local clergy or residents. Their aim is to be, first, the friends of the people, and only secondly a terror to evil-doers; and their worth is gratefully acknowledged alike by the governors and the governed.[7]

Peto had to devise suitable programmes of training for the ladies who attended the school and required experience of the conditions they would be facing. There was no tougher place for a policewoman to prove herself than on the streets of Liverpool. The city that had the highest crime rate in the country and the problem was increasing, with the war against juvenile crime proving a particular issue. 'In Liverpool a census has been taken and it was found that on a single day 13,000 children under thirteen years of age visited cinemas alone,' one correspondent wrote of the troubles, which were caused by vast numbers of unsupervised children haunting the streets. One flustered reader responded that it was clearly all the movies these children were seeing that were causing the problem:

...Liverpool [has] long since decided that the picture palace is working more mischief than good amongst the school children.... It has been clearly proved in Court that the crime film engenders crime. I saw a band of little children the other day in a back street playing at shooting and hanging.... They told me they were 'horse-thieves.' It was probably an echo of a 'cowboy' film.[8]

Juvenile crime became a hot topic in the papers from 1916 onwards, and Liverpool seemed to be at its hub. The authorities appeared to be struggling to get matters under control, and a news article from October 1916 hints at their desperation:

In the opinion of a joint committee of magistrates and members of the Education Committee which has been considering the question of juvenile crime in Liverpool and its punishment, much good would result if the powers of justices to order the birching of boys were enlarged so as to extend the whipping age from 14 to 16. The committee was appointed in view of the striking increase in 1915 of the number of offenders brought before the Liverpool City Juvenile Court. During the year 2,049 cases were dealt with, and in addition there were 397 cases of juvenile delinquency in which the police took no action beyond warning the parents of the children. The excess of cases over the numbers for 1914 was 625, or an increase of 32 per cent ... the committee say that it is desirable that the class of offences punishable by whipping should be enlarged so as to include wilful damage, throwing missiles, stealing growing fruit, and practically all other malpractices.[9]

Sir Leonard Dunning had been Chief Constable for Liverpool between 1902 and 1911 and was well aware of the problem:

I went to Liverpool in 1895 and one of the first things that struck me as a stranger to Liverpool ... was the enormous number of ragged, bare-footed children in the streets ... begging under the pretence of selling newspapers, matches and so on. The first step to deal with at all events one part of that was the establishment of the police-aided Clothing Association which was initiated in 1895 by the then Lord Mayor of Liverpool, Alderman Watts.... The principle is this. The Society lends clothes to children. It does not give them; it lends them. It lends the clothes to those children who come under the notice of police, who pick them up as being ill-clad. After enquiry which satisfies the police that it is not the fault of the parents, but that the parents are not in a position to give the children clothing, they recommend that the child should be clothed, and the child is clothed. The clothing remains the property of the Society, and I must say that the police had most loyal support from the pawnbrokers, who utterly refused to take the clothing in pawn, which was, therefore, left to the children and not disposed of, as it would have been if it had been given to the parents of the children.[10]

Poverty was the main reason for the high crime rates among children in Liverpool, and tackling this rapidly became part of the police's attempts to try and achieve order in the city. The licencing of child traders was eventually moved under the control of the police; children could only be licensed for street trade if an inspection proved that there was no other work available to them. Once licensed the child could then apply for clothing, which was provided at the cost of a sixpence per week. The money was collected weekly by a police officer, with the idea being that it would teach children about keeping their obligations. It also provided the police with a legitimate reason to keep an eye on the children, and enabled them to prevent the children falling into bad ways or being encouraged to join one of the many active gangs in Liverpool. The idea was sound, but Dunning did not include women, either as police officers, adults, or children, under the scheme. This was because no one had suggested women should be employed in that stage of police work—and young girls were not included because male police could find themselves quite vulnerable to charges of immorality when dealing with them. In 1917 Dunning admitted that, on reflection, this was an area where women police would have been useful (*The British Policewoman*). They might also have spoken kindly to the girls about sexual issues, which was another big problem on the streets—the male police had all but given up on trying to deal with prostitutes.

Dunning, unlike some, recognised the value of having women on the force. One of his most memorable experiences as a policeman, largely because it was so embarrassing for all involved, was when he had to interview a pregnant girl—aged under sixteen—and take a sex statement. When he became a chief constable, Dunning made it a priority to find a woman who could take such statements and prevent the humiliation of both victim and constable. Peto found a wealth of material for her training courses in Merseyside, not least in the Liverpool Police handbook (compiled by Dunning) from which should took the admittedly long-winded school motto:

> Anything which helps the very poor, and so relieves them from the temptation to crimes; and anything which helps to take the children of the criminal classes away from evil surroundings and companions and, while there is yet time, implants in them the instincts of honesty and virtue, is true police work; and a policeman should throw himself, heart and soul, into such work as readily as he does into the ordinary work of preventing and detecting crime.[11]

The idea of women police had arisen in Liverpool before the war, probably encouraged by Dunning's openness. In March 1914:

Miss Higson of Liverpool, who is engaged in rescue work, [suggested] that women police should be employed ... The proposal has aroused considerable interest. For many years there have been discussions regarding the dangers to young girls of the public parks and streets at night, and attempts have been made to close the principal public park at dusk. Miss Higson contends that women police could guard young girls by patrolling in civilian dress the public thoroughfares, places of amusement and dancing halls...[12]

The debate continued in July:

The Liverpool Select Vestry yesterday, on the motion of Mrs MacDonald, expressed in a resolution the opinion; 'that the engagement of women police to discharge refined duties is essential in the interest of women and the community generally.' Mr T. White who seconded, spoke strongly of the 'miserable reptiles who infested the streets of Liverpool to the danger of women and girls.' Mr John Quinn protested against the appointment of more officials and suggested the formation of voluntary bands of male and female workers. The motion was passed by 11 votes to nine.[13]

Miss Higson was no doubt delighted. Liverpool was certainly at the forefront of the women's police movement, spurred on by its many problems with crime. Thus, by the outbreak of war, the Liverpool Women's Patrol Committee was in operation and women were already on the streets. Mabel Cowlin joined in January 1915, leaving her career as a social worker. Liverpool now headed into its worst period of criminality during the war, and within a year its juvenile crime rate rose by over thirty per cent. There were a number of reasons why problems suddenly reached fever pitch: fathers were going to war and working mothers left children with little supervision, the increase in port activities drew people to the city for work, and poverty was ever-increasing. Families were often stripped of their breadwinner by the war, and the arrival of American soldiers added even more to the influx of unfamiliar faces. This attracted the usual opportunists and prostitutes. Mabel Cowlin was convinced that it was essential female police recruits saw for themselves the conditions people were living in, and it became part of the BTS course to visit poorer districts and understand the difficulties these families faced. As Dorothy Peto recalled:

Patrol duty in the Liverpool streets certainly called for both courage and initiative. The dockside alleys, where children might be found accosting seamen on behalf of their mothers; Pitt Street, with a Chinese population at the city end and a West Indian and African population at the other, punctuated by seamen's dosshouses and dubious cafes; Scotland Road, with its Irish and Italian residents ready to boil over at the least provocation. These, with Lime Street and its environs, offers a wide and varied field of work, and of invaluable experience.[14]

The first time the women patrols ventured into Scotland Road they were pelted with stones by the unwelcoming residents. Retreating, with a mob at their heels, they regrouped and returned in plain clothes, able to talk to women on their doorsteps. They explained their intentions, asked local charitable organisations to do the same, and slowly came to be accepted.

A large amount of work came in dealing with prostitutes—an area of city life that had gone unchecked by the male police, who were wary of being accused of improper conduct. Miss Higson had envisioned rescue work such as this, but she must have been equally aware of the tough class of prostitute Liverpool created. Mabel Cowlin certainly was:

> The patrols were given powers to inspect lodging houses frequented by common prostitutes and were enabled to take younger ones away and do really constructive work in re-establishing them. In this they were helped by the older women living on their earnings in the streets; for example, one of them brought a young girl to the office and begged the patrols to save her from the life she herself found so difficult to leave.[15]

Cowlin also organised a weekly debrief for the women patrols:

> There, every person or situation dealt with on the beat was examined—their background, their individual needs and the possibilities of helping them; whilst with her trained perception and deep concern for the individual, Cowlin led the patrol concerned to seek and find the best solution. In the years between the two World Wars I met both policewomen and social workers who told me that they owed their whole conception of constructive work to Mabel Cowlin's teaching; and I know how much I learned myself whenever I had an opportunity of sitting in at one of her case-meetings in the Liverpool Patrol Office.[16]

Liverpool had proved the efficacy of women police and that they could be used advantageously. In 1917 Liverpool decided to set up its own school, which was subsequently linked with Peto's BTS. Four years of work could not quite turn the tide against the criminality of the city, but it gave the women an opportunity to shine. They undoubtedly made a difference, and the women certainly had the intention of becoming a permanent part of Liverpool life.

Facing the Future

Back in London, Margaret Damer Dawson was pushing the issue of the long-term employment of women police. It was now early 1917, and she wrote to Sir George Cave asking for an audience. He declined, but the sympathetic Sir Leonard Dunning—now Inspector of the Constabulary—agreed to see her and Mary Allen. He later wrote:

> The truth is, that Miss Damer Dawson cannot get rid of her ideas of the Women Police Service as an independent body and does not realise that the real thing to be aimed at is the employment of women by police authorities as an integral part of the police force, in which case the Chief Constable will be able to find plenty of work for them without coming across any of the difficulties which she sets out. But as a matter of fact most of her difficulties are imaginary.[1]

This was centre of the rift between the WPS and the government. It was simply not feasible to have a separate women's policing body, but men like Dunning were willing to consider the possibility of adding women to the existing force. The trouble was Damer Dawson and Mary Allen were not ready to give up their control over the women police, and this hampered the negotiations. Dunning also felt the ladies were exaggerated the advantages of employing women, and he was unsure that the benefits would outweigh the ensuing controversy.

Home Secretary Sir George Cave was even less impressed and, although he felt that the issue would have to be resolved sooner rather than later, he was not convinced that women were suitable for police work. Dorothy Peto and Flora Joseph also paid a call to the Home Office to press the issue, and were equally fobbed off with vague answers. However, Peto and Joseph did make a better impression than the WPS ladies: they met with the Under-Secretary of State, Sir Edward Troup, who remarked 'I saw these two very sensible ladies'. Troup was informed that the need for policewomen was outstripping supply, largely due the fact that the officers were poorly paid. Only middle class ladies could afford to fill the roles, and though there were many who would have preferred to make policing a career, they were uncomfortable committing themselves to career with no pension and such poor wages. Peto and Joseph also assured Troup that, should women be amalgamated into the police force, they would relinquish all their control—the complete opposite suggestion of the WPS.

Policewomen had become an intrinsic part of wartime life and the government could no longer ignore them. They had fulfilled vital roles, maintained order, and freed up men to join the army. As much as old-fashioned members of parliament might have thought that women could be easily removed from their work after the war, the reality was very different. There was a shortage of fit, able men who could return to the police and other posts, and the special work that had been done by women was not something that could be carried out by male officers. However much people might baulk at the idea, the women police were here to stay.

The success of women patrols had affected all levels of society, and had inspired numerous unaffiliated societies:

> Members of the Bournemouth Women Patrols assembled at St. Peter's Hall and were addressed by the Mayor, who said that from what he had gathered he was sure that the Patrols had been able to carry on their difficult work without provoking resentment, and had gained the confidence of the girls with whom they came in contact. He was glad to hear that the girls' clubs which had been started as an outcome of the Patrol work had proved a great success, and provided rational and harmless amusement for the girls of an evening.
>
> At the annual council meeting of the Women's National Health Association of Ireland in Dublin yesterday, Lady Aberdeen presiding, Mrs Anna Haslam explained the work done by women patrols in Dublin. Twenty patrols, holding cards signed by the Chief Commissioner of Police, went out every night from 9 to 11 in the principal streets. Mrs Cosgrove said that patrol work to be effective should have clubs as a background.[2]

The military also felt the benefits of the women's patrols, as proved by the Queen Mary's Auxiliary Army Corps:

> A new branch of the Q.M.A.A.C., which has just been formed, is a service of patrols, the members of which will work at the camps and hostels. The service is being formed by Mrs Esslemont (late administrator of the Connaught Club), who is now Controller of Patrols at headquarters, and who, before joining the Q.M.A.A.C., worked for two years with the women's patrols in connexion with the London police.
>
> Service in this new force will be voluntary, and the girls will be chosen on account of their good record of work and exceptional character. They will rank as Head Patrols and Patrol Forewomen, and their duties will be to safeguard the members of the corps, to see that they keep the necessary

discipline, and to give counsel and help to those needing it. They will be required to see that the girls do not form undesirable companions, and that they keep within the bounds and report at the proper hours.

The distinctive marks of the members are to be shoulder straps of lemon yellow with a brassard of the same colour stamped Q.M.A.A.C., in black, with a whistle attached to a white lanyard worn round the left arm. They will also be provided with special high boots and mackintosh capes which can be rolled up and attached to their belts. The girls chosen must be over 5 ft 4 in and over 23 years of age, and will be required to pass a special medical board for fitness. They will be selected from existing members of the corps, and must have three months' perfect record of service and will be given one month's training with the Women's patrol Service, after which they will be enrolled for one month on approbation. The test of efficiency will be very strict, as only girls with special qualifications of tact, kindness, and firm character will be passed.[3]

Women were suddenly gaining authority everywhere:

WOMEN OFFICERS FOR THE AIR FORCE—Control of Camp Hostels. The Air Ministry announce that they wish to recruit at once a large number of women officers for the Women's Royal Air Force. The duties of these officers will be to supervise and control the WRAFs employed at various camps in the United Kingdom.[4]

Despite the clear praise the future of policewomen was far from guaranteed. Two months before the war ended, efforts were made to assess the impact of women constables and whether or not there was any point in maintaining them after the war:

The question of the employment of women police is certainly not one that has been ignored, but it is one that cannot be settled offhand, in two or three days. As a matter of fact, Sir Nevil Macready saw representatives of one or two of the women police organisations last week, and would have completed that part of the inquiry, which is proceeding, if the representative of a third body of women police, whose evidence would be of importance, had not been prevented by illness from attending. She is to be seen this week, and in all probability arrangements will be made for employing women much as they are employed in the parks. It must, however, be remembered that the powers of the women will be subject to the same limitations as those of the male police. One can imagine what would happen to a policewoman who attempted to remonstrate with rowdy young girls in the Strand, against whom no proofs of prostitution were forthcoming.[5]

In response to such an unenthusiastic statement, the women pressed their case:

> Dr Sloan Chesser presided last night at a dinner in the Lyceum Club in commemoration of the fourth anniversary of the establishment of the Women Police. Lady Nott-Bower expressed the hope that before long the women police would be officially recognised in London and in all parts of the United Kingdom, as they had been already in more than 20 provincial districts. Much good work had been done in dealing with young women in the streets and elsewhere, and it was desirable that women police should be given full official status.
>
> Commandant Damer Dawson said that the women police had justified their existence. The pioneer work had been successful beyond expectation. They had trained women who had been most usefully employed by the Ministry of Munitions and in other ways in the provinces, but they desired to be more than 'semi-officially' recognised. They had trained some 2,000 women for the work, and had ceased to be a mere philanthropic organisation dependent on charity. It was time that the country realised their use and that they were recognised by the Home Office.[6]

A sort-of triumph came in November 1918:

> The Home Secretary has sanctioned the formation of a small body of women patrols under the control of the Commissioner of Police of the Metropolis. For some time past the Commissioner has employed a number of the women patrol of the National Union of Women Workers, who have done very useful work, but this arrangement will now be discontinued. The women will not be sworn in as constables and will not have the special powers which are given to constables under certain statutes. They will, however, patrol streets and open spaces in the same way as the regular constable, for the purpose of preserving order and assisting the public, more especially those of their own sex. They will wear uniform dress, with the badges of the regular force, and be under the control of a superintendent and other women officers.
>
> The scheme is an experimental one. Only about 100 women will be enrolled for the present, and preference will be given to candidates who have had experience of similar work in Government or other forces. The pay of the rank and file will be at the rate of 30s per week, with a war bonus of 12s per week, but provision will be made for a progressive rise of pay in the event of service extending beyond a year.[7]

This article is notable for the way in which it completely ignores the WPS. Despite the struggle of Damer Dawson and her comrades they would have no further part to play in the legitimisation of female police officers.

Post-War Women

As peace grew nearer the future of the women police began to clarify. In the summer of 1918 discussions began between the Home Office and Ministry of Munitions concerning the future role of women in law enforcement. A committee was formed to investigate the matter and the relevant people from the WPS and NCW were interviewed—the NCW, National Council of Workers, was the new name for the NUWW. The NCW interviews made it plain that the WPS should not be involved in the formation of a women's police unit—the antipathy that had existed between the organisations, simmering away quietly for years, now bubbled to the surface in an all-out attack on each group's purposes and aims. The ladies interviewed could not even agree on whether women police should be allowed full powers of arrest. Mrs Stanley, who was in charge of the special patrols, thought it was entirely unnecessary, while the NCW argued it would only be needed in certain circumstances. The WPS, meanwhile, was adamant that women police should have the same powers as male police. Considering the backlash they had just received from their counterparts, the WPS was rather magnanimous on its views concerning the potential of women police:

> They welcomed the scheme. The present unsatisfactory conditions of opposing Associations could not continue. While very proud of their own share in the matter and anxious to maintain their own Association, they would, in the national interest, be quite satisfied to merge themselves in a Home Office Corps and be taken over, because they recognise that this would be of public advantage, but nothing less than a Home Office Corps, officially recognised, would compensate them for all they would give up in sinking their individual positions and the position secured by the Women Police Service.[1]

The committee came to the conclusion that Women Police Patrols, based in London, should be formed under the supervision of female officers but remain under the main control of the chief constables or commissioner of the regular police. Shortly after this a deputation of high-ranking Church and military personnel went to see Sir George Cave to argue the case for women police. In their eyes this was not just about women's rights but also the need to protect men from prostitution—and this was best done by women. Assistant Home Secretary Harry Butler-Simpson made the suggestion:

> I venture to suggest that the apt. of some energetic but discreet lady to an *official* position in the Metropolitan Police—say as an additional Asst. Commr. or some purely honorary post—would put you in a better position to urge the more backward of the county and borough authorities to appoint policewomen. The deputation was mainly interested in London, and it appeared that their views would be met by some visible recognition of the police work and semi-police work done by women, which besides emphasising its importance at the present time might also lead to its further development. At all events a lady of practical experience of the London streets might be of great assistance to the Commr. in dealing with this subject—of which we are likely to hear more.[2]

The deputation came at a critical time. The end of the war was approaching fast, and women were rising to ensure they did not lose the freedoms and responsibilities they had gained in the last four years. Women had proved themselves, and now felt they should be rewarded with equality. In the midst of it all the regular police went on strike over pay, immeasurably complicating the situation. This calamity coincided with Sir Edward Henry's holiday, and although he hastened home it was only to discover that his time as Commissioner of the Metropolitan Police was over; General Sir Nevil Macready had taken his place. Macready was quick to make his mark on the police force, stripping out what he saw as unnecessary bureaucracy and shaking up the chief constables, who he felt had too long been chosen by rampant nepotism. At first the women police were not sure what to make of Macready, or whether he could improve on the friendship shown to them by Sir Henry. However, they were soon to discover Macready would be their greatest ally. In November 1918 *The Times* reported:

> The Home Secretary has sanctioned the formation of a small body of women patrols under the control of the Commissioner of Police of the Metropolis. For some time past the Commissioner has employed a number of the women patrols of the National Union of Women Workers, who have done very useful work, but this arrangement will now be discontinued. The women will not be sworn in as constables, and will not have special powers which are given to constables under certain statutes. They will, however, patrol streets and open spaces in the same way as the regular constable, for the

purpose of preserving order and assisting the public, more especially those of their own sex. They will wear uniform dress, with the badges of the regular force and be under the control of a superintendent and other women officers. The scheme is an experimental one. Only about 100 women will be enrolled for the present, and preference will be given to candidates who have had experience of similar work on Government or other forces.[3]

Clearly someone had been listening to Butler-Simpson's suggestions. The *Daily Mail* also commented on the news, though in a much less formal tone:

A force of women police is to be created for London, officially recognised, under the control of the Commissioner of Metropolitan Police, and subject to the same discipline as the men. This is another 'break through' by women of that long line of positions that were assumed only to be fitting for men. Women are likely to be firm and efficient constables ... our urban life will be cleaner by the presence of the woman constable. In the woman constable's dealing with the venal minor male offender against the law, she is likely to be less lenient than the policeman, and to be less inclined to 'look the other way.' Man is apt to be merciful with man—and woman. Woman is not to be cajoled. When a woman has a sense of duty, she is inflexible. There is some amusement in the prospect that those who hear the chimes o'midnight will have to be wary of women police. These would be ill days for Sir John Falstaff.[4]

It was a promising beginning, although without powers of arrest women were still unequal to their male counterparts. However, for the WPS this was a mere inconvenience when compared to the way in which they were totally ignored during the formation of a new women police patrol board. Mrs Stanley was chosen, as was Mrs Carden, but the WPS remained unrepresented. This was a blow to Mary Allen, who had always felt that Damer Dawson's relationship with Sir Henry ensured the WPS a role in an official organisation. She failed to recognise not only the damage that criticism of other patrols had caused her organisation, but also that on occasion the WPS staunchness had come across as militantly contrarian. The government was too wary of giving them additional power. Besides, a number of their members were former militant suffragettes who had clashed with the police. Mary was also disturbed that the other organisations had accepted the terms laid out for women police so easily, when quite clearly they could prove to be a handicap. Just days after the announcement, Damer Dawson became rattled and abandoned her usual tact when giving an interview on the subject:

I suppose you want to know what I think of all this correspondence on 'the state of London Streets'.... It's all so one-sided, so unjust to women. They

talk as if men were innocent angels, helpless in the hands of wicked women
... many of them have worked for the starvation wages women used to get,
and they have found a way of earning as many pounds in a night as they
used to earn shillings in a week. If there were no demand there would be no
supply.[5]

She went on to rail about poor social conditions which, she insisted, were to
blame for most evils. Then she got back to the burning question:

It is strange that nearly all those who have taken part in the discussion,
whether they defend the character of London or not, are agreed as to the
general responsibility of women for all wrong doings. That equality of men
and women which has made so much headway in the world of labour is
unknown here. In the realm of morals we have not advanced beyond Adam
who was tempted by Eve.[6]

Damer Dawson had a point. Men seemed to feel certain worldly evils were
solely the fault of women, and that they should shoulder full responsibility.
However, she was also bitter that there would be no place for her or Mary
Allen even if the WPS women eventually joined the Metropolitan patrols. As of
December 1918 women police became officially employed by London; in May
1919 they made their first large public display, which was in attendance at a
memorial service for those who had died in the war. The WPS was dissolving
in the background, as might have been expected. Former members who sought
a career in policing attempted to gain employment by the commissioner, while
others simply returned to their previous lives. Damer Dawson held onto the
reins for as long as possible, but her time too was short; six weeks after the
last witness had been heard by the Baird Committee, which was called to
discuss the employment of women on police duties, she dropped dead of a
heart attack. She was forty-five years old.

However, Frederick Mead, the arch-enemy of the women patrols, was still going
strong, and testified to the Baird Committee that it was wholly dangerous to have
men and women working together on the police patrols. He suggested it would
lead to the temptation of sexual relations. Mead sometimes gives the impression
of having sex on the brain; however, although his opinions were shared by other
men he could not prevent the swell of enthusiasm for women police. Many who
gave evidence to the committee saw only advantages, and argued that women
deserved a wage and a pension that were equal to their male colleagues. The
committee finally agreed that women had to have a role in policing:

There is a note of hesitancy in the report of Major Sir John Baird's Committee
on the employment of policewomen which suggests that the male members

entertained some private doubt but sat in wholesome dread of their fellow-members in petticoats, Lady Astor and Dame Helen Gwynne-Vaughan. Their report is unanimous but records wavering opinion on certain points. They mention important and weighty evidence against policewomen, including that of the most experienced Metropolitan Magistrate [Frederick Mead], but finally decided cautiously that their employment is probably desirable for crowded urban areas on special duties connected with crimes by or against women and children.... The question of uniform or plain clothes should in the committee's judgement be left to the local authorities, like that of their actual employment at all and most of the other points that present any difficulty.[7]

Snide though some of these comments were, it was plain that women could not be ousted from their roles; they were here to stay. However, the Home Office had no qualms about informing its various constabularies to ignore the committee's recommendations for better pay and powers of arrest. Still, they could not stem the tide—it would take time, but women would eventually become integral members of the police service. This story certainly did not end in 1920, nor has it ended for the women who still find themselves facing opposition, 'glass ceilings', and unequal pay, but, compared to the issues our female ancestors had to overcome, modern problems seem suitably surmountable.

'We had always meant our Service to go on after the war,' Mary wrote in later life, 'we had supposed somehow that, when the Germans were beaten, our activities with the khaki armies would cease, and we should be drafted straight into civil police routine.'

They may have thought this, but the government saw things differently. The WPS was politely asked to disband as soon as possible. Police Commissioner Sir Nevil Macready told the WPS that the continuation of policewomen would needle the policemen under his command. This was disingenuous as Macready was, at this point, already working on plans to form his own female police force. In October 1918 the newspapers reported that 'a force of women police [were] to be created for London, officially recognised, under the control of the Commissioner of Metropolitan Police'. The WPS had been officially snubbed—much to their amazement, considering how stringently they had patrolled the munitions factories and upheld DORA. It seemed Macready wanted to bypass the WPS altogether, telling the *Daily Mail* that he was not inclined to hire women who had already served in the voluntary patrols. In reality this was an untenable position, and when the Metropolitan Women Police Patrols (MWPP) was formed it did hire several ex-WPS women. Despite these machinations the WPS remained active for a time, and in December 1918 it was reported:

WOMEN POLICE IN THE STRAND—Canadian Officer's Tribute. At Bow Street Police Court yesterday before Mr Graham Campbell, Charles O'Malley, a young Canadian soldier, was charged with assault. Miss Lena Campbell, of the Women's Police Service, said that about 10.15 p.m. on Saturday she was on patrol duty outside the Beaver Hut in the Strand and saw the prisoner, who was the worst for drink, trying to engage two women in conversation. She went up to the women and asked them to move on. Thereupon the prisoner struck her a violent blow on the right side of her face, hurting her very much. She remonstrated with him. He swore very much and struck her again on the face with his clenched fist, causing her to stagger across the pavement.

Miss Jean Campbell, Inspector of the Women's Police Service, said that she witnessed the disturbance, and when she tried to get between the patrol and the prisoner the latter hit her in the chest, causing her to fall. Some soldiers and sailors tried to get the prisoner away, but he would not go.

The prisoner said that he remembered nothing of what happened. He had been in hospital suffering from erysipelas in the head and when he came out on leave he took too much whisky. An officer of the Canadian Forces said that he was in attendance to corroborate, if necessary, the evidence of the women police. He wished to take the opportunity of saying how much the Canadian military authorities appreciated the services of the women police, who had been doing magnificent work. Mr Graham Campbell ordered the prisoner to be imprisoned for six weeks with hard labour. Maud Clark was fined 40s for obstructing the police while they were conveying the soldier to the police station.[8]

Macready would not have WPS women patrolling in his city for long, but his command to disband was really only effective for the Metropolitan region, as was his foundation of the MWPP. Constabularies further afield were still contacting the WPS and asking for women officers to join their forces; the organisation had over 1,000 well-trained women who were not content to go back to a mundane domestic existence, and who wanted to carry on as policewomen. Some of these women could be deployed to various counties and paid by their respective constabularies, but many more were at a loose end. With the Ministry of Munitions funding gone the WPS limped along, barely able to cover its costs.

A few high-ranking men remained supportive of the WPS, and allegedly even the Prince of Wales spoke to Mary at a garden party in Buckingham Palace, where he stated his enthusiasm for the policewomen. Whether this was his true opinion or merely royal politeness, Mary believed that he was firmly on their side. Sir Leonard Dunning, Inspector of Constabulary, offered firmer support: he was convinced there was much good that the women police, and the WPS in particular, could do outside of London. He was steadfast in his opinion that women should form part of the regular police service.

Unfortunately the WPS's critics far outnumbered their supporters. Everything came to a head in 1920, when Assistant Commissioner of the Metropolitan Police Sir William Horwood informed the WPS that their uniforms too closely resembled those of the MWPP. This was a bitter pill to swallow considering that the WPS had designed its uniform and had it officially approved many years ago, in the early days of the war. They were now told that if they did not change their uniforms they could be fined for impersonating a police officer.

The main male objection to the WPS was that many of its leaders or high-profile officers were former militant suffragettes. Mary Allen was an especially well-remembered name; four long years of war had not whitewashed the politician's memories of violent clashes between the suffragettes, the police, and the House of Commons. The discord had been ignored during the national emergency, but now it could not be forgotten. As Macready told the Bridgeman Committee in 1924, 'The main point was to eliminate any women of extreme views—the vinegary spinster or blighted middle-aged fanatic.'

Macready added fuel to the fire by condemning the actions of the WPS in the 'drunken man' incident. In 1919 Mary Allen and Margaret Damer Dawson decided to create some publicity stills to promote the WPS, in an attempt to draw more funding. They mocked up various scenes in which Mary and Margaret came to the assistance of civilians in distress. One photograph showed a drunk man slouched in the sidecar of a WPS motorcycle, driven by Mary, with Margaret in the background. The identity of the drunk man caused some consternation; a couple in Edinburgh, unaware that the photo was staged, came to believe the man was their missing son, and contacted Macready about it—erroneously thinking that the picture portrayed Metropolitan Policewomen. Macready responded with unnecessary outrage, using the image as a clear example of the confusion the WPS was causing to the general public. Macready caused even more consternation by claiming that the 'drunk man' was in fact a woman in costume. Margaret Damer Dawson countered this by stating that the drunk was a young male actor from a well-known company, and that he could be called as a witness to the photograph if necessary. It actually seems more likely that the drunk was Isobel Goldingham, who was rather fond of dressing up in male clothes.

Macready's venomous dislike for the WPS comes into context when his hatred against suffragettes is taken into account and Margaret and Mary's close relationship—not to mention their way of dressing in a masculine fashion—had earned them his wrath. He was convinced they were homosexual, and was disgusted that they had a woman dress up as a man in one of their photos, but the final straw was that their uniforms meant they might be mistaken for Macready's women; this tarred his force with the same brush. Macready completely overlooked the fact that it was him who had copied the WPS uniform and, if anything, that it was his female force who were impersonating WPS members. There was yet another black mark against the WPS: they were a women's force, run by women, cutting out male authority entirely. Macready couldn't accept this, with his women coming firmly under the control of *men*. The WPS were outsiders, operating by their own rules and refusing to bow to male authority. He could not allow them to continue to exist.

The WPS was dangerously balanced on the precipice of disintegration, and yet another blow was struck against them when Damer Dawson died from heart disease in May 1920. Her illness came on rapidly and her death was sudden. Mary was shattered, and the WPS the only thing left behind to sustain her.

A month after Margaret died, Mary went to Scotland to set up new headquarters and a training school in Edinburgh. This venture did not last long, due to lack of funds, and meanwhile in London Macready had made way for Sir William Horwood, who was determined to deal with the stubborn WPS ladies once and for all. In early 1921 he took the WPS to court for impersonating women of the MWPP. Horwood's attack on the WPS was almost farcical; he claimed, in a speech to the defence, to have no knowledge of the role the WPS had performed during the war or the fact that they had been employed by many forces across the country. He admitted that he would be satisfied if the WPS changed their uniform sufficiently for it to be impossible to confuse them with the MWPP. In truth, however, this was not the case—Horwood would not be satisfied until the WPS was no more. The courts eventually imposed a light fine on the women, making it plain they felt Horwood was being overzealous in his agitation. Horwood then tried to refer the matter of the uniforms to the home secretary, who refused to get involved. Despite Horwood being apparently isolated in his criticism Mary decided to try appeasement rather than protest, and not only modified the WPS uniform but also changed the organisation's name to the Woman's Auxiliary Service (WAS).

Though Mary liked to think the prestige of the WAS had been improved because of the case their money problems persisted, and finding work outside of London proved difficult. The only ray of hope was interest from abroad— in June 1920 British Army Colonel Ormande de l'Eppé Winter paid a visit to Scotland Yard, where he requested fifty trained female officers to work with the Royal Irish Constabulary. Scotland Yard turned him down and directed him to the WPS instead.

Chief Inspector Campbell, a sergeant, and seven female police constables were immediately sent to Ireland, where they would help Winter in his fight against the IRA. Colonel Winter was Chief of the Combined Intelligence Services for Ireland, and was responsible for tracking down IRA agents and

Sinn Féin leaders. His biggest problem was the cocky way IRA operatives used women—in particular wives and girlfriends—to mask their activities. When Winter's forces raided a house, any incriminating evidence (such as guns) would be handed to a woman for concealment on her person. It would stir more trouble, and generate increased resentment towards the British, if male soldiers or military police manhandled a woman when looking for evidence. Winter needed policewomen because they could conduct these searches on females. The WAS could get him out of a tight spot.

The arrival of the policewomen was not what he expected, however. The tensions within Ireland at the time made the Dublin policemen recoil in shock when they saw the WAS ladies clad in full uniform. Walking around in uniform invited trouble, and the women were quickly persuaded to dress in plain clothes from that point onwards. Before long the policewomen were serving their purpose and helping in raids.

The success in Ireland opened new doors for the WPS via the British Army of Occupation in the Rhine Provinces. Large numbers of troops were attracting hordes of prostitutes to the area, and the WAS suggested it was advisable to send policewomen to control the problem. In 1923 Mary paid a visit to Cologne to assess the situation for herself. She failed to recognise the impression she made on the stunned crowd when she turned up in her full uniform, with her cropped hair and monocle. By now Mary was cultivating a very masculine image, presenting herself as militaristic and manly. When the crowd first saw her there was debate over her gender which turned swiftly into a debate over her sexuality. Mary was an extreme parody of a woman trying to fit into a male world. She had abandoned femininity to gain power, without realising that it was her loss of femininity that lead to the detriment of her cause. Even by today's standards Mary's appearance is comical and sinister—similar to the uniform of the *SS* twenty years later—but while her image was controversial it was also distinctive and memorable; no one could forget Mary once they saw her. By June 1923 WAS policewomen were present in Germany, and Mary embarked on her first tour of America. The WAS may have fallen out of favour in Britain but, against the odds, it was making progress abroad.

Conclusion

The war had demonstrated the positive impact that women could have. It took the strain of the conflict for the complacency of centuries to be challenged, and for the authorities to see that women could stand alongside men and contribute. The women police were just part of that contribution: they stood up for women, but they also stood against them, they served their country, but not always their gender, and they saw the war as both a tragedy and an opportunity. The story of the rise of policewomen cannot be presented in black and white; there were too many convoluted turns in the tale, and too many differing opinions and arguments. The patrols were stricken by class divides that would haunt society long after the war had first battered the privileged hierarchy. The women police service was begun by wealthy women because only wealthy women could afford to volunteer, and their practices were inevitably shaped by this. Fortunately there were also those who recognised this disadvantage, and refused to be swayed by antiquated cultural views.

This journey disrupted more than just the old principles of sexual divide: class was also called into question, and the way that criminals were perceived was challenged. Prostitution was understood, not just persecuted, and men revealed themselves as something less than perfect. For some of those men the terror induced by the rise of women was almost palpable, with some believing they would have no use in a society where women were equal. Fear governed much of the resistance—fear of change, and fear of being proved worthless. Fear drove resentment, but in the end this could not prevent the inevitable.

In 1914 the policewoman emerged, perhaps not yet fully formed, but recognisable to us today. She was countless years in the making, and she strode forward ready to change the world one step at a time. Four years later she was a permanent fixture on the London streets, walking alongside the revolutionary women who had pushed for the vote the women who wanted reform, who would stop at nothing to their goals. As much as her story stands alone, it is also a cog in the vast machinery of the women's rights movement. One hundred years on, the beginnings of policewomen are half-forgotten, overshadowed by the other dramas of World War One. While regrettable, this is actually perhaps for the best because it shows how finally women are accepted, and even expected, on the police force. The WPS and NUWW could not have asked for more; despite hardships and sacrifices they had fought their way through. Today, the story of the first policewomen is a remarkable piece of socio-political history; those ladies in the felt bowler hats and armlets must never be forgotten, because they paved the way for the freedoms we now enjoy.

Endnotes

Introduction
 1 Metropolitan Police, History of Policing.

Chapter 1
 1 Lytton, C., *Prisons and Prisoners* (1914).
 2 *Ibid.*
 3 *The Suffragette Movement: An Intimate Account of Persons and Ideals* (1931).

Chapter 2
 1 Lytton, C., *Prisons and Prisoners* (1914).
 2 *Ibid.*
 3 *Ibid.*
 4 *Ibid.*
 5 *Ibid.*

Chapter 3
 1 From Boyle, *Suffragette to Fascist: The many lives of Mary Sophia Allen* (2013).
 2 *Ibid.*

Chapter 5
 1 Holton, *Suffrage Days: Stories from the Women's Suffrage Movement* (1996).
 2 Damer Dawson, *Lady in Blue* (1936).

Chapter 6
 1 Lock, *The British Policewoman* (1979).
 2 *The Times*, 20 August 1914.
 3 *Ibid.*, 9 October 1914.

4 *Ibid.*, 31 December 1914.

5 *Hansard*—House of Commons Debates Transcripts.

Chapter 7

1 Boyle, *From Suffragette to Fascist: The Many Lives of Mary Sophia Allen* (2013).

2 Damer Dawson, *The Pioneer Policewoman* (1925).

3 *People* periodical, 29 November 1914.

4 *The Vote,* 1914.

Chapter 8

1 Damer Dawson, *The Pioneer Policewoman* (1925).

2 *Ibid.*

3 *Magazine of The Friends of The National Archives* April 2012, Vol. 23 No. 1.

4 Damer Dawson, *The Pioneer Policewoman* (1925).

5 *Magazine of The Friends of The National Archives* April 2012, Vol. 23 No. 1.

6 Damer Dawson, *The Pioneer Policewoman* (1925).

7 *Ibid.*

Chapter 9

1 *The Times*, 11 June 1915.

2 *Ibid.*

3 *The Daily Express*, 3 April 1915.

4 *The Times,* 11 June 1915.

5 Lock, *The British Policewoman* (1979).

6 *Ibid.*

Chapter 10

1 *The Times*, 12 Feb 1915.

2 *The Times*, 3 February 1916.

3 *The Times*, 7 June 1918.

4 *The Times*, 3 October 1917.

Chapter 11

1 *The Times*, 29 September 1914.

2 *The Times*, 12 February 1916.

Chapter 12

1 *The Times*, 13 October 1915.

2 *The Times*, 4 March 1918.

3 Lock, *The British Policewoman* (1979).

Chapter 13

1 Lock, *The British Policewoman (1979)*.
2 *The Times*, 27 February 1915.
3 *The Times*, 26 January 1916.
4 *From Suffragette to Fascist: The many lives of Mary Sophia Allen* (2013).
5 Lock, *The British Policewoman* (1979).
6 Boyd, *From Suffragette to Fascist: The many lives of Mary Sophia Allen* (2013).
7 Hammerton, *The Great War: I Was There* (1939).
8 Lock, *The British Policewoman* (1979).

Chapter 14

1 Lock, *The British Policewoman* (1979).
2 *The Times*, 26 November 1916.
3 *The Daily News*.
4 Damer Dawson, *The Pioneer Policewoman* (1925).
5 *The Times* 14 September 1917.
6 Lock, *The British Policewoman* (1979).

Chapter 15

1 *The Times*, 24 February 1917.
2 *The Times*, 26 February 1917.
3 Damer Dawson, *The Pioneer Policewoman* (1925).
4 *Hansard*.
5 *Ibid.*
6 *Ibid.*
7 *Ibid.*
8 *Ibid.*
9 Damer Dawson, *The Pioneer Policewoman* (1925).
10 Lock, *The British Policewoman* (1979).
11 *The Times* 15 March 1916.

Chapter 16

1 Damer Dawson, *The Pioneer Policewoman* (1925).
2 *The Suffragette,* 1912.
3 *The Times*, 6 April 1915.
4 *Ibid.*
5 *Ibid.*
6 *Hansard*—House of Commons Debates Transcripts.
7 As quoted in Damer Dawson, *The Pioneer Policewoman* (1925).

Chapter 17
1 *The Times*, 27 March 1915.
2 Smith, *The Second Battlefield: Women, Modernism, and the First World War* (2000).
3 *Sussex Daily News*, 1914.
4 *The Times*, 17 April 1917.
5 *The Times*, 10 June 1918.

Chapter 18
1 Lock, *The British Policewoman* (1979).
2 *The Times*, 24 October 1916.
3 *The British Journal of Nursing*, January 1918.
4 *Ibid.*
5 *Ibid.*
6 *The Times*, 20 February 1918.
7 *Ibid.*
8 *The Times*, 11 October 1916.
9 *The Times*, 18 October 1916.
10 *Hansard*—House of Commons Debates Transcripts.
11 Lock, *The British Policewoman* (1979).
12 *The Times*, 23 March 1914.
13 *The Times*, 22 July 1914.
14 Lock, *The British Policewoman* (1979).
15 *Ibid.*
16 *Ibid.*

Chapter 19
1 Boyd, *From Suffragette to Fascist: The Many Lives of Mary Sophia Allen* (2013).
2 *The Times*, 15 April 1915.
3 *The Times*, 30 May 1918.
4 *The Times*, 30 July 1918.
5 *Hansard*—House of Commons Debates Transcripts.
6 *The Times*, 1 October 1918.
7 *The Times*, 21 November 1918.

Chapter 20
1 Lock, *The British Policewoman* (1979).
2 *Hansard*—House of Commons Debates Transcripts.
3 *The Times*, 21 November 1918.
4 *The Daily Mail*, November 1918.

5 Boyd, *From Suffragette to Fascist: The Many Lives of Mary Sophia Allen* (2013).

6 *Ibid.*

7 *Hansard*—House of Commons Debates Transcripts.

8 *The Times*, 17 December 1918.

Bibliography

Atkinson, Diane, *The Suffragettes in Pictures* (The History Press, 1996)

Bartley, Paula, *Emmeline Pankhurst* (Routledge, 2002)

Boyd, Nina, *From Suffragette to Fascist: The Many Lives of Mary Sophia Allen* (The History Press, 2013)

Bush, Julia, *Edwardian Ladies and Imperial Power* (Leicester University Press, 2000)

David, Hugh, *On Queer Street; a Social History of British Homosexuality 1895–1995* (Harper Collins, 1997)

Harwood, Jeremy, *The End of a World* (Reader's Digest, 2009)

Hattersley, Roy, *The Edwardians* (Little Brown, 2004)

Holton, Sandra Stanley, *Suffrage Days: Stories from the Women's Suffrage Movement* (Routledge, 1996)

Jivani, Alkarim, *It's not Unusual: A History of Lesbian and Gay Britain in the Twentieth Century*
(Michael O'Mara Books Ltd, 1997)

Liddington, Jill, *Revel Girls: Their Fight for the Vote* (Virago Press, 2006)

Lock, Joan, *The British Policewoman* (Robert Hale, 1979)

Lytton, Lady Constance, *Prisons and Prisoners: Experiences of a Suffragette* (EP Pubishing Ltd, 1976 [first published 1914])

Naphy, William, *Born to be Gay: A History of Homosexuality* (Tempus, 2004)

Pankhurst, Emmeline, *The Suffragette Movement: An Intimate Account of Persons and Ideals* (Longmans, Green and Co., 1931)

Phillips, Melanie, *The Ascent of Woman: A History of the Suffragette Movement and the Ideas behind It* (Little Brown, 2003)

Raeburn, Antonia, *The Suffragette View* (David & Charles, 1976)

Smith, Angela K., *The Second Battlefield: Women, Modernism and the First World War* (Manchester University Press, 2000)

Weeks, Jeffrey, *Coming Out: Homosexual Politics in Britain, from the Nineteenth Century to the Present* (Quartet Books, 1977)